CHURCH
in the
WORLD

Paul's First Letter to the Corinthians:
A Commentary

PHILIP F. CONGDON

Church In the World

Paul's First Letter to the Corinthians: A Commentary

Copyright © 2016 by Philip F. Congdon
Cover image and title page image by Ben Congdon
Published by Grace Theology Press.

Unless otherwise noted scripture quotations taken from the New American Standard Bible® (NASB), Copyright © 1960, 1962, 1963, 1968, 1971, 1972, 1973, 1975, 1977, 1995 by The Lockman Foundation Used by permission. www.Lockman.org

ISBN-10: 0998138509
ISBN-13: 9780998138503
eISBN-10: 0998138517
eISBN-13: 9780998138510

Special Sales: Most Grace Theology Press titles are available in special quantity discounts. Custom imprinting or excerpting can also be done to fit special needs. Contact Grace Theology Press at info@gracetheology.org.

Printed in the United States of America

ENDORSEMENTS

Rare indeed do you find a commentary that is exegetically astute, theologically engaging, pastorally insightful and homiletically valuable. Phil Congdon has provided such a tool to guide pastors and serious students of the scriptures into a rich and robust quest through First Corinthians. Although many have written on the Corinthian Church caught in a culture of corruption in the first century, this commentary exposits the Apostle Paul's care and concern for any church in any culture especially in the twenty first century.

Fred Chay, Ph.D., Professor of Theology
Dean of Doctoral Studies, Grace School of Theology

I am excited about Church in the World for several reasons. First, Phil Congdon has done an admirable job of considering the larger context of the book and each section so that they bear expertly on his interpretations of individual passages. It is hard to argue with contextual interpretations! Second, though he writes with a pastor's heart and passion, the commentary does not dodge the technical issues. Phil has managed to appeal both to the scholar, the pastor, and the untrained Christian who just want to understand First Corinthians. Third, and very significantly, Phil views the epistle through a consistent and clear view of the gospel of grace—this alone captures both the pastoral and theological concerns of the apostle Paul that are so often missed in this wonderful epistle. I could not imagine teaching or preaching First Corinthians without using this book!

Charles C. Bing, Ph.D.,
Founder and director of GraceLife Ministries, Burleson, TX

What a wonderful contribution Phil Congdon has made to the tools available for anyone wishing to make a serious study of 1 Corinthians. With his comments on translations stemming from his knowledge of the original text and textual criticism to his homiletical suggestions, this work bridges the gap between the seminary and the pulpit. Added to that are his theological sidebars that alert the student to issues he may not have known were even there. It is also the only commentary I know on 1 Corinthians that navigates the calm waters between the rough waves of Calvinism on one side and Arminianism on the other. Well done!

David R. Anderson, Ph.D.,
President and Professor of Systematic Theology & Biblical Languages,
Grace School of Theology

Dedicated to the memory of three men:

My father, Dr. Roger D. Congdon,
who implanted in me a love for God's Word

My father-in-law, Charles F. ("Charlie") McAlpine,
who modeled for me the love of Christ

My seminary instructor, Prof Zane C. Hodges,
who instilled in me an appreciation for God's grace.

TABLE OF CONTENTS

INTRODUCTION

THE VALUE OF STUDYING 1 CORINTHIANS

The New Testament contains instruction on a variety of themes, doctrines, and practices. Some authors are very exclusive in their purpose; for example, John wrote his Gospel explicitly to lead his readers to believe in Jesus Christ as God's Son for eternal life (20:30f). James' epistle instructed early Christians how to respond to trials (1:2ff). John's first epistle provides tests of fellowship—ways to gauge our walk with God (1:3, 6-7). Other writings cover different practical and theological topics: Ephesians and the Pastoral letters are examples. First Corinthians falls into this latter category. It is a practical letter dealing with a variety of specific, down-to-earth problems in the church at Corinth.

It is little wonder that, considering the moral and economic climate of Corinth in the first century, this letter is so applicable today. Corinth, with its commercial status, its religious variations, its preoccupation with sex, its emphasis on sports and leisure, its love of knowledge, and its judicial system, has much in common with our modern world. The Christian minister who desires to be both faithful to God's Word and relevant to modern society will find much to draw from in this letter. Parenthetically, this may also explain why, with the possible exception of Acts, no other New Testament book has been more picked apart, "proof-texted," and misused as much as 1 Corinthians. Fringe religious groups often look to this letter for support.

THE SETTING OF 1 CORINTHIANS

There is little doubt—even among the most liberal theologians and critics—that 1 Corinthians was written by Paul. Early external evidence is compelling (Mare, 179). The letter also shows every sign of being original and unified, not a compilation of writings. Its seemingly unrelated subjects are tied together by a fairly transparent historical context which can be largely reconstructed from details provided in the letter itself, and from the Book of Acts.

The relevant facts, with scriptural source, are these:

1. Paul visited and evangelized Corinth following his 'Macedonian Call' during his second missionary journey (Acts 18:1-17).
2. After leaving Corinth, Paul wrote a letter back to the fledgling church, the letter referred to in 1 Corinthians 5:9 (this letter is lost).
3. Subsequently—perhaps after arriving in Ephesus during his third missionary journey—Paul became aware of three things concerning the Christians in Corinth:
   a. They did not understand some things he wrote in his first letter (see 5:9-11);
   b. There were divisions in the church (as informed by Chloe's people; see 1:11);
   c. Members of the assembly had specific questions (see 7:1; these may have been brought by Stephanus, Fortunatus, and Achaicus; see 16:17).
   d. As a result, while in Ephesus (cf. 16:8)—from where he was forced to leave prematurely (cf. Acts 19:23-20:1)—Paul wrote this letter (sometime in 55 or 56 A.D.). Stephanus, Fortunatus, and Achaicus are as likely as any to have delivered the letter to Corinth (see 1 Cor. 16:18b).

Other factors are debated. Some think Paul's 'sorrowful visit' (2 Cor. 2:1; 12:14; 13:1-2) preceded the writing of 1 Corinthians (Findlay, 736-38; Orr/Walther, 129); most think it followed. Some equate the 'sorrowful letter' (2 Cor. 2:4; 7:8-9) with 1 Corinthians, but most view it as a later non-extant epistle. 2 Corinthians was probably written after this 'sorrowful letter,' and followed by Paul's visit to Corinth on his way to Jerusalem for the last time (Acts 20:4).

In summary, then, we approach this letter as Paul's instruction and exhortation to believers in the local church context concerning theological and practical problems.

THE PURPOSE OF 1 CORINTHIANS

Because it contains teaching on a variety of subjects, 1 Corinthians does not lend itself to a single statement of purpose. Indeed, few commentators even attempt one. Rather, Paul's purpose is often equated with instruction on the problems in Corinth—to confront divisions, depravity, and other difficulties in the church. Added to this are other sub-purposes; to clarify the gospel, to affirm his apostolic authority, and to instruct the Corinthians on personal freedom and spiritual gifts. While these describe the contents of the epistle, they do not provide a cohesive statement of Paul's purpose. Did Paul have a broad design in writing this epistle—and if so, what was it?

Lowery (506) suggests that Paul wrote this letter "to make positional sanctification practical." No doubt this is true, yet one wonders if it is not too general. A helpful purpose statement should be concise and precise. To this end, it is first clear from a topical overview of the letter's contents that Paul wrote to *provide instruction promoting Christian unity and moral purity.* Sometimes this instruction is *based on and motivated by believers' common spiritual heritage in Christ.* This theme is found in Paul's introductory comments concerning the Corinthian believers' blessings (1:4-9), his discussion of the gospel (1:17-25; 15:1-11), his recounting of the circumstances surrounding their conversion (1:26-2:5; 4:14f), and his repeated appeal to their spiritual wealth (2:12f; 3:16,21-23; 5:7f; 6:3,11,15,19f; 8:6; 10:1-4,6,11,13; 11:23-26; 12:4-30; 15:11,20-28; 51-57). Paul's instruction is also *based on and motivated by believers' future spiritual accountability before Christ.* This is seen in his repeated allusions and specific references to future judgment (cf. 1:8; 3:8, 10-17; 4:1-5; 5:5; 6:9ff, 14; 7:29; 9:24-27; 13:12; 15:32, 58; note also references to past (10:5-10) and present (7:32, 34f; 9:17f, 23; 10:12; 11:19, 30f) judgment).

The purpose of 1 Corinthians may thus be stated: *To provide instruction promoting Christian unity and moral purity based on and motivated by a reminder to believers of their common spiritual heritage in Christ and their future spiritual accountability before Christ.*

THE CONTENT OF 1 CORINTHIANS

Paul's instruction in this letter can be summarized as his responses to two types of prompting from the church in Corinth. In the first half of the letter (1:10-6:20), he responds to problems in the congregation about which he has been informed. In the second half of the letter, he responds to questions from the congregation which he has been sent, each successive topic denoted by an introductory Περι δε (*peri de,* "Now concerning"; 7:1; 8:1; 12:1; 16:1) or δε (*de,* "Now"; 11:2; 15:1) in Greek. A basic outline of the letter is as follows:

I. Introductory Salutation and Thanksgiving (1:1-9)

II. Disorders in the Church Reported to Paul (1:10-6:20)

    A. Divisions in the Church (1:10-4:21)

    B. Depravity in the Church (5:1-6:20)

III. Difficulties in the Church Raised to Paul (7:1-15:58)

    A. Questions Concerning Marriage are Discussed (7:1-40)

    B. Questions Concerning Christian Liberty are Discussed (8:1-11:1)

    C. Questions Concerning Public Worship are Discussed (11:2-34)

    D. Questions Concerning Spiritual Gifts are Discussed (12:1-14:40)

    E. Questions Concerning the Resurrection are Discussed (15:1-58)

IV. Concluding Responses, Comments, Exhortations, and Salutation (16:1-24)

AIDS FOR INTRODUCTORY AND BACKGROUND STUDY OF CORINTH AND 1 CORINTHIANS

In addition to Bible dictionaries, Bible Encyclopedias, and any other books dealing with the times, the following specified sources provide valuable background information for a study of this letter.

Barrett, C.K. *A Commentary on the First Epistle to the Corinthians* (New York: Harper & Row, 1968), pp. 1-29.

Bruce, F.F. *New Testament History* (Garden City, N.Y.: Doubleday & Company, Inc., 1980), pp.314-326.

Fee, Gordon D. *The First Epistle to the Corinthians* (Grand Rapids, Mich.: William B. Eerdmans Publishing Company, 1987), pp. 1-23.

Findlay, G.G. *The First Epistle of Paul to the Corinthians* (London, 1900), in The Expositor's Greek Testament, 5 vols., ed. W. Robertson Nicoll (Grand Rapids, Mich.: William B. Eerdmans Publishing Company, 1980 reprint), 2:729-754.

Guthrie, Donald. *New Testament Introduction*, 3rd ed. (rev.) in one vol. (Downers Grove, Ill.: Inter-Varsity Press, 1970), pp. 421-449.

Mare, W. Harold. *1 Corinthians* in The Expositor's Bible Commentary, 12 vols., Gen. ed. Frank E. Gaebelein (Grand Rapids, Mich.: Zondervan Publishing House, 1976), 10:175-87.

Orr, William F. and Walther, James Arthur. *I Corinthians*, The Anchor Bible (New York: Doubleday, 1976), pp. 1-131, esp. 81-83, 118-122.

Tenney, Merrill C. *New Testament Times* (Grand Rapids, Mich.: William B. Eerdmans Publishing Company, 1965), pp. 268-277.

COMMENTARIES REFERRED TO IN THIS STUDY

Barrett, C.K. *A Commentary on the First Epistle to the Corinthians* (New York: Harper & Row, 1968).

Bruce, F. F. *1 and 2 Corinthians* (The New Century Bible Commentary) (London: Marshall, Morgan, and Scott, 1971).

Calvin, John. *Commentary on the Epistles of Paul the Apostle to The Corinthians*, trans. by the Rev. John Pringle (Calvin's Commentaries, Vol. XX; 2 vols. in one: 1 Cor. 1 through 14, and 1 Cor. 15 through 2 Cor. 13) (Grand Rapids: Baker Book House, 1979, reprint).

Conzelmann, Hans. *1 Corinthians* (Hermeneia) (Philadelphia: Fortress Press, 1969).

Fee, Gordon D. *The First Epistle to the Corinthians* (Grand Rapids, Mich.: William B. Eerdmans Publishing Company, 1987).

Findlay, G.G. *The First Epistle of Paul to the Corinthians* (London, 1900), in The Expositor's Greek Testament, 5 vols., ed. W. Robertson Nicoll (Grand Rapids, Mich.: William B. Eerdmans Publishing Company, 1980 reprint), 2:727-953.

Grosheide, F.W. *The First Epistle to the Corinthians* (Grand Rapids, Mich.: William B. Eerdmans Publishing Company, 1953).

Hodge, Charles. *Commentary on the First Epistle to the Corinthians* (Grand Rapids, Mich.: William B. Eerdmans Publishing Company, reprinted 1976).

Ironside, H.A. *Addresses on the First Epistle to the Corinthians* (Neptune, N.J.: Loizeaux Brothers, 1938).

Kistemaker, Simon J. *Exposition of the First Epistle to the Corinthians*, New Testament Commentary (Grand Rapids: Baker Books, 1993).

Lowery, David K. *1 Corinthians* in The Bible Knowledge Commentary, 2 vols., Eds. John F. Walvoord and Roy, B. Zuck (Wheaton: Victor Books, 1983), 2:505-549.

MacArthur, John F. *1 Corinthians*, The MacArthur New Testament Commentary (Chicago: Moody Press, 1984).

Mare, W. Harold. *1 Corinthians* in The Expositor's Bible Commentary, 12 vols., Gen. ed. Frank E. Gaebelein (Grand Rapids, Mich.: Zondervan Publishing House, 1976), 10:173-297.

Martin, Ralph P. *The Spirit and the Congregation: Studies in 1 Corinthians 12-15* (Grand Rapids: William B. Eerdmans Publishing Company, 1984).

Morris, Leon, *The First Epistle of Paul to the Corinthians* (London: The Tyndale Press, 1958).

Orr, William F. and Walther, James Arthur. *I Corinthians*, The Anchor Bible (New York: Doubleday, 1976).

Wilson, Geoffrey B. *1 Corinthians, A Digest of Reformed Comment* (Edinburgh: The Banner of Truth Trust, 1978).

ABBREVIATIONS FOR COMMONLY CITED WORKS

BAGD W. Bauer, W.F. Arndt, F.W. Gingrich, F. Danker, *Greek-English Lexicon of the New Testament* (2nd ed., Chicago, 1979).

CrT "Critical Text," a designation for Greek New Testaments which generally follow in the Wescott-Hort textual tradition. These include *Novum Testamentum Graece*, by E. Nestle and K. Aland (26th ed.), and the United Bible Societies Greek New Testament (3rd ed.).

DNTT Colin Brown, ed. *The New International Dictionary of New Testament Theology*, 3 vols. (Grand Rapids: Zondervan, 1975).

MajT Zane C. Hodges and Arthur L. Farstad, eds. *The Greek New Testament According to the Majority Text* (2nd ed., Nashville: Thomas Nelson, 1985).

NASB New American Standard Bible

NEB New English Bible

NIV New International Version

NKJV New King James Version

I CORINTHIANS

COMMENTARY

I

INTRODUCTORY GREETING AND THANKSGIVING (1:1-9)

1-3   *Paul's opening greeting describes both author and audience and gives a salutation.*

1   Paul's opening self-identification is important, as he reminds his readers of the position of authority from which he writes, *an apostle* (ἀπόστολος; 12:28, 29) *of Jesus Christ*. This standing will be called upon repeatedly as he strongly confronts the Corinthian Christians concerning their church problems (e.g. 5:5). Evidently they had lost some of their respect for the position of apostle (4:6-13), but Paul here claims it as his authority in writing to them. That Paul is referring to the office of an apostle and not simply a "messenger" (cf. Phil. 2:25) is clear from the adjective "called" (κλητὸς; cf. Rom. 1:1). A less aesthetic but more accurate translation (than NIV, NKJV) of this phrase is, "…a called apostle of Jesus Christ" (not simply one who is called an apostle; cf. 15:9). Paul took his office and its responsibilities seriously; in all but one of his letters (Philippians) he makes a point of referring to it.

The phrase *by the will of God* refers to God's *sovereign* will, by which Saul was converted on the Damascus Road, became Paul, and went from persecuting Christians as a representative of the synagogue to proclaiming Christ in the synagogue (Acts 9:1-22)! Paul's authority comes from his divinely originated vocation as an apostle of Jesus Christ.

Sosthenes is, quite probably, the former leader of the synagogue (Acts 18:17) who was beaten by Greeks following the Jews' failed attempt to indict Paul before Gallio. At that time he was probably the one seeking to bring charges, but Paul's ministry in Corinth had a dramatic effect on that city—especially on the Jews. His "ministry headquarters" next door to the synagogue in the house of Titius Justus (Acts 18:7) is one sign, and the conversion of Crispus, Sosthenes' predecessor in the office, is another (Acts 18:8)!

2   Paul's descriptions of his audience is pointed and precise. They are *the church of God which is at Corinth* (ἐκκλησία here is not a reference to the universal church, but the local assembly of

believers), *sanctified in Christ Jesus* ("set apart" to be holy; cf. 6:11; clearly this refers to "positional" sanctification—they are 'saved' (1:30)—not "progressive" sanctification!), *saints by calling* (i.e., called-by-God saints; the NIV/NKJV translation "called to be holy/saints" is needlessly interpretive), and finally, they are among those *in every place who call upon the name of our Lord Jesus Christ* (i.e., part of the Universal Church). Paul could hardly be clearer; he is writing to redeemed individuals.

Paul's inclusion of the members of the Corinthian church in the universal body of believers (*their [Lord] and ours*) is purposeful. Some in the Corinthian congregation were independent—wanting to go their own way, disregarding other churches (see 4:17; 11:16; 14:33, 36; the entire discussion on gifts and their purpose to meet the *mutual needs* of the body in ch.12 reflects the prideful independence of some in Corinth). So Paul gives them "a gentle nudge to remind them that their own calling to be God's people belongs to a much larger picture" (Fee, 33).

Theological Note: Lordship Salvation theology views works as 'validation' that "professing believers" are really saved (no good works, no salvation). For Paul, such a view was ridiculous. The members of the Corinthian church are redeemed individuals, but as we will see, Paul indicts them for their spiritual immaturity (see especially 3:1-3; their lives showed little or no difference from the unsaved). Yet Paul pointedly states that they "call upon the name of our *Lord* Jesus Christ, their [*Lord*] and ours." The same *Lord* who Paul, Sosthenes, and Christians everywhere call on is the one the Corinthians call on. They were Christians, not because of the works they did, but because of Christ's work for them (1:4-9).

---

3   This is Paul's customary salutation, but hardly meaningless. For Paul, God's *grace* is His freely giving to His creation, something He loves to do (cf. Matt. 7:7-11; Jas. 1:17f), and something He did supremely in Jesus Christ. True *peace* is also something given by God, and supremely so in Christ Jesus; it was announced at

His birth (Luke 2:14), and is a benefit of His grace (Phil. 4:7; Col. 3:15). The deity of Christ is implicit in His cooperation with the Father in providing grace and peace.

Homiletical Ideas

The opening greetings of Paul's epistles provide an excellent beginning point for a series, with clues to issues within the letter which can be applied to a contemporary setting (e.g., the authority of Paul as an apostle points to the authority of God's Word; the Corinthian Christians' need to see themselves as part of the wider Body of Christ is also a need in many in-grown churches today; grace and peace are *always* subjects Christians need to be reminded about.

Another way to begin an expository series on this letter would be to give a dramatic monologue as Sosthenes. His story could be used to tell of the corruptness of Corinthian society, Paul's ministry there (and his conversion), and how he came to be with Paul in Ephesus as this letter was written (you would have to "fill in the blanks" here).

4-9 *Paul gives thanks for the effects of God's grace in the lives of the Corinthian believers.*

4-7 [Paul gives thanks for God's gracious supply of spiritual gifts to the Corinthians (4-7).]

4 Paul's customary *I thank my God always concerning you* is never mere form, but especially not so here. Paul calls himself their "father" (4:15; 15:1), and views them as his work (9:1; the *field* he planted [3:6-9a], the *building* or *temple* he built [3:9b-17]). They were, to Paul, "the seal of my apostleship in the Lord" (9:2). Like a cantankerous child—intractable, obdurate, yet still loved by his father—the Corinthians were always on Paul's mind. This is a poignant picture of the bond between a caring evangelist and his converts—and exhibits the emotions which drive true discipleship.

Paul's thanksgiving is for *the grace of God which was given you in Christ Jesus,* the pertinent details and description of which follow. It is notable that Paul thanks God only for those things which God has given, and for *His* faithfulness. But even so, it is surprising that Paul thanks God for some of the very things which were causing upheaval in the Corinthian church (speech, gifts). Obviously, Paul sees the problem not in the gifts themselves, but in the abuse of those gifts. His way of expressing thanks is not frivolous or dishonest, but sincere.

Lexical Note: Grace (χάρις; see BAGD, 885-86) is something inherently given freely, as meanings like *favor, gracious care/help, goodwill, gift, thanks,* and *gratitude* show. There was no other way for the grace of God to reach those who needed it. The efforts by many to earn such grace is a reflection of ignorance concerning the meaning of the word. (It is also logically absurd.)

5   This grace is evidenced firstly in that they were *enriched.* Although correct to think spiritually when encountering this word, we may undervalue its significance. The idea is that God has given us immense wealth (πλουτίζω; BAGD, 674) *in Him* (Jesus Christ). The term often denotes a financial object (cf. Gen. 14:23). Josephus writes of Herod making his sister Salome "very rich" (*Ant.* 17.147). Would that Christians responded to the eternal riches freely given by God with the same enthusiasm with which they chase temporal riches which only corrupt.

The Corinthians had been enriched *in all speech* (λόγος) *and all knowledge* (γνῶσις). These terms are probably a pointed allusion to the many special gifts with which God had blessed the Corinthian church (Fee, 41). But the Corinthians, who were prideful about these abilities, would quickly be brought down by Paul's initial distinction in the body of the letter between clever speech and foolish preaching (1:17-18), and between worldly wisdom and the foolishness of God (1:19-25).

6   The conjunction καθὼς (*even as*) suggests a parallel between enriched speech and knowledge and *the testimony concerning Christ* being *confirmed* (βεβαιόω). Perhaps the reference is to the special abilities being confirmation of God's presence in their lives, showing the indwelling Spirit (cf. Rom. 8:9). While noting their special gifts of speech and knowledge, however, Paul does not limit them to that.

7   The testimony of Christ was confirmed among the Corinthian believers by the embarrassing riches poured out on them, so that they were *not lacking in any gift!* If ever there was an evidence that spiritual riches do not guarantee spiritual success, this is it! The spiritual gifts they were not lacking are those listed in 12:8-10 and 28. Paul here states in a negative way what he has said positively in v.5; the Corinthian believers had been greatly enriched as a result of the grace of God which was given them in Christ Jesus.

In the second half of the verse, Paul's focus begins to change. He gives thanks that, by the grace of God, the Corinthians are *awaiting eagerly the revelation of our Lord Jesus Christ.* Even if the believers in Corinth were not as ready to meet the Lord as Paul would like (cf. 4:8; 15:12), he seeks to awaken this hope in them. Perhaps he wanted to use ἀποκάλυψις (revelation) to remind his readers that whatever other revelations or disclosures of God they had already received, and which they highly valued, would be eclipsed by the future appearing of Jesus Christ.

8-9   [Paul gives thanks for God's gracious promise to keep the Corinthian believers to the end (8-9).]

8   In Jesus Christ, the believer is secure to the end. Paul repeats βεβαιοω (*confirm*; cf. v.6) to denote that just as their spiritual gifts were sure signs of God's gracious enrichment, so too that grace would keep them *to the end.* [The NIV rendering "keep you strong" gives the wrong impression here; this is communicated by the Gk. στηριζω in similar contexts (Rom. 1:11; 1 Thess. 3:2, 13; 2 Thess. 2:17; 3:3).] In Christ, our standing before God is clear: We are *blameless.* This will be our standing *in the day of our*

Lord Jesus Christ, a reference to the coming Day of the Lord, and the judgment which will then be realized (cf. Mt. 24:30f; 26:64). It is this coming judgment of Christ which is repeatedly seen as the motivation for the preaching of the gospel in the New Testament (Acts 10:42f; 2 Tim. 4:1f; 1 Pet. 4:5f).

9   Why are the Corinthian believers secure? Certainly not because of their stellar spiritual testimonies! Not because of their exhibited spiritual maturity! And not because of their gifts. No. It is because of the grace of the *God* who *is faithful*.

Believers have been *called* (aorist passive of the verb καλέω here, unlike the adjectives in vv.1-2 above) by God *into fellowship with His Son, Jesus Christ our Lord*. This "fellowship" (κοινωνία) is 1) that positional relationship which comes by virtue of being saved, and also 2) that progressive walk which is available to all who are in Christ. But there is yet another aspect; 3) that fellowship which is available uniquely between believers growing together in the Body of Christ. While all three may be represented in Paul's meaning here, he certainly is giving thanks for the first, exhorting them to experience the second, and—in the verses which follow—dealing with a lack of the third.

Homiletical Ideas

Sermons on the content of biblical prayers are always good, reminders of those matters which should fill the prayers of Christians in every generation. Paul's thanksgiving here is for 1) the giftedness of believers, and 2) the security of believers. The grace gifts of God, as great as they are, are not as great as the gift of salvation; for the Corinthians, they were evidence that they had been enriched in Christ. The use of spiritual gifts by believers can be a living testimony to the presence and working of Christ in our day. However, the presence of gifts is no guarantee of spiritual success; in fact, Paul implicitly exhorts his readers to use their gifts to confirm God's working in them in light of the coming day of the Lord, and to live in fellowship with one another.

II

DISORDERS IN THE CHURCH REPORTED TO PAUL (1:10-6:20)

A. DIVISIONS IN THE CHURCH (1:10-4:21)

In these chapters, Paul confronts divisions within the Corinthian church, and shows that this problem is a result of some fundamental misunderstandings. They misunderstood the gospel, thinking it to be the highest human wisdom, instead of recognizing it as the 'foolishness of God' which is wiser than the wisdom of men! They also misunderstood the apostolic messengers, treating them as orators in a speech contest, or as power-brokers looking for the top spot. Paul declares that those preaching the gospel and building up the Body are God's servants—each one a part of God's growth program for the Church.

10-17 *The presence of divisions in the Corinthian church was contrary to Paul's ministry there.*

10   The translation of Paul's opening verb is understated in the NASV ("Now I *exhort* you"). The NIV improves this to "I *appeal* to you." Better yet is the NKJV: "Now I *plead* with you." Παρακαλῶ, while capable of each translation, is best given its full weight in important contexts (see Rom. 12:1; 2 Cor. 5:20). Paul is *earnestly imploring*, even *begging* (BAGD, 617) the Corinthians to heed his words. The emotional rendering is justified by his extended response to this problem.

The seriousness of Paul's exhortation here is emphasized by the phrase *by* (δια) *the name of our Lord Jesus Christ.* Paul used this to add weight to a command (2 Thess. 3:6), and here does so with an appeal (since a command to unity, which presupposes the willful agreement of the warring parties, would be senseless). What Paul says comes not only with apostolic authority, but through Jesus Christ. Christ, of course, is not and cannot be divided (1:13). Perhaps Paul is referring to Jesus' earthly teaching (cf. John 13:34f; 15:12-17; 17:20-23), which he may have heard about from the Apostle John himself (cf. Gal. 2:9). Beyond this, however, his personal meeting with the risen Christ and instruction by the Spirit (Gal. 1:16f) would be enough. In 7:6, 10, 12, 25, and 40, Paul carefully distinguishes between his own teaching and the Lord's—both carrying the weight of Scripture, but for the sake of Paul's audience, the addition of the name of Jesus Christ served to secure authority.

The content of Paul's exhortation is threefold (denoted by three subjunctives, λέγητε, ἦ, and ἦτε). First, he admonishes them to *all agree* ('to speak the same;' cf. NKJV), or say the same thing (λέγητε πάντες), something they were not known for (1:11). How ironic that these highly gifted (in speech, 1:5!) Christians should need to be exhorted to quit using their gift as a tool to dissect the body. With their oratorical skill, one can only wonder what verbal exchanges accented their disagreements (cf. Jas. 3:9f).

Secondly, there are to *be no divisions* (σχίσματα) *among you*. While harmonious speech (cf. the NIV's interpretive "so that") might help prevent divisions, Paul's appeal here stands on its own. There will always be differences, but there should not be divisions. Paul's only other uses of this term in his epistles are in this letter (11:18 and 12:25). In 11:18ff, the different factions resulted in an inability to have united worship at the Lord's Table. In 12:25, divisions are the source of a lack of care for (μεριμνάω, being concerned about) one another. Both these results are mortal wounds to the functioning of the local body. Remove worship and fellowship, and teaching becomes a dead-end street to head knowledge and pride (8:1).

Thirdly, the Corinthians are to (instead of arguing and being divided; δε) *be made complete* (κατηρτισμένοι) *in the same mind and in the same judgment*. The NKJV/NIV "perfectly joined/united" is acceptable, though not so literal. This verb is used to describe the *mending* of nets (Matt.4:21), and is figuratively applied to the mending of lives (cf. Gal. 6:1). Luke used it to refer to a pupil being *fully trained* (Luke 6:40). Taking these technical uses into consideration, Paul's idea may be that his readers should "mend" (put in order) and "train" their minds, so that instead of focusing on differences and judging one another, they will preserve and nurture unity.

11   Paul adds that he has *been informed...by Chloe's people* (ὑπὸ τῶν χλόης). Who are these people? It is likely (see Fee, 54), in light of the factions within the Corinthian church, that these 'informants' were Christians living in Ephesus who were employed by Chloe, a wealthy Asian woman who had business dealings in Corinth. On business in Corinth they would have visited the church, and been known to the Christians there. As outsiders, they would have been able to give Paul an unbiased picture of what was going on in the congregation.

The indictment is *that there are quarrels* (ἔριδες) *among you.* The charge is a serious one: Paul identifies quarrels as a mark of carnality (3:3), and includes it in his lists of vices (cf. Rom. 1:29; etc.).

12   The factions in the Corinthian church identified themselves under the names of different 'leaders.' Whatever prompted their divisions, each group claimed a leader by which to identify themselves, a leader who, for some reason, could be made the standard-bearer for their cause. Whether or not the various groups formed 'cliques' is not clear, but they were clearly "taking sides" with, or claiming to be in accord with, Paul, Apollos, Peter, or Christ.

13   Three impossibilities show the absurdity of divisions in the church. Each question in this verse demands a strong negative response.

The first question is: *Has Christ been divided?* This does not refer to the possibility of Christ being physically divided, or even the Church as the Body of Christ being divided (since Corinth itself showed that divisions do exist in the Body). The question was: *Is Christ the Messiah of only part of the Church? Is Christ to be put on a par with others as church leaders?* Absurd! Christ, of course, is over the whole church.

The verb (μερίζω, to divide, apportion; in the middle voice, it means "to share") is a perfect middle/passive. The tense is correctly rendered by "Has Christ been divided?" (NASV), but the emphasis on present results of past action (perfect tense) is implicit, making the translation "Is Christ divided?" (NIV/NKJV) also possible. The ambiguity between middle and passive allows for some play in the meaning; certainly Christ hasn't been divided, neither is he distributed like shares to groups of believers. And finally, He shares His sole authority and headship over the church with no one!

How can anyone put a man—even Peter or Paul—on a par with the Savior? Paul drives home this fact in the two remaining questions. *Paul was not crucified for you, was he? Or were you baptized in the name of Paul?* The use of the particle μη ("not") *requires* a negative response: *Of course* Paul was not crucified, nor was he the one in whose name they were baptized (*water* baptism, as the following verses make clear). While Paul played a significant role in their spiritual birth and growth (cf. 4:14f), he is a minister of Christ (4:1), and only one of many through whom God is causing growth (3:6f).

> **Theological Note:** Some commentators have suggested that the joint references to crucifixion and baptism here show that water baptism is the means of appropriating the work of the cross—of getting saved. This is not taught here or elsewhere in the New Testament. The context (v.17) clearly shows that in Paul's mind baptism was not tied to justification *in any way*. His great relief at not having baptized many in Corinth, while he clearly claims to have "fathered" them through the gospel into faith (4:15), shows his distinction between the two.

14   Paul could not be accused of creating a following among the Corinthian Christians: *I thank God* (εὐχαριστῶ τῷ θεῷ; cf. 1:4) *that I baptized none of you...!*

> **Textual Note:** The NIV follows the Alexandrian manuscripts Aleph and B in omitting τω θεω here, but the divided Alexandrian witness (A and C include it) coupled with MajT endorsement is weightier (cf. NKJV/NASV).

On Crispus, cf. Acts 18:8; on Gaius, cf. Rom. 16:23.

15 The Corinthians may have viewed baptism as having some spiritual significance or power (see 10:1-6; 15:29), and that this benefit resulted from the one doing the baptizing. The fact that Paul baptized only a few is intended to quell this idea once and for all.

16 Paul's almost careless *Beyond that, I don't remember if I baptized anyone else* (NIV), puts water baptism into its proper place in relation to the death of Christ on the cross and believing the gospel. In comparison to those, it is insignificant. This becomes even more transparent in v.17.

If the Stephanas mentioned here is the same one referred to in 16:17, perhaps Paul's memory was jogged as he wrote. Paul is not saying that baptism is *unimportant*; but in the present context, it clearly is immaterial to him.

Theological Note: The question of infant baptism is raised by some because of the reference to the *household* (οἶκον) of Stephanas. But this cannot be supported from the text. To be blunt, neither this verse, nor any New Testament reference, ever teaches infant baptism. Just as Acts 16:31 does not teach that an entire family including infants are saved by virtue of the father's faith (but only those who believe), neither does this verse infer that the whole family including infants were baptized (but only those who were ready for baptism). See Fee, 62, n.72.

---

17 A pivotal verse: Paul sums up his comments about baptism by affirming that it was not his divine mandate. *For Christ did not send me to baptize, but to preach the gospel.* Paul is an Apostle of Christ (1:1), sent by Him (ἀπέστειλέν) to preach the gospel (εὐαγγελίζεσθαι). But as he 'closes the book' on baptism, Paul takes the opportunity to introduce a major source of the Corinthians' divisiveness.

The Corinthians loved wisdom—the earthly variety. They were Greeks, with a heritage of philosophers like the world had never known, and they wanted the preaching of the gospel to be accepted alongside this earthly wisdom. But they needed to cling to the apostolic gospel, the message of the cross, which was diametrically opposed to the wisdom of the world (1:18-25). Paul transitions into this critical discussion by adding that he preached the gospel *not in cleverness of speech* (σοφία λόγου; lit. "wisdom of word/speech"); he will distinguish between man's wisdom and God's wisdom later (2:6ff).

In down-playing the verbal skill and intellectual acumen with which he preached the gospel (cf. 2:4), Paul puts the preacher of the gospel in proper perspective. It's not that preaching the gospel is unimportant; just the opposite is true (see Rom. 10:14-15; 2 Tim. 4:1-2)! Paul's point is that in preaching the gospel, what matters is *not* how dynamic, educated, or golden-tongued a preacher may be, but the *content* of the message! In evangelism, each is a servant of Jesus Christ (4:1), and the 'preaching of the cross' is what changes lives, *not* the oratorical skills of the preacher.

Most significant here is the final phrase: *that the cross of Christ should not be made void* (NASV). "Made void" (κενωθῇ) can mean to empty, destroy, or render of no effect (κενόω; BAGD, 428). For Paul, to preach the gospel in such a way that his preaching is what gets the praise would "make void"—'render of no effect' that preaching! The most graphic demonstration of Paul's meaning here is seen in his use of the same word in Phil. 2:7 of Christ emptying Himself in the incarnation. *To the same degree that the glory of God was veiled in Christ's earthly existence, so too the gospel is veiled when we allow our words to get in its way.*

The connection between the source of the wisdom and the words used is unavoidable. A gospel adorned with human wisdom and presented in flowing style may bring praise to the preacher, but it cannot but reduce the power of the gospel message, and distract people from believing in Christ. This is abhorrent to Paul. There are many gifted preachers whose messages, while well-written and spoken, have little power. They are "clouds without rain" (Jude 12). What matters is the clear presentation of the gospel, to which Paul now turns his attention.

Homiletical Ideas

The closing phrase of this paragraph provides a natural crescendo in a sermon; Paul is not going to get involved in church divisions, since they invariably do violence to the gospel. The ever-contemporary problem of church factions and cliques makes this passage extremely practical. A simple breakdown of this paragraph is:

1. Paul urges the Corinthian Christians to be united (10-11).
2. Paul shows that disunity results when church leaders are exalted alongside Christ (12-13).
3. Paul thanks God that in his ministry he has not promoted divisions in deed or word (14-17).

There are two ways Paul could have contributed to divisions. First, by creating a personal following in his deeds (here, baptizing converts, 14-17a), and secondly, by preaching the gospel in such a way that he drew attention to himself. He strongly asserts that he has never undermined the supremacy of Christ over the church through his actions, or muzzled the message of the gospel through his words.

Obviously, a number of potent and timely messages can be presented from this paragraph. For example, in a church where there is (or is the perception of) unity, since disunity is always only an opportunity away, it would be good to preach on *Signs of Unity in the Church,* or something more imaginative like *What Makes a Church Come Apart at the Seams?*

In a church where divisions have wounded the body, the emphasis needs to be on healing. A message on *Cures for a Broken Body*, or *How to Become One Again*, might be positive. Perhaps a light-hearted approach would help in a case of deeply entrenched divisions: *Humpty Dumpty and the Church* (trying to put all the pieces back together again), or *The Church Puzzle: One Picture, Many Pieces* (emphasizing how divisions in a church actually divide up Christ) might help. Always stress the Lordship of Jesus Christ over the Church, and the importance of individually and corporately being submissive to Him.

Paul has introduced the problem of divisions in the Corinthian church, made it clear that such schisms are unreasonable, and exhorted believers to unity (1:10-17). He has alluded to two misconceptions which contributed to their divisions. First, they misunderstood the significance of the messengers of the gospel (such as Paul, Apollos, and Peter), exalting and following them, thus diminishing the prominence and influence of Christ (1:12f). Secondly, they misunderstood the substance of the gospel message, thinking it could mesh with human wisdom, and that its effectiveness could be improved through eloquent delivery. In his response, Paul now sets about dismantling these two misconceptions (1:18-4:5).

He first gives instruction on the *message of the gospel* (1:18-3:4). This message is not the wisdom of man, but is diametrically opposed to human wisdom (1:18-2:5). It is, in fact, the *foolishness of God*, yet wiser than men! The *wisdom of God* is something only the spiritually mature can fully grasp (2:6-3:4).

In 3:5-4:5, Paul emphasizes that the *messengers of the gospel*, far from being placed alongside Christ or made objects of boasting and rival church factions, are actually all servants of Christ. They should never be compared and evaluated for honor by men, since such honor can and will only be given by Jesus Christ when He returns.

Paul's entire response can be outlined this way:

1.   The message of the gospel, Christ crucified, is the true wisdom of God (1:18-3:4).

      a.   The message of Christ crucified is a direct contrast to human wisdom (1:18-2:5).

      b.   The message of Christ crucified reveals the true wisdom of God (2:6-3:4).

  2.   The messengers of the gospel are Christ's servants and accountable to Him (3:5-4:5).

      a.   Messengers of the gospel are Christ's laborers, doing His work (3:5-9).

      b.   Messengers of the gospel will give account to Christ for their work (3:10-17).

      c.   Messengers of the gospel must avoid self-deceiving pride in their wisdom and the boasting of men (3:18-23).

      d.   Messengers of the gospel should not be rated by men, since they will be evaluated in the future by Christ (4:1-5).

We begin with Paul's response to confusion about the gospel message in 1:18-3:4. Paul wants us here to understand that 1) the message of Christ crucified is the antithesis of human wisdom (1:18-2:5), and 2) to those who accept it by faith, more of God's hidden wisdom may be revealed (2:6-3:4).

1:18-25 *The content of the message of Christ crucified is foolishness and weakness to the unbeliever, but the power and wisdom of God to the believer.*

18   Paul made a distinction (in v.17) between human wisdom and the message of Christ crucified, and now develops this theme. The Corinthians thought the gospel was compatible with human wisdom and could even be improved by it. Just the opposite is true! Paul's preaching was not *in cleverness of speech* (ἐν σοφίᾳ λόγου, v.17); it was *the word of the cross* which is *foolishness to those who are perishing*. This is the message the Corinthian Christians had believed and by which they were *being saved*. Nothing could be further from human wisdom; it was, in fact, *foolishness* (μωρία).

Why "foolishness"? Because it makes no sense to man! Why would God become a man, to save mankind? How do you gain victory over sin by taking sin on yourself? Who defeats death by dying? This message is foolishness to men, but it is the wisdom of God. Beyond this, the idea of salvation being totally free, the price paid for by God's own sacrifice, flies in the face of human 'common sense.' 'Man's way' involves *doing something* to earn salvation, to prove that we have it, to show that we deserve it. Salvation as a free gift to all who believe? "Nonsense," says the natural man; "That is foolishness!" The 'gospels' of this world require allegiance, time, effort, and sacrifice. *The hardest gospel for the natural man to believe is that a crucified Christ is the full payment for sin.* That is foolish.

On the contrary, for the believer the gospel *is the power of God.* A repeated theme is that the gospel is foolishness to the unsaved, but it is the wisdom of God to the saved (cf. vv.24, 30). Paul is contrasting what men do to the gospel, and what the gospel does to men. In the 'packaging' of human wisdom, the gospel is "emptied of its power" (v.17, NIV). But when it is proclaimed in its pristine splendor, it possesses the life-changing power of God. So while the pure gospel is foolishness to the world, it is the power of God to those who believe.

That which seems weak and foolish to the world is nothing to be ashamed of. One cannot help but echo Paul's words from Rom. 1:16:

> *For I am not ashamed of the gospel, for it is the power of God for salvation to everyone who believes, to the Jew first and also to the Greek.*

19 The phrase, *For it is written*, is Paul's way of introducing Old Testament proof of his assertion. He cites Isaiah 29:14, where Israel was guilty of making her religious worship a mere formality, a collection of traditions learned by rote. They were wise in their own eyes, secure in their own power, instead of trusting in the Lord. God declared He would *destroy* (ἀπόλλυμι) *the wisdom of the wise, and the cleverness of the clever* (the shrewdness and

insight of those who are wise in their own eyes; cf. σύνεσις and συνετός, BAGD, 788) He would *set aside* (thwart or confound; cf. ἀθετέω, BAGD, 21). The parallel with the situation in Corinth is transparent. The Corinthians need to see that their wisdom has no *part* in the gospel message.

Those who hold to human wisdom instead of (or alongside) the gospel will perish with their wisdom. In the wisdom of the world the message of the cross is foolish; yet by that message the wisdom of the world is destroyed.

20 In mocking tone, Paul challenges his readers to give evidence of human wisdom that echoes the gospel message. *Where is the wise man? Where is the scribe? Where is the debater of this age?* The brazenness of the challenge is reminiscent of Elijah on Mt. Carmel (1 Ks. 18:27) or Isaiah in his prophecy against Egypt (Isaiah 19:11f). In the effective message of the gospel, God has once and for all rendered the world's wisdom foolishness.

How ironic! The gospel message is foolishness to the wise in Corinthian society, yet through it *God* has *made foolish the wisdom of the world* (the final question implies a positive response). Why is this so?

21 Because (γαρ) *in the wisdom of God* [the wisdom which God possesses, His omniscience] *the world through its wisdom did not come to know God*. God has so ordered creation that human wisdom, on its own, does not and cannot lead to a knowledge of Himself.

The evidence is irrefutable. Mankind responded in his own wisdom in Eden; Satan promised Eve divine knowledge, but the result of The Fall was spiritual blindness. The way to salvation is not through human wisdom. This is not a denial of natural revelation which gives a knowledge of God (Rom.1:18ff), but an indictment of the heart of man which, when faced with that evidence, rejects it (Rom.1:21f, 25).

On the contrary, *God was well-pleased* (it seemed good to Him;

cf. εὐδοκέω, BAGD, 319) *through the foolishness of the message preached to save those who believe.*

22   The Jews had long considered themselves on the inside and Gentiles on the outside of God's blessing; both now search in vain for the answer in their traditions. It matters not what kind of intellectual satisfaction one looks for; the *Jews ask for signs* (Mt.12:38f) to interpret endlessly. The *Greeks search for wisdom* (Acts 17:21) to debate perpetually.

23   The message Paul preached was acceptable to neither standard. *To the Jews* it was *a stumbling block* (σκάνδαλον; a 'scandal;' cf. 1 Pet. 2:8). *To the Gentiles* it was *foolishness* (1:18, 21).

Why didn't God give these unbelievers what they were looking for? Is He in effect "hiding" the truth from them? Not at all. What sign could be clearer than the resurrection (cf. Mt. 12:40)? What wisdom could be higher than God's wisdom? The implicit message here is that unbelievers look for what they want to see and hear, not what God has revealed and spoken. The gospel, Paul says, simply is not geared for the wise and powerful of this world.

24   But *To those who are the called* (NASV best here; the term simply refers to those who have believed, not to those who have received some special invitation; vv.9, 21, 26; cf. Rom. 8:30), *both Jews and Greeks* (regardless of ethnic origin; cf. Eph. 2:11-22), the message of Christ crucified is the wisdom and power of God. It makes sense not because they were clever and 'figured it out,' but because they believed it. It is the power of God because it is from God—not man. "Christ crucified" (v.23) becomes *Christ the power of God and the wisdom of God* (v.24) to those who believe in Him.

25   Paul climaxes his argument with the paradoxical axiom in this verse. What Paul is saying is that God's way is *wiser than* man's way, and God's strength is *stronger than* human strength. But he says it in a way which would be more memorable to his audience.

After all, they had gotten the message wrong; they thought it sounded too preposterous, too wimpy, too foolish. They figured a little sprucing up would do it some good. But God didn't need their help; He did it His way—the only way it would work.

Thus played out before human eyes is the scandalous and contradictory wisdom of God. Had God consulted us for wisdom we could have given him a more workable plan, something that would attract the sign-seeker and the lover of wisdom. As it is, in his own wisdom he left us out of the consultation. We are thus left with the awful risk: trust God and be saved by his wise folly, or keep up our pretensions and perish. Better the former, because this "weakness of God is stronger than [human] strength;" it accomplishes that which all human pretensions cannot do. It brings one into "fellowship with his Son Jesus Christ our Lord" (v.9). (Fee, 77)

Homiletical Ideas

Every Christian who has shared the gospel knows that it can seem foolish to many unbelievers. Some Christians shy away from personal evangelism because they fear their message will not 'make sense'! Some have 'revised' the gospel message, adding conditions to faith. In the face of these difficulties and problems, this passage provides an excellent opportunity to communicate three things to the average believer:

1) To explain why the gospel, which makes perfect sense to the believer, makes no sense to the unsaved;
2) To warn believers not to change the gospel to make it more sensible to the unsaved, and to reject those who do;
3) To remind believers to faithfully share the gospel of Christ crucified, and leave the results to God.

1:26-31 *The message of Christ crucified is shown, through the lives of the Corinthian converts, to be the power and wisdom of God, not man.*

26   That the gospel is a direct contrast to human wisdom is first evident from the message itself; but it is also evident from the effects of that message in the lives of the Corinthian believers. Paul directs the Corinthians to *consider your calling*, to look back to their spiritual roots. If the gospel was something that jived with human wisdom and strength, how had it reached them? According to human standards (cf. σάρξ, BAGD, 744, 6.), the Corinthian Christians were not educated (*wise*) or powerful (*mighty*) or aristocratic (*noble*). They had no special standing. Yet they were the ones who received the gospel message. Why?

27-28   Because of God's already-explained plan, whereby the things that are wise and strong to this world are overturned by the things which *seem* weak and foolish to this world, but which are in reality God's wisdom and strength (v.21). *God has chosen the foolish things of the world* (a message foolish in the world's eyes) *to [put to] shame the wise* and reach those who are foolish. *God has chosen the weak things of the world to [put to] shame the things which are strong* and reach those who are weak. Finally, *the base things* ("insignificant;" cf. ἀγενής, BAGD, 8) *and the despised* ("of no account;" ἐξουθενέω, cf. 6:4) *God has chosen* to put to shame those who cling to them, and reach those who are outcasts. Of course, man wouldn't have done that, but this speaks volumes about God and His grace! Man would have put up a high standard, and only those who reached it would be saved. God puts the lowest standard—you have to give up (Rom.4:4f)!—so that all can reach it, but also so only those who recognize their need, instead of their own sufficiency, will receive it.

To put it another way, God chose *the things that are not, that He might nullify the things that are*. That is, He has chosen people and things that are not valued by the world to nullify (do away with, 6:13; 13:8, 10; set aside, 13:11; abolish, 15:24, 26; cf. καταργέω, MM, 331) the things that are valued by the world. Human wisdom and the message of Christ crucified are so in opposition to each other that when human wisdom is added to the gospel, it empties it of its power, but when the pure gospel is believed, it renders the wisdom of the world null and void.

The contrast between what the Corinthians *now* wrongly viewed as important and what they themselves *had been* when they responded to the gospel is clear. What they had been back then didn't measure up to their own standards now! In vv.26-28, they come up short in three categories. In the Corinthian circles of higher learning, they had not been considered wise, but foolish. In social influence, they were not powerful, but weak. And in the "gene stakes," the criterion of ancestry, they were not noble (lit. well-born), but despised. Obviously—and thankfully—the gospel was in no way tied to any human qualifications, efforts, pedigree, power, or intelligence. It was available to all, and thus, it had come to them as well.

29 Used as a conjunction, ὅπως means "so that" and expresses purpose. God ordered His plan of salvation so *that no man should boast before God* (cf. Eph. 2:9).

30 Rather, it is *by His doing* (NKJV "of Him" is literal but unclear) that we are in Christ Jesus. The meaning is that, in contrast to the world where 'you are what you make of yourself,' it is because of what God has done that we are who we are spiritually. And everything we are now, we are *in Christ Jesus.* (One cannot help but see an allusion back to Paul's introduction to the epistle here; in 1:4-9, as here, it is God who gets all the credit for what the Corinthians are and have, and it is all because they are in Christ.)

This verse explains, finally, how it is that when we believe the message of Christ crucified, that message suddenly changes from foolishness to wisdom. The answer? We are in Christ Jesus (cf. 2 Cor. 5:17). Now *His wisdom* has been imparted to us.

The content of this *wisdom* is *righteousness*, holiness (*sanctification*), *and redemption* (these three nouns should be read [as the NIV] in apposition to "wisdom from God" instead of in addition to it). Paul's message is this: In Jesus Christ, we have been made righteous, we have been made holy, we have been redeemed. These terms all point to the moment of salvation, when the wisdom of God became ours, and we, having experienced the fruits of that wise plan of God, now knew it to be true. For this reason, any boasting by the Corinthians in themselves had no foundation.

31 But if someone was to boast, the evidence allows only one object: The Lord. The quote comes from Jeremiah 9:23f, which reflects this passage beautifully:

> Let not the wise man boast of his wisdom or the strong man boast in his strength or the rich man boast of his riches, but let him who boasts boast about this: that he understands and knows me, that I am the Lord, who exercises kindness, justice and righteousness on earth, for in these I delight. (NIV)

God delights to show His wisdom and power in the lives of those who come to know Him through faith in Christ. Let us boast *only* in Him!

Homiletical Ideas

The gratitude of believers to God for their salvation is enhanced by a reminder of their hopeless and helpless condition before being saved. Far from being the "cream" of humanity, we see that we received God's grace only because He reached low! These verses are a reminder that "spiritual pride" has no place in the Christian life! We have one great eternal boast: "Praise God! Jesus saved me!"

2:1-5 *The message of Christ crucified is shown, through the preaching of Paul, to be empowered by God, not sourced in human wisdom.*

Paul began this section (1:18-2:5) by directing his audience to the *content* of the gospel message (1:18-25). The message of

Christ crucified had nothing to do with human wisdom, since to unsaved man, that message was foolishness! Only to those who accept the "foolish" message does it become the wisdom and power of God.

Paul then focused his pen on the *converts* of the gospel message (1:26-31). Again, the message of the gospel was clearly seen to have nothing to do with human wisdom; it found its most receptive audience among the lowly—the weak and unlearned, not the blue-bloods of society. In God alone could any convert boast!

In this final paragraph, Paul points to himself, the *communicator* of the gospel message. Here he finds further evidence that human wisdom is unrelated to the message of Christ crucified. His proof is his own preaching, which was not geared to woo listeners through dazzling logic or personal appeal, but through the person and work of Jesus Christ alone.

2:1   Paul's opening Κἀγὼ ("And I") is emphatic; he is introducing himself as the third proof of the incongruity between the message of the gospel and human wisdom. In v.26 he directed his readers back to the time of their conversion; he now directs them back to his preaching which led to that conversion. The way in which he presented the gospel message in no way exhibited human wisdom, but depended wholly on the power of God in the message.

Two ways Paul did *not* come to Corinth were *with superiority of speech or of wisdom* (ὑπεροχὴν λόγου ἢ σοφίας; lit. "prominence" of word or wisdom). Paul is saying that he did not come as a superior person to whom the Corinthian converts (who for the most part were not superior, 1:26) could not relate. He did not put himself—or allow others to put him—on a pedestal. The *way* he spoke (eloquence), and *what* he spoke (elevated reasoning) were not contrary to the foolish/weak message which God intended to reach foolish/weak people; Paul himself came bearing nothing but the foolish message and exhibiting weakness (2:3).

> **Textual Note:** The message of the gospel is here called *the testimony of God* (τὸ μαρτύριον τοῦ θεοῦ). Some early manuscripts (p⁴⁶אAC) read μυστήριον (*mystery* of God). Some see this as anticipating 2:7 (see the discussion there on this term), but this argument cannot be sustained. Both external textual (MajT, BDFG) and internal evidence (cf. 1:6) favor μαρτύριον (see Fee, 88, n.1).

2   Paul *determined* (an intentional decision; cf. κρίνω, BAGD, 452, 3.) *to know nothing* (i.e., to speak of nothing else) ...*except [the message of] Jesus Christ, and Him crucified* when he came to Corinth. Why? Of course, this was the message he had been called to preach (1:17). But also, his discouraging visit to Athens (cf. Acts 17:16-34), where he tried to present the gospel to the wise, and discerned that such a presentation did not help the cause of the gospel, may have contributed to his decision. Regardless, Paul chose not to concern himself with any other issues, but to be absolutely focused on the gospel.

3   Paul adds (κἀγώ; cf. v.1) that he is a 'walking exhibit' of the character of the gospel. First, he was weak (ἀσθένεια), not inferring timidity (BAGD, 114), but some physical problem (sickness or disease; cf. Gal. 4:13f; 2 Cor. 12:7) which affected him during his time in Corinth.

Second, he came *in fear and in much trembling*. According to Acts 18:9-10, after some time in Corinth, Paul was told by the Lord to "not be afraid any longer." What had caused his fear is unknown. Perhaps early in his ministry in Corinth, because of well-known converts like Crispus, the leader of the synagogue, there were threats on his life. Whatever the cause, his point is clear. His own behavior reflected well the character of the gospel—not that of the wise and powerful of Corinthian society.

4   Paul reiterates and expands on his previous assertion concerning his *message* and his *preaching* (cf. v.1), declaring that it was *not in persuasive words of wisdom*.

Interpretive Note: It could be argued that Paul is using excellent speech and persuasive argument to affirm that he did not use excellent speech and persuasive argument! Clearly, Paul is *not* saying that the gospel should be presented in poor speech and dissuasive arguments. He is confronting the mixture of the gospel with the popular rhetoric of the day. As this speech reflected the human wisdom of the world, it was to be avoided. Human wisdom voids the gospel (1:17) and does not lead to a knowledge of God (1:21); therefore, to mix any form of it with the gospel is counterproductive.

Instead of rhetoric, Paul's preaching was accompanied by a *demonstration* (ἀποδείξει; used only here in the NT; lit. *proof*) of the Spirit's power. What was this demonstration? It may have been something miraculous—some sign of his apostleship (cf. 2 Cor. 12:12), but in this context it probably refers to the conversion of the Corinthians, who were then greatly gifted by the Spirit. Paul did not need to rhetorically show the effectiveness of the gospel; what the Spirit did in those who heard and responded to it was more than enough proof of its power!

5   As in 1:26-31, Paul finishes this paragraph with a purpose clause (introduced by ἵνα). His reason for writing about his own ministry was so *that their faith should not rest on the wisdom of men, but on the power of God.* They must never waver between trusting in what God has done and what they themselves can do. From the beginning salvation has all been of God, not of man. They must never deviate from their total faith in the power of God.

Homiletical Ideas

These three paragraphs (1:18-2:5) are linked together by a common purpose—to show that the gospel message and human wisdom are incompatible. But under this umbrella they each introduce a different approach, and these three points provide a tailor-made mini-series on the gospel.

First, the content of the gospel message itself is foolishness to the unbelieving (1:18-25). A title like "Why Doesn't the Gospel Make Any Sense?" or "Why the Unsaved Think You're Nuts" might grab attention. The point is that God in His wisdom has made the gospel message foolishness to the wise of this world, so that it will appeal to all people—not just to those who are educated, and so that those who believe will not be tempted to think it was something they figured out on their own.

Second, the converts of the gospel message show it to be of God and not of man (1:26-31). The point to drive home is that Christians, of all people, should not think too highly of themselves; what we are, we are because of Christ, not because of ourselves. A title like "Who Do You Think You Are?" or "When It's OK to Boast" would fit with a message on this paragraph. On a lighter note, a title like "How Frank Sinatra and Christians are Different" might raise a few eyebrows; Sinatra sang "I did it my way;" for the Christian, the refrain must be, "I did it God's way."

Finally, the communicators of the gospel message show it to be of God and not of man (2:1-5). Here, the point to make is that the gospel is the one message that needs to be presented without anything to distract from it. The person going out to witness must not trust in his own wisdom or ability because he does not want his listeners to trust in his wisdom and ability! He should take the gospel of Christ crucified and nothing else, trusting in it as the power of God that can transform a life, and in so doing demonstrate that the faith of his hearers needs to be in Christ alone, too. A title like "Who Are You Trusting in?" or "How To Be A Persuasive Witness for Christ" might set the stage here.

There are other good messages within these paragraphs. For example, 1:21 provides the material for a message on God's love for the lowly of the world, and this being the reason He made believing the *only* condition of salvation. A title like "Jesus Loves the Little Children...and Other Fools" might get their attention. A doctrinal message answering the question "Why Does the World Think the

Gospel is Foolish?" might be good. Finally, an overview message of Paul's entire response could answer three related questions:

1) What is my message?
2) In what do I boast?
3) In whom am I trusting?

However you do it, preach this passage!

After three paragraphs emphasizing that the gospel message is *contrary* to human wisdom, Paul announces that he speaks wisdom—a mystery-wisdom reserved for the spiritually mature. Those who believe the gospel have received the Spirit of God, through whom they can know this wisdom. However, it is only for those who are spiritually mature, a fact which had prevented the Corinthian Christians from receiving it.

To summarize, Paul writes in 2:6-3:4 that the message of Christ crucified reveals the true wisdom of God. God's wisdom is hidden from men—no matter how wise they are (2:6-9), and this wisdom is only apprehended by those who have received the Spirit (2:10-13) and are spiritually mature (2:14-16). Paul calls the Corinthian church to spiritual unity by pointing out that their divisions are both the cause and an evidence of spiritual immaturity, which is keeping them from grasping God's wisdom (3:1-4). Paul is a master teacher and motivator here; after informing his readers that the gospel has nothing to do with human wisdom, he draws on the desire he knows they have for wisdom to encourage them to grow up spiritually.

2:6-9 *The true wisdom of God originates in God and is hidden from the world.*

6 Paul's opening phrase could hardly be more unexpected at this point! After so lengthy a section dedicated to showing the emptiness of human wisdom (1:17, 19, 20, 25, 27, 28; 2:1, 4a), especially with reference to spiritual matters (1:18, 21-24, etc.), his abrupt assertion that *we* (himself, and other spiritual leaders) *do speak wisdom* draws on his allusions to God's wisdom in the

previous section (1:21, 24, 30); unlike Corinthian wisdom which is merely human, Paul speaks a wisdom that is 'out of this world.' Literally, this wisdom is not of this age or of the rulers of this age (here possibly a general pejorative reference to worldly leaders, perhaps having great wisdom which the Corinthians treasured; in v.8, their wisdom is shown to be greatly limited). The final phrase links Paul's thought to the preceding context; God chose the "nothings" of this world to do away with the "somethings" (1:28). That is, those who are foolish/weak/base in the eyes of the world are the ones God has chosen; they are those who do not depend on their own wisdom/strength/status. Paul here equates the rulers of this age (and their wisdom) with those things which are being wiped out. They are being rendered powerless and ineffective; their day is passed (καταργέω, BAGD, 418).

Paul's reference to *the mature* (τοῖς τελείοις) anticipates his discussion beginning in 3:1. It is not that Paul has hidden truths which only a select few can understand, but that their spiritual immaturity prevents them from comprehending the wisdom which they should have known. The fact that they were side-tracked on human wisdom (which was coming to nothing) highlights this immaturity.

7   The contrast here is between the wisdom of this age and its rulers, which is temporal, and God's wisdom, which is secret and hidden from these worldly wise men, and is sourced in eternity.

What is meant by ἐν μυστηρίῳ ("in a mystery")? Certainly it means that this wisdom is something hidden. But the use of the term μυστηριον may indicate even more.

1) Paul uses μυστήριον to describe something hidden from man's knowledge until God wants it to be known. In many references (Rom. 11:25; 16:25; Eph. 1:9; 3:3f, 9; 6:19; Col. 1:26f; 2:2; 4:3), μυστήριον refers to the Gentiles being included in the Body of Christ, something God has accomplished through Jesus Christ which is now revealed through the agency of the Spirit (see v.10 below; cf. Eph.

3:5). Note: In dispensational theology, this 'mystery' is the dispensation of grace (the "times of the Gentiles;" cf. Luke 21:24; Rom. 11:25), the present age in which eternal life and its blessings—including union in the Body of Christ—is for Jews and Gentiles alike. This was not known to Old Testament prophets, though they prophesied its coming (cf. 1 Pet. 1:10-12), but it was disclosed in Christ and through the apostles (cf. Eph. 3:2-13). In favor of understanding μυστήριον here as alluding to the 'dispensation of grace' is (1) the discussion of the gospel in this context; (2) the Corinthians' need for unity, which the creation of the Body incorporates (notably between Jews and Gentiles; cf. Eph. 2:16; 3:4-6, 8-9; it is probable that some of the divisions in Corinth were exacerbated by racial tension, considering the strong Gentile and Jewish backgrounds of converts; cf. Acts 18:7f); and (3) the statement that *if they* (the rulers of this age) *had understood it* (God's hidden mystery), *they would not have crucified the Lord of glory* (cf. v.8 below; see also John 10:16; Acts 2:23; Rom. 11:12; they would not have crucified Him because they would not want to fulfill God's pre-determined plan and put the Messiah to death.)

2) God's wisdom is a mystery because it has been hidden since before time and even now is hidden from "the rulers of this age" (the wise).

3) God's wisdom is a mystery because it is from God. He determined before time to allow Christ to be crucified—it was His plan, hidden from men (cf. Acts 2:22-24). If they had known, they wouldn't have done it (v.8)!

4) Finally, God's wisdom is a mystery because it is foolishness to the world; it simply doesn't make sense (see above on 1:18).

8   This wisdom of God is that *which none of the rulers of this age has understood; for if they had... they would not have crucified the Lord of glory.* By seeking the wisdom of this world instead of God's wisdom, Corinthian Christians were joining themselves with

those who crucified Christ! Men looked at Christ in unbelief and saw a menace, not the Messiah, and crucified Him. Corinthian Christians, in contrast, had believed the message of Christ crucified. A return to human wisdom now was a contradiction of their faith in Jesus Christ, and a collapse back into the world out of which they had been saved.

9   Paul substantiates his point with a reference to Scripture. His text is unclear; most likely he is referring to parts of Isaiah 64:4 and 65:17, possibly from a collection of various Old Testament texts in use in Judaism. While not quoted from one passage, the material is sourced in Scripture, and its message is simple: Those in the world did not see, hear, or comprehend God's wise plan. What they are missing is *that God has prepared* a salvation *for those who love Him.*

Interpretive Note: This verse is often interpreted eschatologically. Although the terms themselves can be used in this way, the context does not lead to such a conclusion. Paul is talking about the wisdom of God which is unknown to the world, in which God planned the death of His Son to gain the salvation of mankind. The reference to those things which God has prepared (ἃ ἡτοίμασεν; cf. ἑτοιμάζω, BAGD, 316) is to *His wisdom* which has been and is only revealed by the Spirit.

Paul's argument is complete: True wisdom of God originates in Him and is hidden from the world. To be enamored with the world's wisdom is to follow that which is passing away. To know God's wisdom is to share in the benefits of that which God has planned since before time for those who love Him.

2:10-16 *The true wisdom of God is revealed by the Spirit of God to those who have received Him.*

10   In direct contrast to the *rulers of this age* who could not comprehend God's mystery, Paul and all the Christians in

Corinth *could*. But the emphasis is not on the people involved, but on the way that God has made His wisdom suitable to man. This answers the implicit question, "How?" That is, *how is it that the wise of this world do not comprehend the foolishness of God, but the Christians in Corinth—and Paul—do?* It is all because of the spiritual enabling of God. This is what *God has prepared* (9) and now revealed through the Holy Spirit.

Paul now presents a brief logical argument showing why spiritual knowledge can *only* be revealed by the Spirit. It is because only "like can know like." That is, since spiritual things are outside the natural realm, we are dependent on the Spirit to reveal such things to us. It was a similar point on which Jesus challenged Nicodemus to believe His witness (John 3:11-13). Paul subtly suggests here that those Corinthians who thought his message of Christ crucified was "foolish" should take note; these are the *deep things* of God!

11   This should come as no surprise. Human experience is no different. The only one who can truly know what a person is thinking is that person himself; so too the only one who knows the things of God is God Himself.

It is interesting how humanism and New Ageism conflict directly with Paul's teaching here. By making man into a god—the creator and controller of his own universe and destiny—humanism encourages every person to pursue their own wisdom. (One wonders how Mormon theology, in which men become gods by human effort and the passage of time, is any different.) New Ageism, along with astrology and much of modern psychology, claims the ability to see into a person's mind, to see into his past (even past lives), to unveil that which is unknown. This is not unlike a claim to self-deity. Of course, these movements reveal *not* the God of creation, but the god of this world, who is not a revealing God, but a concealing one (2 Cor. 4:4; cf. 1 John 5:19).

12   The Corinthians had *received, not the spirit of the world, but the Spirit who is from God*. Obviously, any spirit of this world is not

of God and is opposed to Him, but Paul's point here is that the wisdom of man cannot apprehend the wisdom of God's foolish gospel because it is bound to this world. Those who have received the Holy Spirit (all believers; cf. Rom. 8:9; 1 Cor. 12:13), have within them all they need to *know the things freely given...by God*. In other words, one who receives the message of Christ crucified also receives the Spirit of God, who reveals to the believer the wisdom of God in the gospel which was formerly hidden.

Theological Note: The reference to *things freely given to us by God* refers not to the abundant spiritual gifts the Corinthians had received. It is a reference to their salvation, freely given (χαρισθέντα) through the foolish message of Christ crucified (1:23-24; 2:2). This message had saved them, and if they would 'grow up' spiritually, they would understand ever more about the amazing and wonderful salvation plan of God in Jesus Christ!

---

13   The things concerning God's wonderful plan of salvation are those things Paul speaks. They are anything but foolishness! They are not *taught by human wisdom, but...by the Spirit*. Far from being God's basic or beginning information, they are His *deep things* (v.10). These are what Paul referred to in his letter to the Ephesians as "the unfathomable riches of Christ" (3:8; cf. Rom. 11:33).

Textual and Interpretive Note: The precise meaning of the final phrase here is not certain. NKJV reads "comparing spiritual things with spiritual;" NASV reads "combining spiritual *thoughts* with spiritual words" (italics theirs); the NIV has "expressing spiritual truths in spiritual words" (margin: "interpreting spiritual truths to spiritual men"). The verb (συγκρίνω; BAGD, 782) is hard to nail down. The repetition of πνευματικός (spiritual) is ambiguous. What did Paul intend us to understand here: spiritual thoughts, words, truths, men? Perhaps the following reference to the natural man (v.14), and the opening statement of Paul in v.6 that this wisdom is spoken among the mature, support a translation like *explaining spiritual things to spiritual men*. In any case, the point is that spiritual truth comes only to those who have received the Spirit, and are taught by the Spirit.

14   The 'flip side of the coin' is that those who have rejected the Spirit think God's wisdom is foolish, and find it incomprehensible. Paul has said this before (cf. 1:18, 23), but he now identifies the one who does not accept God's wisdom as *a natural man* (ψυχικὸς ἄνθρωπος). This person is described in Jude 19 as devoid of the Spirit and divisive. Paul does not charge the Corinthians with being natural (i.e., unbelievers), but he will shortly point out that though they are saved, they are acting like those who are natural—spiritual babies and filled with strife and divisions (3:1-4).

The natural man is here described in a series of clauses. He *does not accept the things of the Spirit of God* (in contrast to believers in v.12; "we have received...the Spirit who is from God"). Why? Because *they* (the truths of the gospel) *are foolishness to him, and he cannot understand them*. Why? *Because they* are in the spiritual realm—and thus *are spiritually appraised* (only grasped spiritually).

Here then is graphic evidence of the plight of an unsaved person who has rejected the gospel and is depending on his own wisdom to come to know God. He is literally caught in his own 'human wisdom trap;' he cannot understand God's wise plan, which can only be discerned with the aid of the Holy Spirit, and it remains to him, therefore, foolishness. Such a person does not need a more eloquent or intelligent presentation of the gospel; he needs a simpler one!

15   Paul now introduces a second kind of person, the spiritual man (πνευματικὸς). It is tempting to think of this person as an extraordinary Christian, but the contrast is between one

who has the Spirit, and one who does not. The repetition of ἀνακρίνω (appraise) in vv.14 and 15 clearly shows the difference. The ψυχικὸς (natural man) does not understand anything that requires spiritual *appraisal;* he cannot even *appraise* the spiritual man! The πνευματικὸς (spiritual man), on the other hand, *appraises* all things. While it is true that Paul will shortly confront the Corinthians for being saved, yet living like the unsaved (3:1-4), he is in no way suggesting that these are two options in the Christian life. As far as Paul is concerned, the only 'normal' Christian is *he who is spiritual.*

The phrase *he himself is appraised by no man* means that the spiritual man is above judgment by the world (perhaps anticipating 4:3-4 and 6:1-8). Clearly, the believer is not to lower his analysis of spiritual things to the level of the world, but this is what the Corinthians had done! Paul also seems to be saying that the spiritual person who understands what God has done in Christ crucified is not subject to judgment by those who are worldly. And this anticipates Paul's words in 3:1-4; his Corinthian audience had judged him and his message as inferior, but as one who was spiritual, he was not subject to their analysis.

16 Scriptural support comes from Isaiah 40:13. The question is rhetorical, and calls for a negative response: *Who has known the mind of the Lord, that he should instruct Him?* Answer: No one! Paul's point is this: Since no one has known the mind of the Lord, since no one has instructed Him, then no one devoid of the Spirit should be instructing those who *have the mind of Christ* (cf. Phil.2:5-8) either.

3:1-4 *The true wisdom of God is not fully received by carnal believers, who have stunted their spiritual growth and remain spiritually immature.*

Paul's extended discussion about foolishness and wisdom reaches its climax in this paragraph with an exposé of the Corinthian Christians' spiritual lives. Their confusion over the message of Christ crucified had caused divisions and rendered them spiritually immature. Their injection of human wisdom into both the content and presentation of the gospel not only weakened their message, it bred divisions! While they had received the Spirit, they were not spiritual at all, but were rather thinking and acting like natural men.

At the same time, this paragraph is a hinge in Paul's response to the Corinthian church. His instruction to this point has been given to correct their misunderstanding concerning the message of the gospel. He sums up this discussion here by showing that their pursuit of human wisdom has resulted in spiritual babyhood, a limited spiritual capacity which has made them unable to fully apprehend God's wisdom. And what is the *symptom* of this spiritual immaturity? Divisions in the name of their leaders! This leads Paul directly into his instruction concerning their misunderstanding of the significance of the messengers of the gospel (3:5-4:5) and his closing argument against their divisions (4:6-21).

3:1   Paul's opening classification of his readers as *brethren* (ἀδελφοί) puts to rest the suggestion by some that Paul's readers were actually unsaved. The term is used throughout the epistles as a designation of Christians (BAGD, 16). The further suggestion of some that Paul knew there were unsaved as well as saved in the church at Corinth and was implicitly directing his comments to the former cannot be sustained from the text. Paul is addressing the whole church (Fee, 123), and addressing them as believers. To suggest otherwise would make him a tacit contributor to their church divisions!

Beyond this, the idea that Paul is writing to unsaved people in the church would make his charge that they are unable to take in solid spiritual food (3:2) meaningless. Obviously, no unsaved person can understand the things of the Spirit (cf. 2:14)! Paul's argument in these verses *demands* that his audience be saved; he says that while they have received the Spirit, they are not spiritual men (πνευματικοῖς; spiritually mature). They are spiritually like they were when they were first saved. *Then* they were *babes in*

Christ, needing to grow. *Then* Paul gave them spiritual *milk to drink*. But whereas through the passage of time they should have grown and been eating *solid* spiritual *food*, he still could only give them spiritual milk. The problem here is the stunted spiritual growth of the Christians in Corinth, caused by their confusion over the message of the gospel, and evidenced by their divisions.

Two issues need to be addressed here, one concerning the text, and the other involving the implications of Paul's teaching for the doctrine of sanctification.

Textual Note: CrT reads σαρκίνοις (fleshy, made of flesh; cf. σάρκινος, BAGD, 750b), while MajT reads σαρκικοῖς (fleshly, carnal; cf. σαρκικός, BAGD, 750a). External evidence is not decisive for either reading. However, the internal evidence seems to favor the latter reading for the following reasons:

1) If the CrT reading is followed, Paul simply accuses the Corinthians of being like men of flesh (having the character of flesh, humanness). But what is the indictment here? All believers have characteristics of humanness, but this does not normally inhibit their ability to apprehend solid spiritual truth.

2) Paul seems to be pointing back to the beginning of the Corinthians' spiritual pilgrimage in vv.1-2a. His point is that while they, as new converts, were *excusably* fleshly *at that time* (the residue of carnal Corinthian society ingrained into them), it is *inexcusable* that they still are now. Indeed, his emphasis on them *still* (ἔτι) being fleshly (σαρκικοί; v.3) calls for a correlation in the preceding context. Unless the MajT reading is taken, there is none.

Conclusion: Regardless of which reading is chosen, the difference in meaning should not be exaggerated. Paul's other uses of σάρκινος show that it can carry the idea of being simply made of flesh (2 Cor. 3:3) or having the character of sinful flesh (Rom. 7:14). It seems that this latter designation, which is certainly the meaning of σαρκικός, is intended here.

Theological Note: Paul here describes the Corinthians as what we might term "unspiritual Christians." This does not mean that they did not have the Spirit. Paul refers to them as having the Spirit, but also being carnal. All Christians have received the Holy Spirit (Rom. 8:9). At the outset of Christian experience, each believer has a different amount of carnality to deal with. It is normal for this worldliness to progressively be put away, and for spiritual truth to progressively fill and control those areas previously ruled by the flesh. The Corinthians exhibit a Christian experience of failure to deal with pre-conversion fleshly thoughts and actions; for this reason, they are "unnatural" (or abnormal, since it is 'normal' for a Christian to grow spiritually), like babies, even though they are old.

Paul's use of νηπίοις ἐν Χριστῷ (infants in Christ) as figurative of spiritual immaturity is not uncommon. In fact, his fourfold use of the term in 13:11 virtually echoes his idea here; an infant may speak, think, and act like a child without arousing any disapproval (after all, it is expected of a child). But when, through the passage of time, one becomes a man, he is expected to put away childish things. (Cf. Eph. 4:14; 1 Thess. 2:7; also note Jesus' words in Matt. 11:25 and Luke 10:21.)

2 Paul's imagery continues; the Corinthians had been given *milk to drink* at first, *not solid food*, since they were spiritual babes. Cf. Heb. 5:11-14 (where the sense echoes Paul here) and 1 Pet. 2:2. N.B. Spiritual milk always pertains to salvation, and leads to deeper appreciation of Jesus Christ.

The end of v.2 commences Paul's indictment of the Corinthians, and deserves a verse break. The disjunctive here (ἀλλ') is strong, and is intended to startle his listeners. In fact, it seems that Paul purposely refers back to their early days in the faith, much as they themselves would have, as times when they were immature and foolish. The problem was that the Corinthians thought they had become wise by combining human wisdom with the gospel message, but the opposite was true. They had in fact seriously retarded their spiritual growth. The shock value here is in Paul's sudden declaration that they are *not yet able* to take in solid food—their condition at the beginning.

3   Why is this? Because (γὰρ) they *are still fleshly* (σαρκικοί). They are still showing the effects of their society; instead of affecting it, they are being affected by it (as becomes abundantly clear in the chapters to follow). And how does Paul know they are still fleshly? Because they have the symptoms: *envy* (NKJV)/*jealousy* (NASV, NIV) (ζῆλος; cf. BAGD, 338, 2.), and *strife* (NKJV, NASV)/*quarreling* (NIV) (ἔρις). Both these occur often in Paul's vice lists; cf. Rom. 13:13; 2 Cor. 12:20; Gal. 5:20.

Textual Note: NKJV, reflecting MajT, adds *divisions* (διχοστασία; lit. dissensions). The support of p⁴⁶ makes this reading likely.

The rhetorical questions require an affirmative answer (οὐχὶ). Yes, they are fleshly. Yes, they are acting (περιπατεῖτε) like men (κατὰ ἄνθρωπον). The use of ἄνθρωπον here is pejorative; as often in his epistles, Paul uses it to denote inferior 'ways of men' in comparison to those of God (cf. 9:8; 15:32; Gal. 1:11; 3:15).

4   The evidence is laid on the table like a smoking gun. "Is there any doubt that you are fleshly? Look at the evidence! *One says, 'I am of Paul,' and another, 'I am of Apollos.'* So there you have it; you are fleshly!" (The grammar of the final question requires a positive answer.)

Textual Note: CrT here has ἄνθρωποί (...are you not [mere] *men?*), while MajT has σαρκικοί (...are you not *fleshly* [*carnal*, NKJV]?). The different readings do not affect the sense of the passage, and both have external and internal support. The MajT is consistent throughout the paragraph (σαρκικός appears four times), which is perhaps an argument against its being original (how did the variations arise?). The meaning is the same either way: Divisive Christians may have the Spirit, but they are not living like it!

Homiletical Ideas: As with all passages which contain teaching critical to the Christian life, it is important not only to preach this passage, but to preach it well. It would be 'homiletical felony' to preach this passage without the audience being motivated to grow spiritually.

The passage breaks down nicely:
1) God's wisdom is hidden from the world (2:6-9)
2) God's wisdom is revealed to Christians by the Spirit (2:10-16)
3) God's wisdom is not fully received by carnal Christians (3:1-4)

A key is to communicate what it means to be a "spiritual man" (πνευματικοῖς). This should be a practical element in every message drawn from this passage.

A spiritual man is not of this age (2:6); that is, he doesn't have his hopes, dreams, goals, or interests tied up in this age. He recognizes that everything this world has to offer is temporal—and those who wrap their lives in it are passing away, too—but the things of God are eternal, from God.

A spiritual man is a 'normal' Christian; he is no oddity. This is not something only for preachers and teachers; it is for everyone. If you are a Christian, you have 'tapped into the source.' The question is, will you turn it on? Focus on the need to be taught by the Spirit—who explains things to the spiritual person. If a man's heart is in the right place, if his desires are for the Lord, then he will be taught by the Spirit.

Finally, a spiritual man is not fleshly. He is not characterized by the same attitudes and actions as one who is unsaved. Since Paul's application is in a local church body, this is a good place to start. Is there dissension? Strife? Jealousy? How dare we bring that into a spiritual gathering?!

Perhaps the bottom line here is pride (love for ourselves) versus love for Jesus Christ. If we decide to love Him, and cultivate that love, we will be receptive to the Spirit in our everyday lives. If not, we will shrivel up spiritually. Will we be normal or abnormal? Wise or foolish? Immature or mature? Spiritual or carnal? These are the decisions that make a life.

The first part of Paul's response to divisions in the church at Corinth is now complete (1:18-3:4). The Corinthian Christians were confused about the message of the gospel; they thought it could be improved by incorporating human wisdom into it. Paul has informed them that not only does human wisdom have nothing to do with the gospel, it is the antithesis of it! Human wisdom may consider the message of Christ crucified weak and foolish, but it is in reality human wisdom which is foolish! The injection of man's wisdom is fatal to God's gospel...and beyond this, it spawns divisions. Just as human wisdom is constantly divided, so too those who buy into human wisdom are divided.

In the case of the Corinthian believers, this division was over human leaders. They, the foolish and weak of Corinthian society, who had responded to Paul's foolish and weak preaching of the foolish and weak gospel, should certainly boast only in the Lord and rest in His power (1:18-2:5). They, who as believers had received the Spirit and thus had access to spiritual wisdom, should certainly leave behind the things of the world and become spiritually mature (2:6-3:4). But they did not. Their lingering carnality and spiritual babyhood was evidenced in their confusion over the place and importance of church leaders.

So in 3:5-4:5, Paul gives instruction concerning *messengers of the gospel.* Their misconceptions about gospel messengers is as much a cause of their divisions as their confusion over the gospel message. Just as they should not boast in human wisdom (*what* they know), but in the Lord from whom true wisdom comes, so too they should not boast in human leaders (*who* they know), but in the God whom all true leaders serve.

As noted above, this section breaks down as follows:

The messengers of the gospel are Christ's servants and accountable to Him (3:5-4:5).

a. Messengers of the gospel are Christ's laborers, doing His work (3:5-9).

b. Messengers of the gospel will give account to Christ for their work (3:10-17).

c. Messengers of the gospel must avoid self-deceiving pride in their wisdom and the boasting of men (3:18-23).

d. Messengers of the gospel should not be rated by men, since they will be evaluated in the future by Christ (4:1-5).

3:5-9 *Messengers of the gospel are servants of God through whom His work is accomplished and to whom appropriate rewards will be given.*

5 Paul's conclusion in 3:1-4 was so pointed that the questions of this verse are unavoidable. Incomprehensible as it may seem to the Corinthians, choosing sides over favorite church leaders is tantamount to spiritual foolishness, and must stop. But *What then is Apollos? And what is Paul?* The answer to these questions is the heart of Paul's instruction: they are *servants* (διακονος; obviously not to be confused with church deacons). They work for God; they are His helpers; they do His bidding. And as befits their role as messengers of the gospel, the result of their service is that people *believed*.

The phrase *as the Lord gave [opportunity] to each one* (NASV; NKJV omits *opportunity*; NIV ["as the Lord has assigned to each his task"] is quite interpretive here) has caused some confusion. The question concerns what the Lord gave, and to whom He gave it. This could be read to mean that God gave each of the Corinthians the opportunity to believe through the ministry of Paul and Apollos. It could also mean that God gave Paul and Apollos opportunities to preach, as a result of which many Corinthians believed. While both are true, the following verse shows that Paul's meaning is closer to the latter. Apollos and Paul are servants of God who have each performed the tasks given them by God, the result being that the Corinthians have come to believe.

6 Paul now begins to develop an extended agrarian metaphor. The scene is a farm or a garden. As servants of the master of the plantation, each worker has his assigned task. Paul *planted*, and *Apollos watered*. But there is nothing between them; neither is any more or less important than the other.

The development of this metaphor in the following verses identifies the parallels in the Corinthian church context. Paul "planted"—he started the church. Apollos "watered"—he nourished the young church. Each performed their given task, *but God was causing the growth*. Finally, the garden plot or "field" (v.9; "building") is the Corinthian Church.

Here and in v.7 Paul states that it is God who causes the growth (αὐξάνω; cf. 2 Cor. 9:10, where a similar metaphor illustrates God's ability to multiply the spiritual harvest of those who give). This emphasizes that church growth is His work, a fact established by Christ Himself during His earthly ministry (Mt.16:18).

7   Paul now summarizes vv. 5-6. Verse 5 began by asking who or what Apollos and Paul were. The answer there was "servants," but the message for those in Corinth who were inclined to put one or the other on a pedestal is, "They are nothing!" It is God who is everything; He is the one who is causing the growth, not the 'nothing servants' who work for Him.

Paul is not trying to denigrate the role of the full time messenger of the gospel. Far from it! It is the highest calling! But just as erudite human wisdom was nothing compared with God's foolishness (1:25), so too even a significant gospel messenger is nothing compared with the God whom he serves.

8   Because all gospel messengers (*he who plants and he who waters*, i.e., Paul and Apollos) work for the same master, they *are one*. That is, since it is God who 'assigns each one his task' (v.5b, NIV), there is a unity in what they are doing. Like a smoothly running engine, each part performs its function, and all perform together. Take away one of the parts and the 'divine machine' would not function properly. Implicit here is the idea that those who distinguish between and divide over leaders like Paul and Apollos are dividing that which, in God's design, is really united.

Is then there any difference between leaders? Certainly, both in function and in quality. But it is only the latter which concerns

Paul. In the future *each will receive his own reward* (μισθός; lit. pay, wages; cf. 1 Tim. 5:18) *according to his own labor.* This reward is not received based on man's evaluation, nor is it given by men. To put it bluntly, this is not something with which the Corinthians should concern themselves. *God determines the reward due His servants (4:1-5).* Perhaps already in Paul's mind is the instruction of vv.10-17; if so, those who were leading the church in Corinth into such divisions should pay close attention to their work... since it will someday be examined, and appropriate reward given.

9   How does Paul know that each one who works as one of God's servants in God's field will receive appropriate reward? Because (γάρ) they belong to God. Paul says that he and Apollos *are God's fellow workers*, both who belong to God (not *with God*, as KJV translates). In the same way, the Corinthian Christians *are God's field*—they too belong to God. Finally, anticipating the following paragraph, Paul changes the metaphor; they are *God's building* (temple; vv.16f). Paul's meaning is clear; this is not *our* work, or *our* church. It is God's. He owns it, and He owns those who are now taking care of it on earth (cf. "stewards," 4:1f; also 1 Thess. 5:12; Heb. 13:17). And as a good servant is careful to do his master's will, so too a wise builder is careful what and how he builds.

3:10-17 *Messengers of the gospel are spiritual builders on the foundation of Jesus Christ, and receive or forfeit rewards based on the quality of their ministry.*

These verses are sometimes used to teach a general doctrine of sanctification. Walvoord writes: "The Christian life is viewed here as a building...the quality of our life will be tested at the Judgment Seat of Christ" (*Prophecy Knowledge Handbook*, [Victor Books], p.459; see also MacArthur, *1 Corinthians*, p.83).

While it is true that each believer's works will be tested at the Judgment Seat (Rom. 14:10-12; 2 Cor. 5:10), that is not what Paul is addressing in this passage. The context here is the

Corinthian's elevation of individual church leaders, and their need to understand that whatever work those leaders did, good or bad, would be evaluated and rewarded by God. Those who build on the church's foundation are measured by a high standard; it might be said that they "have a hard act to follow" (Jesus Christ). We must view this passage in its context, which is focusing on leaders, and understand its message within that context—the importance of how ministers perform their duty.

10   Paul begins by picking up on what he said at the end of v.5 to reiterate that all that is done in the church by its leaders is from God. In v.5, he said that he and Apollos were the Lord's servants, doing the work that He *gave* (δίδωμι) them to do.

Now, referring to himself (he includes Apollos and other ministers of the church in his "any man" of vv.12, 14, 15, and 17), he writes: *According to the grace of God which was given* (δίδωμι) *to me, as a wise master builder I laid a foundation*. For Paul, just as salvation was graciously provided freely by God, so too God had graciously provided good works for each believer as they lived their lives (Eph. 2:10). Indeed, he refers to his own preaching ministry as a grace (cf. Eph. 3:2, 8). God's gracious calling and enabling had given him the opportunity to lay a foundation for the church in Corinth (cf. with his previous description of his work as *planting* in vv.6-8); in no way was this foundation something he had done, or for which he could take credit. It was all of God (cf. 6b, 7b).

It is also notable that Paul describes his ministry by saying that what he did, he did as a *wise master builder* (σοφός ἀρχιτέκτων; English *architect* comes from this). That he was *wise* is a thinly veiled reminder that his preaching of Christ crucified, now considered by some as foolishness, was actually a *wise work*.

The purpose of Paul's introduction is to establish his new metaphor for the church in Corinth, himself, and other church leaders. The *building* is the Corinthian church (cf. Eph. 2:21, where the figure of a building is used for the universal Church), which—as with the figure of the field—is owned by God (cf. 9b), has been founded by Paul, and *another is building upon it* (referring to Apollos, and any other leaders in the church).

Paul's central warning in this paragraph comes at the end of this verse. It is directed toward those who *are building upon* the foundation he has laid; *let each man be careful* (pay close attention, beware; cf. βλέπω, BAGD, 143, 4., 6. and 1 Cor. 8:9; 10:12) *how he builds upon it*. This is a warning, therefore, to all who aspire to build the church of Jesus Christ: They must be careful what they do.

11   And why? Because (γάρ) the foundation upon which they build is none other than Jesus Christ (cf. Eph. 2:20 where the apostles and prophets are the foundation, and Jesus Christ the cornerstone of the Church). Again, they are reminded of the central message of the gospel, and the contrast with their human wisdom is evident in the following contrast.

12   The foundation is sound; certainly no one will find fault with Jesus Christ as the church's foundation. But the rub is this—*if any man builds upon the foundation*, he must run a quality check: Is the building material used appropriate to the foundation (such as *gold, silver,* and *precious stones*)? A *wise builder* would hardly consider using *wood, hay,* or *straw* on such a fine foundation!

13   The key to the various materials listed is their combustibility. There is a time coming when *each man's work will become evident, for the day will show it, because it is to be revealed with fire*. There is a judgment by fire coming, and only what is "fireproof" will survive. The amount of work one has done will not matter; rather, *the fire itself will test the quality of each man's work*. One thing that certainly will not pass the test is any work on the building performed by those following human wisdom, which is of this age and is passing away (1:19f, 28; 2:6)! Anyone's work which is not based on Jesus Christ is illegitimate; it may look good to the

eyes of men, but when the fire of God's judgment comes, there will be nowhere to hide. Gold, silver, and precious stones behave differently in a fire than wood, hay, and stubble!

What is this time of judgment? It is the Judgment Seat of Christ, when each will be recompensed for deeds done in the body (cf. 2 Cor. 5:10). This applies *especially* to those who have *led* the church on earth. While they avail themselves to special rewards (cf. 1 Pet. 5:4), they will also receive a more rigorous judgment (Jas. 3:1), a judgment at which there clearly is the possibility of loss.

14   For any builder whose *work which he has built upon it remains* (it is true to the foundation), the fire will reveal its quality, and *he shall receive a reward* (μισθός; cf. 3:8).

What will the reward be? As in the previous reference, this is appropriate 'pay' (very generous, no doubt!) from God for our work. Obviously, this is not salvation, since eternal life is a *free gift* of God (Eph. 2:8f; see the Theological Note on v.15 below). Perhaps this reward will be hearing the "Bravo!" of Christ (cf. Mt. 25:21a; Alan Hugh McNeile, *Matthew* [Baker], 365) or receiving a crown (cf. 2 Tim. 4:8). Mt. 25:21b may imply additional responsibilities and unique joy in the coming Kingdom (cf. McNeile, op. cit., and Barnes, *Notes on the Gospels*, 2 vols., 1:286).

15   For those who have built with their own wisdom, the fire will also reveal it: It will burn. *If any man's work is burned up, he shall suffer loss.* Like the wisdom of the wise, it will be destroyed (1:19). Furthermore, they will *suffer loss* (ζημιόω; cf. BAGD, 339; lit. = "be punished").

Theological Note: This passage is an important source of information for the doctrine of rewards. Some theologians have trouble differentiating between salvation and rewards (cf. Fee, 143; MacArthur confuses the issue, first saying this reward is "eternal joy and glory" and "future eternal blessedness" [which sounds like a reference to heaven], then saying that a person who has his work burned up "will not lose their salvation;" cf. p.85). But if the "reward" here is equivalent to eternal salvation, it certainly can be lost, and it is 'earned' on the basis of works! This is, of course, theologically faulty. Furthermore, v.15b makes clear that whatever this reward is, it is in addition to eternal life. Paul sees a future judgment coming which has nothing to do with eternal salvation (which is unrelated to works or wisdom, so no one can boast; cf.1:26-31; Eph. 2:8f). Despite the efforts of some to omit the potential of punishment in this judgment (MacArthur, 84), there is certainly the possibility of *gain or loss*. Finally, the temporal setting is clearly outside this lifetime (since the rewards/judgment are distributed on the basis of actions in this life). Evidently, this refers to the Judgment Seat of Christ, and the rewards or punishment (surely an experience of the greatest sorrow) which will be given there. Messengers of the gospel must beware how they build, since their work is going to be revealed and rewarded on the basis of its quality.

There is considerable confusion concerning the final phrase of v.15 (*he himself will be saved, yet so as through fire*). Chrysostom argued that this meant the offender would be preserved in hellfire instead of experiencing annihilation (hardly a desirable option!). But σώζω (saved) here refers to eternal salvation. Others find support for the doctrine of purgatory here. But this fire has no relation to or effect on our attainment of eternal life. Paul is writing to Christians, and announces that if anyone seeks to build on the foundation of Christ with human wisdom and effort, he will *suffer loss* of rewards *through fire* at the Judgment Seat of Christ, *but he himself shall be saved* (it will not affect his eternal salvation).

16   *Do you not know...?* By beginning this way, Paul signals the gravity of what follows. This is the climax of his warning that those who build the church must do so with great care.

The building of vv.9-10 is now more specifically defined as *a temple* (ναός) *of God*, which follows from the materials to be used in its construction (gold, silver, precious stones; v.12), materials which were among the building materials of the Old Testament Temple (cf. 1 Chron. 22:14,16; 29:2; 2 Chron. 3:6). The temple here refers to the *entire church* in Corinth (*you [pl.] are*), not to individual believers as in 6:19. The picture is straight from Paul's Jewish heritage and harks back to the time when God actually dwelt in the temple. Now *the Spirit of God dwells in* (cf. ἐν, BAGD, 258, 3.) the local assembly. That is, the Holy Spirit is present among them when they are gathered together. Perhaps by using this metaphor Paul also reminds the Corinthians of their past worship in temples dedicated to the Greek pantheon of gods. *Then* they had many temples; now there is but *one*, because as they have come to know, there is only one true God.

17 The message of this verse is focused especially on those who are upsetting the unity of the body in Corinth, and their actions are set against the backdrop of Paul's designation of the church as the temple of God. *If any man destroys the temple of God* (the local church), *God will destroy him.* The term "destroy" here (cf. φθείρω, BAGD, 865) commonly refers to men corrupting others through idols or seduction or false teaching, some or all of which may apply here. Its use describing an action of God is unique to this passage. Based on the concept of 'an eye for an eye,' those who destroy the temple will be destroyed by God. This destruction is not eternal damnation (which results from one having not trusted Christ as Savior), but physical judgment, possibly death. (See 11:30, where divisive behavior in the assembly also led to death.)

The significance of the imagery here should not be missed. Jesus referred to His body cryptically as a temple, telling the Jews that if they destroyed it, He would raise it up in three days (John 2:19ff). His death and resurrection showed the prophetic nature of His words. Now the Church on earth is His Body. Those who would destroy the "temple" now are in effect destroying His body. To do so again is to invite the severest judgment, even physical death. (Compare the discussion below on 11:27-32.)

3:18-23 *Messengers of the gospel must not be deceived by human wisdom or be objects of human boasting.*

This paragraph sums up Paul's instruction concerning the leaders in the Corinthian church. The human wisdom which warped their opinion of the gospel and rendered them spiritual babies when they should have been mature was actually an insidious deception which made them think they were wise when they only had the wisdom of this present age, which is doomed (2:6). It further led them to boast in men. This sort of wisdom was foolishness. They had everything they needed in Christ, and needed to return to Him. They must become foolish as far as the world is concerned, stop exalting human wisdom and wise men, and exalt Jesus Christ alone. Paul here gives two reasons why the Corinthians should not boast in human spiritual leaders: Only the foolish are really wise (18-20), and all things, including leaders, are freely theirs in Christ (21-23).

18   Paul's opening 'call to attention' (*Let no man deceive himself*) is ironic, considering the Corinthians' elevated view of their own wisdom. Such deception was characteristic of the naive, however (cf. Rom. 16:18). This self-deception (ἐξαπατάω, BAGD, 273) cheated people out of what was rightfully theirs (cf. Josephus, *Ant.*, 10, 111, who so describes the self-deceit of Zedekiah and Judah's other leaders which led to their captivity). The paradox here is that the "foolish" one (Paul) is telling the "wise" (Corinthians) not to be deceived! These themes, of course, recapitulate the basic paradox between the wisdom of men and the foolishness of God in 1:18-2:6.

The conditional phrase, *If any man among you thinks*, is not meant to question whether anyone in Corinth thinks *he is wise in this age*. Clearly many did! Paul uses this phrase to identify the actual position of his opponents (yet without harshly accusing them), which causes them to listen to what he has to say (cf. 8:2; 11:16; 14:37; Gal. 6:3; Phil. 3:4).

Of course, the deception is that those who think they are wise are actually foolish. The solution? Anyone who *thinks that he is wise in this age, let him become foolish that he may become wise.* Instead of pursuing the wisdom of the world, believers should rather embrace the 'foolishness of God.' A believing "fool" to the world is "wise" to God.

19   The inverse relationship between what the world perceives and what God reveals continues here. Perhaps giving a slightly new angle to the statement of 1:25, Paul states that *the wisdom of this world is foolishness before God.* This motif—the reversal of strength, wisdom, and position—is a direct result of God's wise plan (1:21). He has determined that a crucified Savior gives life, and does so freely through faith. What seems like folly is now wisdom; what seems weak is now strong. Those who seem to be nothing now have everything…all because of Jesus Christ (22-23)!

Paul finds support in two Old Testament quotes, the first from Job 5:13: *"He is the one who catches the wise in their craftiness."* Although this comment comes from the lips of Eliphaz, who misconstrued the issue in Job's suffering, this statement was true. Job needed to submit to God, for no one else, no matter how wise, could compare with Him.

20   The second supporting passage also comes from Old Testament wisdom literature. Paul quotes Ps. 94:11: *"The Lord knows the reasonings of the wise, that they are useless."* To be *useless* (μάταιος; BAGD, 496) highlights the emptiness (fruitlessness) of human wisdom.

21   *So then* (ὥστε), Paul concludes, since those who think themselves wise are really foolish, and only those who are foolish to the world are truly wise, *let no one boast in men.* Any boasting in men is ridiculous! Any true wisdom a spiritual leader may have

is actually just a maturing of the "foolishness of God" (the message of Christ crucified) in his life, so why boast in the man? Much rather let us boast in Jesus Christ (cf. 1:30-31)! The NIV rendering here is good: *So then, no more boasting about men!* The problem which first surfaced in 1:12ff is here openly settled: "Stop it!"

Paul's reason for putting a stop to boasting not only looks back, it looks forward. A second reason why they should not boast in men is introduced by γάρ (*for*). Paul declares the absurdity of siding with one leader over another, when all such leaders—and in fact all things—are theirs through Christ. *All things are yours*, he writes. What things?

22   All church leaders, including *Paul or Apollos or Cephas* (who they argued over; 1:12), are for all of them! The body of Christ is totally inter-related (cf. 12:12-26).

There is one body, not many, and therefore all are part of the *one* body, regardless of their function. To borrow an analogy from chapter 12, an arm cannot "claim" an eye, nor an ear a foot. They are all for one and one for all.

But Paul goes beyond this to touch on the wonder of what God has prepared for those who love Him (2:9). Just as the world could not comprehend this, so too the Corinthians in their human wisdom missed it! As believers in Christ, as God's people, whatever was His was now theirs!

So *the world* is theirs (cf. Ps. 24:1). In this present age the whole world is in the power of the evil one (1 John 5:19), but the world is passing away; Christ overcame it (John 16:33), and One greater than the world is now in them (1 John 4:4). One day they will judge the world (6:2; cf. Isa. 11:9)!

Life is theirs, both the best kind of life now (cf. John 10:10), and eternal life. *Death* is also theirs, since in Christ crucified and risen it has been conquered; it no longer owns them (15:51-57). *All things*—present or future—are theirs.

23   That all these things are presently under the control of a usurper in no way indicates ownership; they are created by God and remain His. And they are also the possession of believers because they belong to Christ, and Christ belongs to God. Truly, these are all part of the unfathomable riches of Christ (Eph. 3:8)! Therefore, since all these things are ours, it is absurd to boast in men (21)!

4:1-5   *Messengers of the gospel are custodians of God's mysteries and are accountable to God, not man, for their faithful service and proper motives.*

In these verses Paul concludes the section dealing with the Corinthian's misconception about church leaders, and again focuses on himself and others in similar roles (presumably Apollos and Peter) as he did at the outset (3:5f). He is addressing the root problem behind their boasting, which was the idea that—in their human wisdom—they would pass judgment on leaders. This action on their part showed they did not understand that spiritual leaders are answerable to God. This is as it must be, for there is no way for those on earth to see the motives of men's hearts, and it is these which reveal the true lasting value of their ministry (cf. 3:10-15).

The tendency to judge and 'rate' leaders is present in every generation. We are given to judging others and ourselves. Usually, our standards are of this world, not of God. There is only one Judge before whom church leaders must stand, Jesus Christ. There is only one standard by which they are judged, and that is God's Word. Divisions in the church at Corinth, and in countless churches today, would be avoided if everyone from elder to spiritual babe would measure themselves only and always according to that standard.

4:1   Paul's opening *"Let a man regard us…as servants of Christ"* harkens back to his identification of himself and Apollos as servants (διάκονοι) in 3:5, but here he uses the Greek word ὑπηρέτας (helper, assistant), the only time it appears in his letters. The term was used when he was commissioned as a minister by

Jesus Christ (Acts 26:16). Perhaps Paul thought of that earlier experience here; the two contexts certainly reflect each other well. In Acts, Luke records Paul in his testimony before Agrippa telling how Jesus had appointed him "a minister (ὑπηρέτης)... not only to the things which you have seen, but also to the things in which I will appear to you." These "things" certainly included the mystery of the inclusion of Gentiles in the Body of Christ (cf. Acts 26:17). Now in his letter to the Corinthians, Paul seems to draw on this memory, and use the same term to identify his stewardship of that mystery.

Paul's identification of himself and other servants of Christ as *stewards* (NASV/NKJV; *those entrusted with*, NIV; see οἰκονόμος, BAGD, 562) refers to a house-manager or administrator. This is one who is left in charge, given the task of keeping things in order, a custodian of something of value (cf. Rom. 16:23, where the term refers to a city treasurer). Here, the care of *the mysteries of God* (cf. 2:7f) is their task.

But what Paul wants his readers not to miss is that this ministry of his is *of Christ* and *of God*, not of them! It is *God's* ministry, and he is *God's* minister. This is how they should *regard* (cf. λογίζομαι, BAGD, 476, 1.b.; consider, look upon) Paul and the other church leaders.

2   It is important to the argument that this point be made clear; *it is required of stewards that one be found trustworthy.* When one is a custodian of something, he must be faithful to the one who entrusted him with the task, and faithful to properly care for what he has been entrusted with. God's stewards must be faithful to God, and must faithfully preach the message of the gospel, Christ crucified.

3   Having established the chain of responsibility (going from himself to God, and pertaining to his faithful preaching of the gospel), Paul now raises the issue of judging. Since he is not answerable to them, he writes: *To me it is a very small thing that I should be examined* (ἀνακριθῶ) *by you*—or, for that matter—*by*

any human court. It is not going to result in any meaningful evaluation, so why do it? (The text here literally reads *by [any] human day*; cf. ἡμέρα, BAGD, 347, 3.b.α. = 'day in court.' Compare the eschatological use of the term in 3:13, and see καιροῦ [time] in v.5 below.) Paul is so unconcerned with the judgment of men that he writes, *I do not even examine myself.* His only concern is the Master to whom he is accountable.

4   Why is self-evaluation of no consequence for Paul? Because although he is *conscious of nothing against myself* (what an admission!), he is not *by this* assessment *acquitted*; that is, this doesn't insure final approval of his work. That determination will be made at the Judgment Seat of Christ; *the one who examines me is the Lord.* The 'final exam' will be given by Jesus Christ Himself.

Paul is not claiming sinless perfection here; he exhibits a consciousness of his sin (see Rom. 7:15ff; 1 Tim. 1:15). What he *is* claiming is that he is not consciously or willfully sinning. For the believer, the battle with sin continues in this life, and the heart of man is very deceitful. We should live our lives, and perform our ministry, with the future judgment of our Savior in view.

Perhaps in addition to the relegation of final judgment to Christ, Paul is here reminding the Corinthian Christians that anyone can be self-deceived (as they had been; 3:18). Ever the gentle tutor, Paul puts himself on their level; he too is subject to self-delusion, so he joins them in refusing to judge himself, leaving that to the Lord.

5   The conclusion (ὥστε; *Therefore*) is that since the Lord is the only legitimate judge, the Corinthians should *not go on passing judgment* (κρίνετε; arriving at a verdict) on his ministry *before the time, but wait until the Lord comes.* This does not preclude any judging at all (cf. 5:3, 5, 7, 12; 6:5), but it does exclude evaluation of those things outside the revealed moral will of God in His Word. The 'rating' of men is something for the Lord alone to

do, since He *will bring to light the things hidden in the darkness and disclose the motives of men's hearts* (1 Sam. 16:7; Heb. 4:12). Any praise for work done must originate with Him. Instead of trying to determine the relative merit of Paul's (or anyone else's) ministry, they should wait for the time (καιροῦ) when the Lord comes to judge.

This 'time' is the Judgment Seat of Christ (Mare, 211; cf. Rom. 14:10-12). Before Jesus Christ the works of every believer will be brought out of concealment, out of darkness, and into the light. Even the motives behind their actions will be exposed! At that time, *each man's praise will come to him from God.* Those who give praise to (or crave praise of) men now have wrong priorities. It's time to serve now. Reward time is when the Lord comes.

It is worth reminding ourselves how highly successful ministers are often put on a pedestal and given the praise of men, only to have it revealed later that they were motivated by financial gain, taught unbiblical doctrines, and even engaged in lurid passions (compare 2 Peter 2:1-3).

Homiletical Ideas: There are two groups being targeted in this section (3:5-4:5). First, it has special relevance to church leaders—anyone with a teaching or leading role. It is a call for total devotion to God and careful avoidance of human accolades. As one of my seminary professors once advised: "Never believe your press clippings!" The lure of men's praise is a snare for any minister.

Second, these verses speak to all believers, who must be careful how they contribute to the building of the body of Christ, and who must avoid the pastoral 'hero-worship' so common in churches today.

In 3:5-9, the message is that the church belongs to the Lord, and everyone who works in the church works for Him. There is no place for anyone to claim a church as their own. A message like "What's Your Job on the Farm?" or "Who Makes the Garden Grow?" reflect Paul's metaphor here.

In 3:10-17, the spotlight moves to the *quality* of work we are doing. The imagery of a building is apt, since people today generally equate a church with its physical structure. In a day when people will do almost anything to realize numerical church growth, spiritual *quality* needs to be emphasized. "What Makes a Church Fireproof" or "God's Building Code for the Church" are catchy titles to drive home this message. Verses 16-17 are worth highlighting, in order to emphasize that the church is a holy temple of believers bound together by the Spirit, and that God will destroy those who destroy it.

The third paragraph, 3:18-23, gives two reasons why no one should boast in human leaders. A message entitled "Is Your Pastor a Fool?" or "Who Are You Proud Of?" might reflect Paul's emphasis here.

Finally, 4:1-5 summarizes many of the thoughts throughout the section. "Don't Put Your Pastor on a Pedestal" reflects an overall theme here. The teaching on judgment in v.5 is important and can be emphasized, too: "Here Comes the Judge!" will certainly get the point across!

Throughout this section, emphasize God's role (and de-emphasize man's) in successful ministry. God is the one who causes the growth, and He will see to it. We are to be faithful to Him. If we are, we will receive our reward—a reward far greater than the praise of men!

The conclusion to Paul's instruction concerning divisions in the Corinthian church focuses on the arrogance and pride which led them to pursue human wisdom and to judgmentally embrace or criticize human leaders. They thought they were superior to others in the church because of their human wisdom. They egotistically exalted themselves, even looking down on the apostles! While Paul has been direct, he has avoided being overly harsh to this point. However, his ire at their disregard for apostolic example and God's Word now comes to the surface. With biting irony, he reveals their arrogant pride as it contrasts with his apostolic example (4:6-13), then exhorts them to follow his example, or face the inevitable results when he comes to them (4:14-21).

4:6-13 *Paul's apostolic example of humiliation and degradation exhibits by contrast the divisive pride and arrogance of the Corinthians.*

6   The opening phrase, Ταῦτα δέ, ἀδελφοί (*Now these things, brethren*) marks off this section as a summary of Paul's instruction concerning divisions. It points back to all he has said in 1:18-4:5, and prepares them for his concluding 'purpose statement' in this verse. Paul states that his instruction to them has been *figuratively applied to myself and Apollos for your sakes.* That is, he has used himself and Apollos as examples in his instruction so as to avoid naming names (of perpetrators) in the church, and also to condition them to look upon him and Apollos as examples worth following. His purposes in giving them this instruction are twofold: 1) so *that* (ἵνα) by viewing the apostolic example (*in us*), they *might learn not to exceed what is written*, and 2) *in order that* (ἵνα) *no one of you might become arrogant in behalf of one against the other.*

The second purpose is transparent: Paul wants them to stop dividing over church leaders! The words "one against the other" may refer to Apollos and himself. A similar problem is reflected by the excessive praise given to some pastors today, especially those in large churches. When Christians identify themselves as members of "so-in-so's church," they may tacitly eclipse Christ as sole Head of the church. In extreme circumstances, an almost 'papal' respect can even 'replace Christ' as the only mediator between God and man (1 Tim. 2:5)! The inevitable result of such human exaltation, Paul has already shown (3:5-4:5), is divisions.

The first purpose is more enigmatic. Even the translation is difficult (lit. "in order that in us you might learn (μανθάνω) the not beyond what is written;" MajT/NKJV adds "to think" (φρονέω), which does not affect the meaning). Some have suggested that the phrase is actually an early copyist's error, and thus does not belong in the text, but explanations for how it became part of the text are far-fetched (see Fee, 167f, n.14 and 15). These words are Paul's, and they fit his train of thought as well.

His purpose is that they might learn not to go beyond what Scripture clearly tells them. His reference is primarily to those scriptures he has quoted. Therefore, they should understand that God's "foolishness" has destroyed human wisdom and made it useless (1:19; 3:19, 20). They should learn to boast only in the Lord (and not in themselves; 1:29, 31). They should recognize that what God reveals to those who are spiritual is far greater than anything the natural man can comprehend (2:9, 16). In other words, Paul is saying: "My purpose in writing all this has been that you might do what the Bible says (instead of contemptuously pursuing human wisdom and what it can tell you) and stop dividing over leaders."

7   Why should they abandon their arrogant self-exaltation and judging of Paul, Apollos, and others? Because (*For*; γαρ) they are no different than anyone else. This is the combined meaning of the three rhetorical questions in this verse. The first question reflects incredulity: *Who regards you as superior?* (Of course, they themselves did!) We might loosely paraphrase Paul, "Who do you think you are? Who made you any different from the rest? Who set you apart as judges of others?" The question answers itself. The Corinthians' self-delusion (3:18) had gone to their heads. They were not 'legends in their own time' (as they were prone to think), but 'legends in their own minds'!

The second question is, *What do you have that you did not receive?* The answer, of course, is "nothing." This points to the fact that all things come from God—a message Paul has driven home in 1:26-31. They had not earned their gifts; they had received them freely, just as they had received salvation freely. To claim an exalted position over other Christians was to deny that anything and everything was a result of God's grace.

This point is driven home with the third question. Paul asks, *But if you did receive it, why do you boast as if you had not received it?* That is, "Why, if everything you have has been freely given to you, do you act as if it is something you have earned?" If we are what we are because of God's gracious provision and work, we should not boast in ourselves, but in God! Instead of boasting before men, Paul says, they should be grateful and humble before God.

8   However, they were anything but humble! The spiritual fullness, riches, and status which they had received were the bases for their spiritual pride. Paul here sarcastically endorses, with biting irony, their evaluation of their own spiritual condition which they were using to puff themselves up. They were *already filled* (cf. κορέννυμι, BAGD, 445; only other NT usage is Acts 27:38). They had eaten their fill of spiritual food! They did not need any more! (How ironic—as Paul has now informed them that they are not even able to take in solid food; cf. 3:1f.) They had *already become rich* (ἐπλουτήσατε). Their spiritual riches (cf.1:5) had gone to their heads; instead of being humbly grateful, they were egotistical. They had *become kings* (ἐβασιλεύσατε), a position they had gained ahead of the apostles (*without us*). They figured that they had everything they could ever need and want. The stewards of God's mysteries (4:1, the apostles) were no longer needed! They had all the treasures—so they must have come into their own kingdom! Paul wishes it were so; in a moment of personal reflection, he shows his longing for the culmination of the age in Christ's earthly kingdom; *I would indeed that you had become kings so that we also might reign with you.* Paul could wish that they did reign (NKJV) not in their own minds, but in Christ's coming kingdom!

But they were wrong—and worse, everything was out of kilter. Wrong because while they were in the spiritual kingdom of God (4:20; cf. Col. 1:13), the experience of the Millennial Kingdom is reserved for the end times (15:24, 50). Out of kilter because any true and lasting experience of fullness and riches and reigning with Christ will only be given by the Lord when He comes (4:5). Following the pattern of Jesus Christ, these rewards are given in response to humility, not boasting (cf. Phil. 2:5-11).

9   What a contrast there is between Paul and the other apostles on one hand, and Corinthian believers on the other! The Corinthians thought of themselves so highly, as Paul has just reminded them. On the other hand, *God has exhibited us apostles last of all, as men condemned to death; because we have become a spectacle to the world, both to angels and to men.* Paul is not belittling the office of an apostle here; indeed, by contrasting apostles with his sarcastic assessment of the Corinthians, he signifies their true significance. The Corinthians should have seen in the apostolic example the character of true discipleship. Paul underscores the error of their prideful thinking by pointing to the trials and humility of the apostles.

The background for this verse is the arena in which convicts and captives were brought to be killed by gladiators or wild beasts as a spectator sport. In order to make these events more exciting, the first "contestants" wore armor. But by midday, the last victims were led naked into the arena so as to quickly satisfy the crowd's lust for blood. This humiliating place, being 'last of all,' was the apostles' lot. The irony from v.8 is carried over: *I wish you had become kings so that we might reign with you, because we apostles certainly don't seem to have any wealth or honor; we are condemned to die!* Not only were they not kings, they were like those condemned to die in a public spectacle before men and angels!

Why "men *and angels*"? Perhaps this alludes to the fact that angels are interested observers of Christians (cf. 11:10; Eph. 3:10; 1 Pet. 1:12). Since believers will judge angels (6:2), our depth of commitment to Christ in this life might surely be a matter of interest to the heavenly hosts (and of shame to the Corinthians, no doubt). Regardless, Paul's point is that the apostles have become a spectacle like that of those condemned to die not only to people in the world, but to the whole universe. Indeed, historical tradition suggests that each apostle in turn bore witness to his faithfulness to Christ in martyrdom. As such, they are witnesses to the mature believer's awareness of the ephemeral nature of this life and the greater value of things eternal (cf. 15:31; 2 Cor. 4:10f, 16-18; Phil. 1:20f). They had made a voluntary decision to follow Christ, whatever the cost. This decision was evident before men and angels.

10   Paul now further emphasizes the graphic irony of vv.8-9 with three direct contrasts. Firstly, the apostles *are fools for Christ's sake* (this is true, since they followed His example, and preached the foolish gospel), while the Corinthians *are prudent in Christ* (a sarcastic compliment). This contrast points back to the subject in 1:18-25 and 3:18-19). Secondly, the apostles *are weak* (again, a true assessment in the world's eyes), but the Corinthians *are strong* (hardly true of those who are existing on a milk diet!). This harkens back to 1:26-2:5. Finally, while the Corinthians *are distinguished* (ἔνδοξοι; glorious; cf. Eph. 5:27; this was certainly true—in their own eyes!), the apostles *are without honor* (ἄτιμοι; insignificant, despised; cf. 12:23). This contrast refers back to the comments concerning position in 1:26b, 28 and 3:5-9.

Of course, the Corinthians were *not* among the wise, strong, and honored; they were chosen from among the foolish and the weak and ignoble of the world (1:26-28), saved by a foolish message (1:23) presented by a weak and foolish messenger (2:1-5)! Furthermore, their spiritual immaturity has already been established (3:1-4)! The absurdity of what Paul is saying is what makes his irony so biting. To the extent the Corinthians thought highly of themselves, they were the opposite. They had wanted to be wise in the world; they should have chosen to be fools for Christ. They had wanted to be strong; they should have instead chosen to be weak. They wanted to rub shoulders with the upper crust of society; in so doing they are separated from the apostles, who are dishonored in the world.

11   Having established the distinction between the apostles and his readers, Paul takes the liberty in vv.11-13 of spelling out in detail just what it means for an apostle to be *without honor*. It is not a pretty sight. It does not describe the kind of situation anyone

would choose if his motivation were at all selfish. It expresses characteristics which a disciple of Jesus Christ, however, should expect (cf. John 15:20; 16:2, 33; 2 Tim. 3:12).

The list begins with five conditions of deprivation (all which are descriptive of Christ sometime during His earthly ministry); they were *hungry* (Matt. 4:2), *thirsty* (John 19:28), *poorly clothed* (cf. John 19:23), *roughly treated* (lit. beaten with fists; Matt. 26:67), and *homeless* (cf. Matt. 8:20). (See Matt. 25:34-46, where these conditions characterize the life of godly Jews during the Tribulation period.)

Beyond the obvious dishonor of such conditions is the fact that this experience is far different to that which the Corinthians envisaged for themselves (v.8). They were *filled*, not *hungry and thirsty*; they were *rich*, not *poorly clothed* and *homeless*. And while they thought of themselves as *kings...*

12   The apostles *toil, working with our hands*. For his part, Paul never made himself a burden to those to whom he ministered, as though he were of a higher class and deserved some special treatment (9:4-18; cf. 1 Thess. 2:9;4:11; 2 Thess. 3:6-13).

Not only were the apostles objects of bad treatment, when they were so treated, they never responded in kind. When *reviled* (λοιδορούμενοι; cf. λοίδορος in 5:11), they *bless*. When *persecuted*, they willingly *endure* (cf. ἀνέχω, BAGD 65f).

13   When *slandered*, they *try to conciliate*. That is, when they are verbally maligned, they try to assuage any hard feelings (on this use of παρακαλέω, see BAGD 617, 5. and Acts 16:39).

Textual Note: The term translated "slandered" is βλασφημούμενοι (cf. βλασφημέω, BAGD 142f) in the MajT, but δυσφημούμενοι in the CrT. External evidence favors the MajT, since the Alexandrian witnesses are divided. How δυσφημούμενοι (only here in the NT) arose is uncertain.

Their condition is summed up in vivid terminology. They *have become as the scum* (περικαθάρματα; BAGD, 653; lit. "that which is removed as a result of a thorough cleansing") *of the world*. The term is used only here in the NT. In Classical Greek, it described a person who was "a polluted wretch." The second phrase echoes the first in slightly different terminology; they are the *dregs* (cf. περίψημα, BAGD 653) *of all things*.

The contrast between the way the apostles and the Corinthians saw themselves in Christ is stark. The arrogant pride of the Corinthians is shown in sharp contrast to the humility and suffering of the apostles.

4:14-21 *The purpose for Paul exhibiting the Corinthian's arrogance and pride was to urge them to imitate his example of humility.*

14   Paul writes in this closing section as a father to a troubled child whom he loves. His tone is both affectionate and firm. His writing them in the form of sarcasm and biting irony is *not... to shame you*; he is not trying to make them feel awful for the way they have been thinking and acting. He wants to *admonish* (NASV) or *warn* (NIV/NKJV) them (νουθετέω) *as beloved children*. He teaches them, admonishing them to take heed, and warns them of the consequences if they do not (cf. v.21).

15   Paul is uniquely qualified to make such an appeal; if they *have countless* (lit. ten thousand; cf. 14:19) *tutors* (lit. boy-leaders) *in Christ*, they do *not have many fathers*. Paul claims a place of special privilege with them, one they should grant him since, as only a father can be, he is both a teacher and a lover of them. He led them to faith in Christ, and thus claims, *I became your father through the gospel*. He is their spiritual father; as such, he has authority to instruct and chastise them (v.21).

16   Because of this position (οὖν; *therefore*), Paul exhorts them to *be imitators of me* (cf. 11:1). This exhibits a confidence in his own obedience to Christ which is awesome. It reflects his confession of 4:4, and serves as a motivation to spiritual leaders of any age to be exemplary in every walk of life, not just in "church affairs."

17   Since Paul (their "father") cannot be with them right now, *for this reason*, he writes, *I have sent you Timothy, who is my beloved and faithful child in the Lord.* Notably, while both the Corinthians and Timothy are beloved (ἀγαπητός; see v.14), Timothy is also πιστὸν ἐν κυρίῳ (faithful in the Lord). Timothy is faithful in that he has not strayed from the truth, and thus is a living example for the Corinthians. He shows how a spiritual child should behave!

His role is not simply as an example, however, but *he will remind you of my (Paul's) ways which are in Christ.* Since they are *in Christ* (15) and yet their ways do not reflect it, Timothy will be a 'stand-in' tutor to refresh their memory concerning that which *I (Paul) teach everywhere in every church.*

But how would Timothy be received by those who needed to change? The implication of 16:10-11 is that Paul expected he might not be welcomed (or worse) by some in the church at Corinth. Paul reminds them that Timothy is a spiritual child of his, just as they are. Perhaps he had some misgivings about sending Timothy; the treatment of spiritually astute children by their less devout siblings was well-known to Paul (cf. Gen. 37).

18-19 So that Timothy would not have to level the hard charges, Paul closes out his call to action by putting himself clearly in the picture. It is not as though he is disinterested and sending a representative to do work he does not have time to worry about; they should know that he is indeed coming. *Now some have become arrogant, as though I were not coming to you. But I will come to you soon, if the Lord wills...* The warning here is probably to a smaller group of people in the church who were spreading the idea that Paul would not return. Perhaps these people are some of the same ones who considered themselves wise, and thought Paul would not come back because by comparison he would seem foolish before them. Paul has long since done away with this idea; he will be coming...and soon!

As an added warning, Paul writes that when he comes, *I shall find out, not the words of those who are arrogant, but their power.*

The combination of words (λόγος) and power (δύναμις) in this context ties together much of what Paul has said in 1:18-4:5. The word (λόγος) of the cross (1:18) was Paul's message—a foolish message (1:18, 23), but also a message which carried with it the power of God (δύναμις; 1:18, 24). In Paul's ministry this power had been demonstrated (2:4-5). Now he will come and see if the arrogant words of those teaching human wisdom carry the same power!

20   The spiritual *kingdom of God* is a powerful one; it changes lives, and the way people live. It is a dynamic kingdom. While Paul often refers to the "kingdom" in reference to the second coming of Christ (cf. 6:9f), this verse refers to the aspect of that kingdom which is already existing. All those in Christ are in the spiritual kingdom of God, and this kingdom is manifested by power that changes lives. Those in Corinth who arrogantly consider themselves "kings" (4:8) will be put to the test. Unless they change their ways, the implication is clear; it will be shown that not only are they not kings, but they are also speaking a message which is not of the kingdom. They may be able to 'talk' with the wise men of the world, but God's truth *does not consist in words, but in power*. That power is not something the world sees or values (1:18; 2:5), because it comes cloaked in the 'foolish' message of the gospel. The power it provides is a mystery to the world.

21   In verses 14-17, Paul spoke as a father to the Corinthians. He changed his emphasis briefly in 18-20 in order to make sure that Timothy was not treated badly, but heeded. Now he finishes his exhortation again as a father. *What do you desire? Shall I come to you with a rod or with love and a spirit of gentleness?* The choice is theirs. Like a father he gives an ultimatum to his children: "Do I need to give you a spanking, or are you going to obey?" The contrast is not between chastisement and love, since the two are properly related (cf. Heb. 12:3-11). The question is, will Paul be required to come in punishment, or in gentleness? Surely Paul's hope, as with any loving father, was that his strong and clear words would provoke the desired change in them.

(Unfortunately, as 2 Cor. 2:1-4 seems to indicate, Paul's "spanking" was required to deal with their behavior.)

Homiletical Ideas

These paragraphs are excellent for concluding an expository series on the issue of divisions in the church. Paul had to dissolve the divisions by getting to the heart of the problem. This he has done by focusing on the message and messengers of the gospel. In closing, he spotlights the need for active response.

The central issue in the first paragraph (4:6-13) is no doubt the Corinthians' exalted self-image. The idea portrayed in the classic children's story "The Emperor's New Clothes" is fitting here: Those who think they are filled, rich, and reigning are wrong. They need to recognize that godliness is evidenced by humiliation and suffering.

In the second paragraph (14-21), the concept of being an imitator of Jesus Christ is compelling. Paul says to imitate him, and Timothy is an example of one who has done this faithfully. The idea here is to *not* be a "Do as I say, not as I do" Christian. We should 'show *and* tell' others what it means to be godly. This has implications for discipleship as well; may we always be those who model—as well as speak—godliness.

B.   DEPRAVITY IN THE CHURCH (5:1-6:20)

In this section, Paul addresses three cases of moral depravity which had been brought to his attention. The first is a case of incest (5:1-8), which gives Paul an opportunity to instruct them on how Christians should associate with unbelievers, and with willful sinners in the church (5:9-13). The second involves believers taking each other to court (6:1-11). The third concerns participation in the pagan temple prostitution of Corinth; some in the church were suggesting such conduct was permissible (6:12-20).

While these problems seem unrelated to the divisions of 1:10-4:21, an obvious connection is that both were brought to Paul's attention by reports from others (1:11f; 5:1f). Beyond this, the implicit threat to Paul's authority as an apostle is common to both sections. Paul calls on believers in Corinth to follow him instead of the arrogant leaders who were steering them off course. In 4:14-21, he claims authority over them and announces his soon coming to test their power. These cases are the issues which he will address. They were not properly judging immorality in their midst; he would do so—and in the power of the Lord (5:4)! They were letting pagan courts settle their internal disputes; he would have none of it. They were justifying immoral relations with prostitutes with contemporary slogans; he would show the foolishness of such reasoning.

In the widest sense, it must be recognized that these three moral problems result from the same faulty human wisdom which led to the divisions of chapters 1-4. In 5:1-13, human wisdom is shown to be full of 'gray areas,' compromise, and cover-ups. God's wisdom has no such hang-ups; it discerns moral decay and roots it out. (It is noteworthy that in their human wisdom, the church in Corinth misconstrued separation as being from the outside world, instead of from the worldly who were in their midst. Such a misconception is endemic in the church today.) In 6:1-11, human wisdom subtly elevates itself so that the wisdom of God within believers is discounted by comparison. The end result is a devaluing of what is of God and a prideful elevation of what is human. In 6:12-20, the presence of human wisdom is most obvious. The participation with temple prostitutes is justified with 'slogans'—pithy sayings of current 'in vogue' wisdom. Such 'politically correct' maxims were stupidity compared to the wisdom of God.

Here then is a three-step dismantling of humanism—the doctrine of human wisdom. Humanism seeks to confuse and compromise moral judgment and thus stifle moral action, then to elevate man's judgment over God's, and finally to replace God's word with man's trite clichés. Paul's application of God's wisdom exposes it all.

5:1-8   *Paul exhorts the Corinthian church to judge openly sinning believers because unjudged sin pollutes the whole assembly.*

Paul's progression through this paragraph must be closely followed. He begins by identifying the problem, which is not only that immorality such as is detailed exists in the church, but primarily that the church has not dealt with it (1-2). They did not judge the blatant sin because they were arrogant and indifferent. In vv.3-5, Paul tells how he would handle the situation; his way is to exclude the guilty party from fellowship. And why would he do this? As verse 5 will affirm, it is to restore the sinner to fellowship, but as vv.6-8 add, it is ultimately to preserve (or restore) the purity of the church. To summarize, the reason why the church should exclude openly sinning believers from church fellowship is because this will preserve the holiness of the church.

1   The opening phrase *It is actually reported* (lit. *It has actually been heard*; passive of ἀκούω) is not intended to be as abrupt as it seems at the beginning of a new chapter. While starting a new paragraph, it is connected to Paul's closing question of 4:21: "Do I need to come with a rod or not? Listen to what I have heard about you!" This is one area in which they need to heed his message, and if they do not, they will be up for chastisement when he comes.

The indictment is made: *there is immorality in the church*. While πορνεία in Paul's epistles can mean any kind of illegitimate sexual intercourse (DNTT, 1:500; cf. 6:13, 18; 7:2), its meaning here is specified. It is characterized as *immorality of such a kind as does not exist even among the Gentiles*; this was an act which went beyond even the depraved acts of pagan Corinth. This heinous evil was *that someone has his father's wife*. That is, a man was taking his father's wife (his own step-mother) and having an ongoing incestuous sexual relationship with her. (For a similar relational use of the verb ἔχω [to have], see 7:2.) For Paul, such behavior was a breach of God's law (cf. Lev. 18:8), but even those who did not know the law should have discerned the inherent evil in this act. This was worse than what the pagans did!

2 But Paul quickly moves on from the sin to those who were tacitly condoning it through their inaction; καὶ ὑμεῖς (*And you*) is emphatic. It is as though he says, "This heinous sin is taking place, and look at you! What are you doing?!" No sooner is the sin identified than it is left behind; the real issue is the failure of the church to respond to the sin in their midst. This reflects their spiritual condition.

They are *arrogant* (πεφυσιωμένοι; cf. 4:6, 18, 19). The NASV *you have become* diminishes the directness of Paul's indictment; "Someone is committing incest, and you are proud!" The insinuation is not that they were proud of the person who committed this sin, nor even that they endorsed his actions. Rather, it is that they remained proud of themselves (the false view of their own wisdom) and their supposed exalted spiritual condition while this was going on. They had *not mourned instead* for the loss of whatever position they might have had. They should have, *in order that the one who had done this deed might be removed from your midst*. If they recognized the spiritual ramifications of such spiritual pollution in the body, they would have also responded properly to one committing such a sin.

The interesting point here is that while the Corinthians were quick to set themselves up as judges of their leaders (1:12; 4:5), when judgment was called for in their own assembly, no one was paying attention! Why? They glibly and self-assuredly viewed themselves as kings (4:8; cf. Col. 2:18). Like the church at Laodicea, they needed eye-salve to anoint their eyes so they could see their own depravity (Rev. 3:18). The warning of 10:12 is exhibited in process here; those who *think* they stand are about to fall.

If they had been remorseful, the guilty offender would have been *removed* (NASV)/*put out* (NIV)/ *taken away* (NKJV). The difference in the Greek between ἐξαίρω (MajT) and αἴρω (CrT) does not affect the meaning, although the former makes for a tidy beginning/ending repetition (inclusio) to Paul's discussion on this problem (cf. comments on v.13 below, the only other use of ἐξαίρω in the NT). This action entails putting the sinner outside the circle of support and fellowship of the church, and is a presage of Paul's determination which follows.

3   The emphatic ἐγώ signals that Paul's response to such sin will be different from theirs, and will show the correct way to deal with it. The Corinthians were so focused on human wisdom, they didn't react to public, heinous sin right under their noses! They had become spiritually blind to what should have been obvious. Paul, even *though* he was *absent in body*, could see the problem, because he was *present in spirit*. Such sinfulness is not merely perceived physically, but spiritually (cf. 1 Sam. 16:7). In the spiritual realm, it was as if he were present. The spiritual power he possessed in Jesus Christ (v.4) was present and effective even if he was absent; his judgment was sure.

Paul did not need to do any background studies, nor evaluate the social and environmental causes of this man's actions. These modern concerns are notably absent, even though a case could be made that the pressures of living in Corinth would contribute to such moral decay. Paul was not ignorant of these social pressures (cf. 7:26). The issue, however, was not what had contributed to the existence of such sin, but what would contribute to its cure! In this regard, Paul has *already judged him who has so committed this, as though I were present.*

4   The judgment is announced with proper gravity. It is prefaced with *In the name of our Lord Jesus*, indicating that He alone who is the Judge of all things is the One behind this decision. (The NIV and some commentators [Barrett, 124] make this phrase adjectival to the assembly ["When you are assembled in the name of our Lord Jesus"]; while possible, this is not preferable.) It follows that the decision also has God's *power* behind it (to which Paul refers in 4:19f). The sin is public; the announcement of judgment too is public (*when you are assembled*).

     The phrase *and I with you in spirit* (the Greek καὶ τοῦ ἐμοῦ πνεύματος is literally "and my spirit") repeats what Paul stated in v.3. Since the Body is spiritual, it is not necessary to be physically present in order to be spiritually present. He is 'in the Spirit,' and the Spirit is among them (3:16); therefore, he too is among them. And he is among them *with* (σύν) *the power of our Lord Jesus* (*Christ*, NKJV).

5   His decision is to *deliver such a one to Satan for the destruction of his flesh, that his spirit may be saved in the day of the Lord Jesus* (NASV).

Interpretive Note: Exactly what Paul's decision entails is debated. Some suggest it signifies giving the sinner over to civil authorities, since Roman law prohibited incest (Orr/Walther, 186). Their punishment would hopefully bring him to repentance. But in light of Paul's instruction in 6:1-11, this idea seems unlikely, and since the incest was public knowledge, any civil action could have been taken anyway. Others think it means literally handing someone over to Satan (as in Job 2:6), but that is not the issue here. Rather, as verse 2 indicates, this judgment involves putting an unrepentant sinner outside the sphere of church support (5:11, 13; cf. 1 Tim. 1:20). In practical terms, this did not mean he could not be present at church meetings, but that the blessings of church comradeship were denied. The exposure to sin outside the protective environment of the church is where the sinning member will come face to face with the results of his sin. Instead of having the love, concern, and support of the body, he will feel the full effect of the evil which he is embracing. The end result of this exposure is the *destruction of his flesh*, which can mean anything up to and including physical death. Death is the ultimate punishment for sin in the life of the believer. Such punishment for sin is evident in this letter (11:30) and throughout the New Testament (Acts 5:1-11; Jas. 1:14f; 5:19f). But this is not the expectation (cf. 5:11) or the aim of the discipline which Paul enjoins.

The desired goal of the incestuous man's exclusion from the church (*that his spirit may be saved in the day of the Lord Jesus*) is also debated. Some commentators take this to refer to final justification; the sin of incest shows that this man has lost his salvation (a denial of eternal security), or never was saved in the first place. This misses Paul's point entirely. Paul has made it clear that their salvation is sure (1:8). Indeed, eternal life, by definition, cannot be lost (or it was never *eternal!*). The goal here is that the guilty person will feel the effects of his actions in the context of the world, repent of his sin, be restored to fellowship, and be thus *saved* from further judgment before Jesus Christ (3:13; 4:5; 9:24-27; cf. 2 Cor. 5:10). That this is intended as a tool of instruction and not just elimination is clear from Paul's parallel usage in 1 Tim. 1:20, where the offenders are delivered to Satan so that they may be *taught* (παιδεύω = to child-train, or raise a child with instruction and discipline (cf. Heb. 12:6f, 10); this verb also describes the desired result of God's judgment in 1 Cor. 11:32) not to blaspheme. Some of the Christians in Corinth clearly needed such child-training (3:1)!

Finally, we can hold out hope that the church heeded Paul's call to action, and that the sinning member was restored to fellowship. If 2 Cor. 2:6f and 7:9-12 refer to this episode, such seems to be the case.

Application: Today, the desire for numerical church growth may cause many churches to avoid the kind of discipline Paul enjoins in this passage. This may contribute to spiritual weakness and participation in worldly pursuits. We are foolish if we try to improve on the biblical instruction here. Modern thinking views such discipline as old-fashioned and harsh, but in the end it is shown to be loving in that it leads to repentance.

6   The harsh judgment he has just announced has not caused Paul to forget the real issue here, which he noted in vv.1-2. The arrogance of the Corinthians resulted in their inaction in response to this sin, forcing Paul to pronounce judgment from afar. Now that he has done this, he focuses again on the church as a whole. *Your* (plural) *boasting is not good.* Boasting never is (unless it is in the Lord, 1:31), and their boasting in their perceived spirituality especially so! Their pride blinded them to their own spiritual need. It resulted in them failing to apply a basic principle they should have known well: *Do you not know that a little leaven leavens the whole lump of dough?*

Leaven signified the presence of sin in Old Testament law. The Feast of Unleavened Bread began on Passover each year (cf. Exod. 12: 15-20; 13:3, 7); the commemoration of the birth of the nation (Passover) was thus followed by a reminder of the need to be holy and pure. Instructions for grain or meal offerings stipulate that they are not to be made with leaven (Lev. 2:4, 11). The significance of leaven was clear in Jesus' teaching (cf. Matt. 16:6, 11f; etc.), where it symbolized the danger of the teachings of the Pharisees which, if listened to at all, would then fester and grow. Paul has already used the symbol of leaven for evil (Judaistic legalism) which must be totally avoided (cf. Gal. 5:9), so his meaning here is clear.

In the person of the incestuous man, the church at Corinth had become polluted with a deadly sin; it was in their "lump" (congregation). But like an inept physician, they looked at a malignant growth, and called it benign! *Do you not know...?* is Paul's rhetorical way of saying, "You certainly should know...!" (3:16; 6:2, 3, 9, 15, 16, 19; etc.). They were so deluded, thinking they were wise and perceptive (3:18), they did not even realize there was an unholy element among them which was destroying their sacred condition (3:17).

7   Continuing with his figure of the Corinthian church as a lump of dough, Paul exhorts them to follow his instructions and get rid of the infected part (cf. vv.2, 5): *Clean out the old leaven, that you may be a new lump.* The reason they should do this is because they *are in fact unleavened.* This is similar to Paul's call for them to recognize that they were in fact holy in 3:17. They must begin to see themselves as they really are in Christ, not as they are in their own eyes. Their own wisdom deceived them into thinking they were well when they were sick. Paul wants them to see that in Christ they are something holy; when they begin to realize this, they will mourn and grieve (5:2) when sin comes into their midst.

Paul makes a brief but explicit parallel between the Passover lamb and Christ to secure his point. On Passover all leaven was removed from the country (Exod. 12:19; 13:7) in preparation for the Feast of Unleavened Bread, which began with the sacrifice of the Passover lamb at twilight. Since *Christ our Passover also has been sacrificed*, it is past time for believers to eradicate evil from their midst! They had been saved by the blood of the Lamb, 'passed over' from eternal death, because His blood was applied in their lives. They should imitate the Old Testament example and clean the leaven of sin from their midst.

8   By doing so, they can *celebrate the feast* as the holy people they are—without sinful contamination: *not with old leaven, nor with the leaven of malice and wickedness, but with the unleavened bread of sincerity and truth.* Perhaps there is an implicit reference here to the Lord's Table—a celebration the Corinthians needed to "get the leaven out of" (11:28-32)! Regardless, the call is for them to

be holy; this will result if they begin to mourn the sin in their midst. If they do this—and expel the sinner (for his purification *and* theirs)—their actions will truly reflect who they are: an "unleavened," holy assembly of believers.

Homiletical Ideas: A case study like this, with its concise statement of the problem and its solution, is invaluable. The clarity of Paul's approach to the problem of sin makes this an excellent passage for teaching on church discipline. But the focus of our teaching should be in the same place it was for Paul—on the church as a whole, and our corporate stand for holiness, not on the individual sinner.

We might entitle this paragraph, "The Case of the Corrupt Corinthians," because while Paul is taken aback with the heinous sin practiced by one in the congregation, his ire is directed at the arrogance of the whole group who have not confronted this evil. The implicit suggestion is that by failing in their duty, they are party to the sinning man's spiritual demise. Paul's apostolic intervention is not a pattern for pastors or other church leaders today; rather, it is a 'last resort' when the other channels have failed (cf. Matt. 18:15-17). Paul's message is, "Church Discipline Starts with You!" Believers in the local church should lovingly hold each other accountable, and in this way preserve the purity and holiness of the body (cf. Eph. 5:25b-27).

5:9-13 *Paul directs the Corinthian assembly to associate with immoral people in the world, but to distance themselves from immoral people in the church.*

These verses can easily be seen as a unit with the rest of this chapter; however, while the subject is the same in effect, and certainly the conclusion (13) harks back to the issue in 5:1-8, the issue of a lingering misunderstanding of something Paul wrote in a previous letter sets this apart as a distinct paragraph.

9   Since leaving Corinth, Paul had already written a letter back to the church there, in which he instructed them *not to associate with immoral people.* The term πόρνος (pornos) refers to people who are sexually immoral. The connection with the preceding context is transparent. Paul expected the Corinthians to understand that he meant they should not associate with those who polluted the church from within. But they had gotten it wrong. Perhaps this contributed to their lack of spiritual discernment, a deficiency exposed in 3:1-2. Now that Paul's intended meaning has been made abundantly clear in the case of the incestuous man, Paul sets about clarifying his meaning in his previous letter.

10   The message he *did not at all mean* for them to get was that they should not associate *with the immoral people of this world, or with the covetous and swindlers, or with idolaters.* They were *not* to avoid sexually immoral people in the world...or sinners of any other description. While his conclusion (*for then you would have to go out of the world*) may reflect the awful moral condition of Corinth (and these sins did describe Corinthian society), it also reflects a universal truth. The church is in the world for a purpose, and that is not to avoid the world as much as possible. It is to 'infect' the world with the love of Jesus Christ, and expose the world to the gospel. This task is hindered by open sexual immorality within the church, and thus it needs to be removed. Sadly, the Corinthians' misunderstanding of Paul's message led to the opposite result from that which he had intended. Instead of being purified and thus having a more potent impact on the world, they remained polluted and distanced themselves from the world!

11   What Paul intended for them to grasp, and what he now makes clear, was that they should *not associate with any so-called brother if he should be an immoral person, or covetous, or an idolater, or a reviler, or a drunkard, or a swindler*—that they are *not even to eat with such a one.* The distinction between the church and the world needed to be clear, otherwise the impact of the church on the world would be nullified.

Translation Note: The expression *so-called* in the phrase *any so-called brother* translates the Greek participle ὀνομαζόμενος (from ὀνομάζω, "to name," BAGD, 573f). The idea conveyed by "so-called" in English, that the person is not "really" a brother, just 'called' one, does not accurately reflect the meaning of the Greek verb (compare the passive participle of λέγω in 8:5 and Eph. 2:11). A better translation here is *anyone named a brother* (NKJV), that is, a fellow Christian.

Theological Note: It may be that the translation "so-called" is motivated more by theological presupposition than exegetical study. Indeed, many commentators conclude that such a sinning man either never was (Mare, 220) or had ceased to be (Fee, 224; Barrett, 131) a "brother" in the spiritual sense (a regenerate person)—based on his behavior. In addition to the havoc this interpretation causes to the doctrine of salvation by grace through faith alone apart from works, or to any assurance of salvation, it further reflects a distorted view of this context. While a person's spiritual condition is known only to God, Paul clearly assumes this person *is* saved. He is not treated like those who he behaves like (unbelievers), who are unsaved (see v.10). It is not the unbeliever, but the one who bears the name 'brother,' who is to be shunned by other believers. In verse 12, Paul will again make it clear that the church is to judge those who are *within* it, not those who are on the outside (unbelievers) of it. Only the most intrusive interpretation would lead to the conclusion that Paul is encouraging the Corinthians to hunt for phony Christians in the assembly! Clearly, the "so-called" brother" in v.11 is a believer, and is treated like any openly-sinning believer should be.

The final admonition *not even to eat with such one* may include fellowship gatherings and home meals. The similar ban in 2 Thess. 3:14-15, however, indicates that exhortation continues.

12   Having cleared up any lingering misconceptions, Paul now ties up his argument with two rhetorical questions, an answer, and a command. These serve to both conclude his response to the case of the incestuous man, and introduce his next topic, taking each other before pagan courts.

For what have I to do with judging outsiders? The reason they are not to distance themselves from the immoral people of the world is because that is not their sphere of judgment; rather, the church is. *Do you not judge those who are within the church?* In other words, they are to judge those inside the church, and leave those outside the church to God (13a).

Two issues arise here. First, hasn't Paul told them they should not be passing judgment in the church (4:3, 5)? Yes, but the issue here is preserving spiritual purity. In the previous context, they were arrogantly judging others, instead of humbly judging themselves—being critical of others, while blind to their own need. Here, the exhortation is to recognize and respond to their own spiritual need.

Secondly, how does saying they are not to judge the world jive with the assertion that saints will judge the world in 6:2? Simply that in the future, when the church age is completed, those saints who are 'overcomers' will have the special privilege of reigning and ruling with Christ in His Kingdom (cf. Rev. 3:21).

13   The reason believers should not be passing judgment on those outside the local church is because *those who are outside, God judges.* Those outside the protective and nurturing environment of the church face the full effect of God's wrath on sin (Romans 1:18-32), and the conviction of the Holy Spirit (John 16:7-11). This is why the willfully and openly sinning believer must be put out.

Paul's final admonition is found often in Deuteronomy (cf. 17:7, 12; 21:21; 22:21; 24:7; in the LXX, as here, the verb is ἐξαίρω, which agrees with the MajT reading in v.2; see above): *Remove the wicked person from among yourselves!* (It is interesting that the NKJV has broken with the MajT here, which takes the quote directly from the LXX, making it a future indicative: "And you shall remove the wicked one from among you.") This phrase provides a fitting summary to Paul's instruction on how to deal with a sinning believer in the church. It calls for an end to the inaction of the body, and an effective dealing with the sinning member. With it, Paul rests his case.

Homiletical Ideas: Perhaps the most telling sign of a weak and ineffective church is that it becomes ingrown, building ever-higher walls between itself and the world, becoming ever-more irrelevant to the issues of the world in which it exists. Paul's calls us back to our 'original charter.' The church is to be 'in the world, but not of the world.' Obviously, the issue of church discipline which is displayed in vv.1-8 is further clarified here, but Paul's fundamental purpose is to correct the Corinthians' misconception from his previous letter that they should avoid association with sinners in the world. Paul did not at all mean that, for these are the very ones they (and we) have been sent to reconcile to God through Christ (cf. 2 Cor. 5:18f). This is a message the church in the 21st century needs to hear and apply. It is no overstatement to say that generations with no knowledge of God's love and grace will be lost eternally if we do not confront them with the gospel now.

6:1-11 *Paul instructs the Corinthian assembly not to take each other before human courts because they are competent in Christ to judge themselves.*

Paul has prepared the way for this instruction in the previous paragraph. He told the church they should have known that when he wrote them *not to associate with immoral people*, he was talking about people in the assembly, since it is not the responsibility of the church to judge those who are outside, but inside. This was the opposite of what they had been doing, as the case of the incestuous man (inside the church), and the present discussion concerning litigation (outside the church) clearly exhibit.

1   With the abrupt rhetorical question, *"Does any one of you...?"* (which implies at least one did), Paul exposes the second depraved action which has come to his attention; one Christian *has a case against his neighbor*, and to settle it, he goes *to law before the unrighteous, and not before the saints.* Some in the assembly had the audacity (τολμάω; BAGD, 829; *dare*, be brave enough, presume; cf. Rom. 5:7) to take a brother to the civil court. In Paul's view, this was a disgrace to the cause of Christ. They failed to properly respond to the sin of incest in the church; now they are unable to even settle a dispute between two Christians without going to an outside court! They are going to the unrighteous (τῶν ἀδίκων) instead of the saints (τῶν ἁγίων). And they think themselves wise?!

In Paul's view, every believer should understand their high position as a Christian. They are recipients of God's grace and gifts (1:4-8), God's power (1:18), and God's wisdom (1:24). They have received the Holy Spirit (2:12), and with the Spirit, a wealth of spiritual insight the unregenerate can never know. They are God's field, God's building (3:9), God's temple (3:16). They are holy (3:17; 5:7). The Christians in Corinth are unthinkably acting no different than those in the world. This is the antithesis of who they are! Clearly, they need to be reminded of their place in Christ, the privileges and responsibilities which are theirs, and their distinctiveness from the world. This Paul immediately sets about doing.

2   As in the case of the incestuous man, Paul quickly moves from the sinning member to the entire church community. This suggests that he knows there is a lack of condemnation of the action of the man, and why not? After all, they exalted human wisdom alongside the gospel; now they were installing it as a worthy judge in their internal affairs! Their humanistic vision,

which led to self-exaltation (4:8), then moral confusion (5:2), now leads to a tacit denial of the value of God's wisdom which they have received.

Having identified the problem, Paul now begins to explain why believers should not be taking each other before pagan courts. In general, this is because of who they are in Christ. Specifically, the first reason (vv.2-4) is because society's civil courts are staffed by people who are nothing in comparison to saints. Imagine two members of the Supreme Court taking a disagreement to a group of first graders to decide! (Ironically, such idiocy occurred during Mao's Cultural Revolution in China, when students were given the power to judge their teachers. The result was a loss of direction, and intellectual chaos.)

Why are Christians more capable judges than the unsaved? The first evidence comes from eschatology: *the saints will judge the world*. Paul's opening *"Do you not know...?"* (οὐκ οἴδατε; cf. 3:16) signals that they should have known this. Paul may have taught them this during his time in Corinth.

Interpretive Note: When will saints judge the world? This must refer to judging that will take place in conjunction with Christ's judgment on the world. It may refer to our participation in His judgment at the Second Coming (Rev. 19:11ff), but more likely is related to the judgment that will be entrusted to saints in the Millennial Kingdom. This role is based in Dan. 7:18, 22, and seen in Matt. 19:28 and Rev. 3:21; 4:4; 20:4.

This statement is not a contradiction of 5:12. There the idea is that Christians should not be judging the world in the present age; instead of condemning the unsaved for their sinful practices, they should be concerned about their own holiness! In addition, the Christians in Corinth should not be judging their leaders (siding with one or another, and dividing among themselves), but they should 'judge' the wisdom of this world to be foolishness. They should judge themselves (11:31) and among themselves—to make sure they are individually and corporately pure—but they are not to judge those outside the church—*yet*. That day of judging will come, and it will follow the Day when they themselves will have been judged by Christ (3:13; 4:5); having been thus fully and finally cleansed of all impurity, they will *then (and only then)* be fit to judge the world with Christ.

But for Paul, this future promise has present ramifications. Since we are already *positionally* that which we will someday be *experientially*, we should live now in the light of that reality. For example, the fact of positional holiness called for practical holiness (3:16-17; cf. 6:19-20). Here, the second rhetorical question builds on the first: *If the world is judged by you, are you not competent to constitute the smallest law courts?* The implication is, since (εἰ denotes a condition of fact; that is, it is assumed to be true) the world is going to be judged by saints, we ought *now* to be able to *at least* judge the petty issues which exist among ourselves!

Translation Note: The NASV (*smallest law courts*) differs from the NIV/NKJV (*trivial cases/ smallest matters*) in the final phrase of v.2. The Greek κριτηρίων (cf. v.4) can mean either law court or lawsuit (BAGD, 454). The NASV translation is difficult, but would mean something like "Can't you even put together a small court to deal with your petty problems?" The second rendering is preferred; for those who will one day judge the world, is it too much to tackle your own petty problems now?

---

3   The second reason Christians are more competent judges than the unsaved is because they *shall judge angels*. This again makes absurd their inability to judge *matters of this life* (βιωτικά). Instead of the second sentence of this verse ending with a question mark,

an exclamation point (NIV) is more fitting. *To say nothing of the things of this life!*

4   Paul now ties up his argument. *If then you have law courts dealing with matters of this life*—or, perhaps better—*If you have disputes* (κριτήρια) *over matters of this life* (which was certainly true of them!)—*do you appoint them as judges who are of no account in the church?* (NIV makes this a command—"appoint judges…"—an interpretive rendering.) The bottom line is this: *Don't let those outside the church make a ruling!* Human judges may be wise, but even if they can handle such a dispute, how much more should the saints be able to?

5   Paul now speaks with stinging irony, and exposes the Corinthians' blindness to their own need; *I say this to your shame* (cf. 4:14). In a church that prided itself on its wisdom, *Is it so, that there is not among you one wise man who will be able to decide between his brethren?* Couldn't they find one person who could adjudicate in this dispute? Of course, the wisdom which they were courting was a wisdom which elevated men, and this tied them to the wisdom of their society.

6   Paul resolutely drives home his point. His incredulity is transparent. You think you are so wise, *but brother goes to law with brother, and that before unbelievers!* It was bad enough that believers were having disputes; that they aired them for judgment before unbelievers was appalling. Verses 5-6 are an argument from shame and shock. The Corinthians are shamed; Paul is shocked. And the stage is set for Paul to pass his judgment on this sort of judging.

7   The only conclusion that can be drawn from the pitiable scene is that the Corinthian Christians have already lost the case—regardless of who wins in court! *Actually, then, it is already a defeat for you, that you have lawsuits with one another.* They settled for an earthly referee—when they themselves are bound for heavenly courts! They hung their dirty linen out for the world to see—when they are in fact holy. Shame!

Perhaps it is implicit here that the wrong committed had so divided the congregation, they were in two factions, and both wanted blood. In an assembly noted for divisions, this is not unlikely. Churches are notorious for disputing and dividing over the most mundane issues, issues at which the world snickers and points with disdain.

The more honorable way? *Why not rather be wronged? Why not rather be defrauded?* That is, why not take the personal loss, instead of spreading it over and around the whole church? The Greek term for *defrauded* (ἀποστερέω, cf. BAGD 99; steal, rob) may indicate that someone had cheated another out of something. In 7:5 this term applies to the denial of sexual fulfilment. In Jas. 5:4 it denotes wages wrongly withheld by an employer. Regardless, no matter how 'within his rights' the plaintiff was, he should have taken the loss instead of taking it to court. In doing the latter, he—and the church as a whole—was a guaranteed loser.

8   Those who supported this course of action are guilty of the same thing they charged others of doing. How? *On the contrary, you yourselves wrong and defraud, and that your brethren.* When they took a brother to court for wronging and defrauding them, they were themselves wronging and defrauding them—and the vicious cycle continued. While they were redeemed saints, they were living like those who were not. It was expected that those outside the church would choose such a course; but that fellow believers would do it was unbefitting of their position as saints. They needed a refresher course on the distinction between themselves now and who they had once been. And Paul gives them one.

9-10   For the third time in this paragraph (vv.2, 3), Paul appeals to their stunning ignorance (*Or do you not know...?*). Surely they must know *that the unrighteous will not inherit the kingdom of God?* Of course, they do, and this picks up the distinction between saints and the unrighteous from vv.1ff. Saints will judge the world and angels—and be in the kingdom. The unrighteous will not. Paul emphasizes his point (and their self-deception) by saying *"Do not be deceived!"* (cf. 3:18). Those things which characterize the unrighteous (they are *fornicators, idolaters, adulterers, effeminate, homosexuals, thieves, covetous, drunkards, revilers,* and *swindlers*; note the inclusion of coveting, a sin which Christians in a materialistic society might not think of as being as bad as the other vices listed here) are not to be descriptive of those who are in the fellowship of saints! The fact that they *are* showing up is cause for alarm. The reference to fornicators (πόρνοι) points both back (5:1-8), and forward to the sexual immorality in 6:12-20.

Theological Note: It is essential to guard proper soteriology at this point. Some commentators recklessly suggest that those who *persist* in sins such as those listed here will be in danger of losing their entry into the kingdom (Fee, 242, 245). Can eternal salvation be lost, after it is once possessed? Or, to borrow Nicodemus' imagery in John 3, can a Christian 'crawl back into the spiritual womb' and be 'unborn'? Obviously, this violates the heart of the gospel message. Sadly, many arbitrarily assume that abhorrent sinners (in our eyes) are not saved. But we must not limit the grace of God on the basis of the sins of men (cf. Rom. 5:20f). We all sin (and battle with sin daily); why are only those who sin *badly* (this usually means sinning worse than the one passing judgment) unsaved? It is patently clear that if any *kind* or *amount* of sin can cause a Christian to lose his salvation (or indicate he was never saved in the first place, which amounts to the same thing), then there is sin that is not covered by the cross. This passage gives a list of sins which are *descriptive of the unsaved*; it is not intended as a test of regeneration! It is given as a reminder of the kind of people the Corinthian Christians once were, and the kind of people they *should* no longer be as a result of their conversions. The motivation for lists like this is not to cause readers to doubt their salvation (a task handled well by Satan), but to stimulate them to holy living.

11   This vice list was once descriptive of those who were now in the Corinthian church (*And such were some of you*; cf. 1:26-29). But they *were washed* (ἀπελούσασθε; cf. Acts 22:16; see theological note below), *sanctified* (ἡγιάσθητε; made holy; refers to positional sanctification; cf. 1:2), and *justified* (ἐδικαιώθητε; cf. 4:4, "acquitted"). That was not their work; indeed, no part of their salvation or spiritual life and abilities could be called a result of their work (1:30-31). It was *in the name of the Lord Jesus Christ, and in the Spirit of God.*

Theological Note: The reference to being washed is sometimes construed as supporting the doctrine of baptismal regeneration. It is true that the only other use of ἀπολούω in the New Testament (Acts 22:16) is in the context of water baptism, and relates to the forgiveness of sins (cf. Acts 2:38). Acts 22:16 involves a *transitional* requirement at the onset of the church age, when baptism preceded the reception of forgiveness of sins and the gift of the Holy Spirit for certain believers (both Jews on the Day of Pentecost [cf. Acts 2:37] and Paul [on the Damascus road] already believed in Jesus Christ). Water baptism was never a requirement for reception of *eternal life*; for a time, it was a condition of fellowship for certain early believers. The use of ἀπολούω here, however, is not directly related to water baptism; like λουτροῦ in Tit. 3:5 and λούσαντι (MajT) in Rev. 1:5, it refers to the reception of eternal salvation by believers.

6:12-20 *Paul instructs the Corinthian assembly to reject sexual immorality with prostitutes because the physical body is for the Lord.*

As in 5:1 and 6:1, Paul changes subjects without any formal transition. This serves as a literary tool (attention grabbing), but also indicates a corresponding relationship with the preceding context. Fornicators (πόρνοι) headed Paul's vice list (6:9); related terms πορνεία ("immorality," 13, 18), πόρνης ("prostitute," 15, 16), and πορνεύων ("one who practices immorality") dominate this section. Also, Paul just affirmed the privileged spiritual position of the Corinthians (11); he did this to motivate them to live a life in keeping with that position. The present paragraph will close with a similar call.

The issue in this paragraph is sexual immorality with temple prostitutes, a practice which some in Corinth were justifying on the basis of slogans like "All things are permissible for me!" and "Food is for the stomach, and the stomach for food, but God will do away with both of them!" Perhaps our saying, "A man's got to do what a man's got to do!" would be similar. These "nuggets" of human wisdom are exactly the kind of thing Paul detests. Now he uses them to confront "the case of the Christians going to prostitutes."

12   *All things are lawful* (or *permissible*) *for me* was most likely a slogan, reflecting the pride and arrogance of the Corinthians. The sense here is, "I can do anything I want to!" They had the right to decide what they would do; no one was going to take that freedom away from them! This attitude led to their immoral liaisons with prostitutes, so Paul begins by dealing with it.

Paul qualifies their right to decide with two conditions; while all things may indeed be permissible (not that he agrees, but for the sake of argument, he grants it), *not all things are profitable* (συμφέρει; beneficial, for the common good). Instead of asking if having sex with prostitutes was permissible, they should have asked if it was profitable. Secondly, while all things may be permissible, Paul states, *I will not be mastered by anything.* They thought they were strong and independent, so they could do what they wanted, even commit sin. They failed to consider how such sin could overpower them. For Paul, these two conditions nullified the supposed logic in their slogan.

13   Another Corinthian saying was: *Food is for the stomach and the stomach is for food, but God will do away with both of them.* This slogan stated an obvious truth; the stomach and food were made for each other, and both are temporal and will be done away with. Perhaps this saying had affected the eating habits of

some (cf. 11:21); it was used to justify the satisfaction of bodily appetites (since God had made them—and they were made for the present age). The net result was to drive a wedge between the actions of this life and any ramifications in the life to come (a distinction which is invalid when it comes to the body; see v.14), or to promote living life like there was no future day of reckoning, as some who denied the resurrection were doing (cf. 15:32). This was a fallacy; as Paul knew from the Old Testament (cf. Isa. 22:12-14; 56:12) and as Jesus taught (cf. Luke 12:19f), present actions do have future results. Paul's point in this verse is to make clear that whatever application the slogan had for food restrictions ("We can eat whatever we want!"; cf. 8:1-13; 10:23-11:1, where Paul limits those actions), it did *not* apply to physical sexual appetites! Paul echoes their saying, but changes the subject-object from food-stomach to immorality-body. They were wrong to equate these two; food may be for the stomach and the stomach for food, but *the body is not for immorality, but for the Lord, and the Lord is for the body.*

Their argument went something like this: "Everything is permissible for us, and God has given us physical appetites (like hunger and sex drives) to be met by what He has provided, and these are for the present age, since they will be done away with in the end...so let's go for it!" They sound like an old beer commercial: "You only go 'round once in life, so grab for all the gusto you can get!" "If it feels good, do it!" was their cry. Though Christians today would rarely condone the Corinthians' sin (having sex with prostitutes), contemporary equivalents—materialism and hedonism, justified with claims of "abundant life" and enjoying "God's blessing"—are common. What was their error (and what is ours)? They had made a basic mistake, an invalid correlation; food was for the stomach, but immorality was never for the body; the body was for the Lord, and the Lord for the body. Why is the body for the Lord? See vv. 14, 19-20. Why is the Lord for the body? Because in His death and resurrection He provided for the bodily resurrection of saints.

14   This verse completes Paul's parallel response to the saying of the Corinthians in v.13a. They said that God would do away with both the stomach and food. Here Paul anticipates what he will argue in chapter 15 concerning the resurrection of the body. The reason the Corinthian slogan was invalid was because *God has not only raised the Lord* (bodily), *but will also raise us up through His power*. All Christians will be raised *bodily*. The dualism of the Corinthians (an odd variation on gnostic thinking) made physical actions in this life of no effect in the life to come, as if the decay of the body indicated that any deeds done in the body would also fade away and be forgotten. Paul's teaching in other contexts (3:10-17; 4:1-5; 5:5; 6:9-11) has already dismantled this argument, and here he does it again. In effect, he says, "Your analogy between food for your stomach and immorality for your body is all wrong! The stomach is for food...but the body is not for immorality! And unlike the stomach and food which will be done away with, the body (and those things done in it) will be raised (for a future judgment)!"

15   As in the case of the litigious saints (6:1-11), Paul uses the introductory phrase *do you not know...?* three times in this paragraph (cf. 16, 19), indicating that this is something they should have already known. The basis for Paul's argument is the correlation between Christ's body and the believer's body (v.14). Christ's body has been raised, and so too (positionally, and eventually) has the Christian's. The future experience of resurrection reality with Christ is already true; it just hasn't been realized yet. The upshot is that the Christian is actually part of that resurrected 'body of Christ' (*members* is from μέλος, which refers to parts of a physical body). With this in mind, Paul asks rhetorically: *Shall I then take away the members of Christ and make them members of a harlot?* The answer is obvious: *May it never be!* This strong adversative (μὴ γένοιτο) is translated "Never!" (NIV) or "Certainly not!" (NKJV); "What a ghastly thought!" reflects Paul's mood well. As far as he is concerned, it is abhorrent for

any believer to consider taking part of the resurrected Savior and giving it to a prostitute to be part of her body!

16   "What do you mean...part of a prostitute? How can we become part of a prostitute just by having sex with her?" It is this question, which Paul anticipates some of the Christians in Corinth might ask, to which he now responds. Again, they should have known (*Do you not know...?*) that by having sexual relations with a prostitute they were becoming part of her. Indeed, *the one who joins himself to a harlot is one body with her*. Why? Because in Gen. 2:24, God says that if a man and woman consummate a physical union, *the two will become one flesh*! When they had sexual intercourse with a prostitute, they were literally joining their body with hers. The abhorrence of such a union is apparent.

17   As believers, they were joined to the Lord. *But the one who joins himself to the Lord is one spirit with Him.* In the spiritual realm, it is impossible to break this union; believers *are* the Lord's possession, one with Him (19b-20; cf. 3:9). Christ *cannot* become party to immorality; when the believer takes part in such sin, he loses part of himself to it. Therefore, believers who are joined to Christ must not indulge in such activities. *Who they are* spiritually is to be reflected in *what they do* physically.

18   Paul therefore commands: *Flee [sexual] immorality* (cf. 2 Tim. 2:22). This does not come as a surprise; everything Paul has said pointed to it. He just makes it explicit now. Their reasoning was flawed, and he has shown this. Their action was also wrong, and it must be changed.

At this point, another issue which shows the foolishness of having sex with a prostitute comes to Paul's mind. The phrase *"every [other] sin that a man commits is outside the body"* may reflect another slogan which the Corinthians used to divorce themselves from any effects for their actions, or it may simply be a proverbial truth which Paul adopts. Regardless, Paul declares that *the immoral man sins against his own body*. The lack of any connective between the command to flee immorality and this instruction suggests a transparent relationship between the two. The idea which seems to follow from Paul's command to "Flee!" is this: "Every sin a person commits is outside the body (it is something you can flee from); but where can the immoral man flee?! His sin is within himself!" As many commentators note, other sins besides sexual fornication are indeed against one's own body (cf. Barrett, 150). But for Paul, sexual sin is unique in that it is bringing that which is impure right into the body of the believer and joining it with him.

19   The reason Paul sees fornication in such a distinctive light is now explained. In vv.15-17 the fact that the believer's body is a member of Christ's body is the basis of his argument. Paul now states that the Corinthians should have known (*Or do you not know...?*) that the individual believer's *body is a temple of the Holy Spirit*. The gravity of Paul's distinction in v.18 is clear; since the body is for the Lord (v.13), it is to always be presentable to Him. This is explained in the fact that the body is a temple of the Holy Spirit *who is in you* and *whom you have from God*. A temple is always to be kept pure and holy (just as the whole church as a "temple" was to be; 3:16f). They justified sexual sin on the basis that the body would be done away with (v.13), forgetting that the Holy Spirit is living there *now!* Paul can therefore add *that you are not your own*; they are the rightful possession of God, who purchased them through the blood of His Son, and who indwells them in the person of the Holy Spirit.

20   The final phrase of v.19 and the beginning of v.20 go together (NIV). As God's temple, the believer has more to think about than only his own wishes; this is because *you have been bought with a price*. Since the Holy Spirit has been given by God to the believer (2:12-13) and dwells in him, we are not free to indulge in any acts we want to. The arguments of vv.12-17 have shown the fallacy of the "wise" Corinthian slogans; now Paul says that not only does such sinning not make sense, it is an affront to the spiritual

resident in our bodies—the Holy Spirit. It is like throwing dirt into the Holy of Holies, for the body is where the Holy Spirit dwells! Beyond this, the Holy Spirit is there by right of purchase. They and their bodies were the Lord's possession as a result of the death of Jesus Christ on the cross (1:30-31); it was the message of Christ crucified that they believed (1:18, 21-23); it was all freely given to them by God (2:12). Only the crassest reasoning could lead one who has received everything to ignore the will of the giver!

The conclusion? *Therefore* (δή; BAGD, 177; gives urgency to the command) *glorify* (δοξάσατε; praise, honor, magnify) *God in your body.* This is the reciprocal command to that in v.18. Believers are to flee from that which dishonors God, and hold fast to that which exalts Him. He has paid such a price for them, seeking to avoid dishonoring Him is not enough; their highest aim must be to make His temple a fitting and welcome dwelling place, where He is exalted.

Homiletical Ideas: Chapters 5-6 are excellent for a series of messages on The Christian and the World. The specific problems dealt with are present in different ways today, but the basic issue throughout is the intrusion of the world and its system and values into the church. The insidious humanistic forces which ever seek to bring the church down to the world's level and elevate the world to the place of God are always attacking believers. It is here that practical answers are given which, when implemented, can begin to restore the two-fold mandate of the church—to be separate from the world (holy, pure), while at the same time being in the world (being salt and light to it).

Another theme of these chapters is the holiness of the church. With the barrage of mocking and insults directed at the church in the media (sadly, often fueled by public disclosures of impropriety by church leaders), Christians need to rediscover a high view of their

---

identity as the body of Christ. If we see ourselves as God sees us, we will be more likely to live the way He desires us to live.

Chapter 6 deals with two always-contemporary subjects: litigation and licentiousness. It may be tempting when teaching this chapter to heap condemnation on those who are involved in such practices—perhaps in the hope that by creating a negative perception, people will avoid them. Unfortunately, this approach is more likely to lead struggling believers to become hypocritical, hiding their sin instead of dealing with it. Paul's approach is to reason with brothers and sisters who he *knows* are practicing such things, so that instead of feeling condemnation, they will be motivated within themselves to change. In teaching these passages, reason with the congregation, show the spiritual rationale for such holiness, and exhort them to join you in pursuing it.

III

DIFFICULTIES IN THE CHURCH RAISED TO PAUL (7:1-16:4)

With the opening phrase *Now concerning the things about which you wrote (to me;* MajT/NKJV*)*, Paul reveals the source for the topics he addresses in the rest of the letter. In response to questions sent to him by members of the Corinthian assembly, he deals with subjects ranging from marriage and divorce to spiritual gifts. The practicality of these issues and their relevance in every age has made Paul's instructions the object of countless studies with varied conclusions. Few who come to these passages do so with an objective mind; most come with a heavy load of presuppositions, looking for a way to support them! This actually increases the importance of Paul's instruction: His words are not his alone, but by inspiration, the words of God as well. We should therefore be all the *more* careful to resist the urge to 'color' Paul's words to agree with theological views. God is speaking, and we must be ready to listen.

A. QUESTIONS CONCERNING MARRIAGE ARE DISCUSSED (7:1-40)

This chapter actually contains two different topics (as denoted by Paul's characteristic Περὶ δὲ, *Now concerning*, introducing each section). First, he advises those who are married or formerly married (1-24); he then turns his attention to those who have not yet married (25-38), with vv. 39-40 being a brief added note concerning the permanence of the marriage bond for life and the freedom of a widow to remarry if she pleases.

The two topics flow in the same current, however, as Paul's underlying theme is for them *to stay as they are* (cf. 2, 8, 10, 12, 17-24, 26ff, 40). For those who are married to believers, they are to remain married in order to avoid falling into temptation (2a, 5b) and to be obedient to the Lord (10f). For those married to unbelievers, they are to remain married for the spiritual benefits which may accrue from such a union (14, 16). For those widowed (8f, 39f), and those who have never been married, they should stay as they are if possible, since this will allow them to be free of temporal problems and concerns (28b, 29-35; cf. 40a).

7:1-7 *Married believers should not abstain from sexual relations because to do so invites temptation to immorality.*

1   It is no coincidence that Paul responds first to a question about marriage and sex. The preceding section (6:12-20) dealt with sexual involvement with temple prostitutes, an action the Corinthians had justified on the basis of meeting physical needs (6:13). Paul points to the marriage bed as the place where such appetites are alone to be met.

The expression *it is good for a man not to touch a woman* may have been a slogan used by Christians in Corinth, possibly based on a general principle Paul had taught them during his time there. In the context of sexual licentiousness for which Corinth was well known, such instruction would hardly be surprising. But whatever agreement Paul had with this principle, it did not apply to married couples! That interfered with sexual relations in marriage—and thus directly contributed to a problem of sexual temptation which was rampant in their society.

Translation Note: The NIV reading (*It is good for a man not to marry*) is not really a translation, nor even a good paraphrase. Reflecting perhaps their own concerns, the third edition includes a note in the margin: *Or "It is good for a man not to have sexual relations with a woman."* The phrase γυναικὸς μὴ ἅπτεσθαι (lit., "not to touch a woman") clearly is idiomatic, referring to sexual relations (cf. BAGD, 102), but to equate such actions with getting married is lexically uncalled-for and simply wrong in this context. Paul is not suggesting that his readers should not marry (he will discuss this later), but focusing in on the act of sexual gratification in marriage. As the following verses show, it was their teaching of sexual abstinence between married couples to which Paul objected.

---

2   Paul's response to the Corinthian slogan is not a denial of its truth, but a clarification of its sphere of application. It does *not* apply within marriage. *But* (δὲ) *because of immoralities, let each man have his own wife, and let each woman have her own husband.* Two issues need to be clarified here: What are the *immoralities* which motivate Paul's instruction, and what is meant by the verb ἐχέτω ("to have") in this context?

Immoralities refers to general sexual temptations present in Corinthian society, particularly the temple prostitution of 6:12-20. Verse 5 further suggests this idea in its reference to a "lack of self-control." Evidently, the idea that sexual abstinence in marriage was a virtue had led some couples to take this path, with the result that husbands were going to the temple for satisfaction. Paul condemned this immoral action and the philosophy which justified it in the previous paragraph, but here he begins his response to their questions concerning marriage by pointing out that sex in marriage is designed to satisfy their physical needs, and that for this reason alone they should not refrain.

The meaning of Paul's instruction for each man to *have* his own wife and each woman to *have* her own husband follows directly from this. The view that Paul is instructing all men and women to get married in light of the rampant immorality of Corinthian society is absurd (see his teaching in vv.8f, 25-35, 38, and 40). Paul is rather saying that those who are married should have sexual relations with each other (cf. the use of ἔχω in 5:1).

3   Paul carefully elaborates on his meaning in vv.3-4: *Let the husband fulfill his duty to his wife, and likewise also the wife to her husband.* More literally, both husband and wife are to give (ἀποδίδωμι, "give away, give up;" BAGD, 90) what is due (τὴν ὀφειλὴν; cf. Rom. 4:4; 13:7) to each other. The way for each partner to *have* the other is for both to consider it a fulfilling of their duty to give what is due to the other.

> **Translation Note:** The MajT here reads τὴν ὀφειλομένην εὔνοιαν (*the affection due;* NKJV). The presence of the noun "affection" probably reflects the original text, since any basis for its later addition is doubtful. The only other New Testament occurrence is Eph. 6:7, which, like the only use of the cognate verb εὐνόεω (Matt. 5:25), occurs in a context of social relationships. While the basic meaning is not affected, the longer reading identifies that which is due as something good.

4 And why should they consider this a *duty?* Because *The wife does not have authority over her own body, but the husband [does]; and likewise also the husband does not have authority over his own body, but the wife [does].* The control of each one's body is not theirs exclusively, but jointly 'managed' with their partner. The NIV reading here continues a very average effort in this paragraph; the question is not one of ownership ("does not belong to her alone..."), but of rights and power (ἐξουσιάζω; BAGD, 278; cf. 6:12). Neither husband or wife has the right to refuse or demand sexual relations; rather, the desires of one's spouse must also be considered. The marriage bond is a balance between rights and responsibilities. Each has a duty to fulfill to the other, and each has rights which they may claim from the other. The emphasis is on giving what is due to the other, and granting rights to each other. Sexual relations are here raised to a place of central importance in the context of marriage.

5 This leads to Paul's explicit response to those who had wrongly interpreted the slogan of 7:1 to be enjoining sexual abstinence in marriage: *Stop depriving* (ἀποστερέω, "rob, defraud," BAGD, 99; cf. 6:8) *one another!* Sexual relations were not to be shunned, *except by agreement for a time that you may devote yourselves to prayer.* The conditions are precise. First, abstinence is only by agreement; this implies a harmonious decision made together. The Greek συμφώνου, used only here in the New Testament, gives us our English word "symphony;" just as the sexual union is to be a

marriage of rights and duties, so too times of abstention are to be decided in concert. Second, abstention is only for the purpose of spending time in prayer (MajT includes *fasting*, suggesting a practice of denying all physical appetites). Only devotion to God should break the physical union between a husband and wife! Third, it is only for a set time (certainly limited if fasting is included!), after which they should *come together again lest Satan tempt you because of your lack of self-control* (cf.v.2).

The spiritual union with God in prayer would of course provide for a natural buffer against the onslaught of Satan's temptations during such a time of sexual abstinence, but even this is not to be drawn out. The implication is that there may be an agreed-on time for separation, but this is to be limited, and sexual intimacy restored, so that the lack of self-control (τὴν ἀκρασίαν; self-indulgence; here it denotes the physical appetite for sexual pleasure) will not become a tool of temptation for Satan.

6   But even this exception is *by way of concession* (συγγνώμη; BAGD, 773), *not of command*. That is, Paul is not commanding seasons of abstinence for spiritual devotion. This is not necessary. However, because some thought that refraining from sexual relations was spiritually desirable, Paul would go half-way with them. He would concede them the right to separate for a time of prayer, but they had to limit it. Paul is dealing with Christians who, in the midst of the lascivious Corinthian society, decided the only legitimate response was total abstinence. This amounted to pious legalism, and actually heightened the lure of that which they wanted to avoid. If they were serious about being spiritual, then let them abstain for a time to devote themselves to the Lord. But this is not a command; it is an allowance to those who feel that abstinence is essential to spirituality.

7   Those who touted abstinence as the spiritual 'high road' may have thought they would find a sympathetic ear in Paul, since he was unmarried. But Paul would have none of it. He confesses, *I wish that all men were even as I myself am*—that is, he wishes they

had the gift of celibacy. *However, each man has his own gift from God, one in this manner, and another in that.* Each man must live in accordance with his gift; some are gifted to be celibate and sexually inactive, others to be married and sexually active.

It is this tandem which is the key. The Corinthians were imposing sexual abstinence on those who did not have 'the gift' of celibacy. Sexual abstinence is not for everyone—and certainly *not* for those who are married. To encourage such a prohibition is to expose them to an area of weakness and temptation. Married believers, therefore, should not abstain from intimate sexual relations, because to do so invites temptation to immorality.

7:8-9   *Although Paul wishes they would remain single, widowers and widows may remarry if they lack self-control.*

Why is this little paragraph here? Perhaps Paul had once been married, a fact suggested by the likelihood that he had been a rabbi, and was now a widower (see below on the meaning of the term *unmarried*). As he writes in v.7 concerning his gift (celibacy), it occurs to him that some of his readers are widowers/widows, yet do not have the gift as he has. He has given a general principle that not everyone is as he is, and therefore sexual abstinence is not a universal rule. It is only for those so gifted. This then raises the question of others whose spouses have died; are they to look for the same gift as Paul now has? What if they don't receive it?

Perhaps because of this relationship with the preceding context, the NKJV includes these verses in a single paragraph (1-9). The subject is sufficiently different, however, to warrant a break. Verses 1-7 are directed to married couples, exhorting sexual fulfilment. Verses 8-9 are directed to surviving spouses, exhorting re-marriage *only if* the physical appetite for sex has clearly not waned.

8   The initial interpretive issue in this verse concerns the identity of the ἀγάμοις—the *unmarried* person. This term occurs only in this chapter in the New Testament, but is sufficiently broad to

encompass a divorced woman (11), an as-yet unmarried young man (32), and an as-yet unmarried young woman (a virgin; 34).

None of these designations fits here, however. Instruction to those never married begins in v.25 with the definitive τῶν παρθένων ("virgins"), and Paul's instruction to a divorced woman to remain unmarried or be reconciled to her husband (v.11) differs from his allowance of marriage here. The *unmarried* here are therefore widowers (see Orr/Walther, 210; Fee, 287f; Findlay, 825). In Koine Greek ἄγαμος was the normal term used to describe a widower. Indeed, this is the meaning we would expect to find opposite ταῖς χήραις (widows). Throughout this section, Paul repeatedly balances his instruction to both husbands and wives; it is most natural to see him doing the same here. Therefore, Paul is here giving instruction to "widowers and widows."

To those who have lost their spouses, then, Paul says *it is good for them if they remain even as I*. That is, it is good if they choose to remain single. As noted above, Paul may have himself been a widower (see Fee, 288, n.7); he was definitely unmarried. In either case, his instruction is clear. To remain unmarried is a good thing.

9 However, this is not a mandate. The principle of v.7b applies here to widows and widowers; *if they do not have self-control, let them marry*. One who did not have the gift of celibacy and lacked self-control (ἐγκρατεύονται; cf. 9:25) should get married. This is because (γάρ) *it is better to marry than to burn*. 'Burning' (πυρόω; BAGD, 731) is a figurative reference to the heat of sensual desires, not to the fires of judgment.

7:10-11 *Christian couples should not seek divorce, and if divorced, should remain single or be reconciled.*

10 For believers, this verse is fundamental instruction on the subject marriage and divorce. Any misconception about the permanence of marriage from vv.8-9 is here dispelled. Paul's instruction is *to the married*, and is the teaching of *the Lord* (cf. Matt. 5:32;

19:3-9; Mark 10:2-12; Luke 16:18). Directed first to the wife, and then to the husband (11b), the teaching is that there is to be no divorce. *The wife should not leave* (χωρισθῆναι; the verb is passive, and can be translated "be separated from") *her husband.* She is not to cause a separation, nor is she to leave.

11   But what *if she does leave?* A parenthesis is provided in the case that the ideal is breached. If separation does occur (the reason is not given; perhaps because of immorality, as in 5:1 or 6:12-20), two new commands take force, in an "either/or" arrangement. Either she is to *remain unmarried, or else be reconciled* (καταλλαγήτω) *to her husband.* As with Jesus' teaching, this presents the absolute ideal established by God (cf. Gen. 2:24), and also clearly prohibits adultery in the case where divorce has taken place. The same ideal applies to the husband as to the wife; *the husband should not send his wife away.* He is not to divorce (ἀφιέναι; let go, send away) his wife.

Why is this such a fundamental and important teaching? As far as society is concerned, it is foundational; God has so designed mankind that when the family is strong, the human community is strong. When the home dissolves, so too does the society which it held together.

But for the believing couple, the significance is even greater. A Christian marriage is a reflection of the spiritual marriage union between Christ (the bridegroom) and the Church (His bride) (cf. Eph. 5:22-27). Just as Christ cannot be divorced from His bride, neither should the earthly union be broken.

Even the directions in case of separation have spiritual significance. Just as a divorced wife is reconciled to her husband, so too all believers have been reconciled to God, and no paramour can take the unique place of the one true partner. Should a believer ever wander from fellowship with the Lord, there is never any other 'mate' with which to join; the only option is to return to the Savior. The standards for Christian marriage are eternal and unchanging, and as a reflection of the spiritual bond in an age in which divorce and remarriage is common, they warrant our sincere obedience.

7:12-16 *Christians married to unbelievers should remain married if possible because their influence may bring the unbelieving spouse to faith.*

12   For the third section in a row, Paul begins with an introductory *But...I say...* (cf. 8, 10), indicating another sub-group requiring special instruction in the issue of marriage. Here, it is those involved in spiritually mixed marriages. His instruction is *not* from the teaching of *the Lord*, but no less inspired. In Corinth, Paul's evangelistic preaching had led many to faith in Christ, resulting in cases where one partner was a believer, and the other not. How should the believing partner respond in this situation? If marriages between Christians were coming to grief in that hedonistic culture, how much more so would unequally yoked partners?!

Paul's basic instruction does not change here. As with widowed spouses and believing couples, *if any brother has a wife who is an unbeliever, and she consents to live with him, let him not send her away.* A believing husband is not to initiate divorce from his unbelieving wife. If she agrees (συνευδοκεῖ; approve, consent) to live with him, he should not seek to dissolve the relationship.

13   In the same way, if there is *a woman who has an unbelieving husband, and* if *he consents to live with her, let her not send her husband away.* The believing wife is not to divorce her unbelieving husband if he agrees to live with her. No further moral stipulation (for example, stopping going to temple prostitutes) is enjoined. Both cases are identical; the saved spouse has one goal—to preserve the marriage. If the marriage is destroyed, the saved member is not to be the initiator. Believers married to an unsaved partner are not to seek a change in their position.

14   Why is this so? Because (γὰρ) *the unbelieving husband is sanctified through his wife, and the unbelieving wife is sanctified through her [believing] husband.* That is, the partner may be led

to faith through the testimony of their mate. Paul's point is simple; instead of a mixed marriage polluting the saved partner, such a union provides a context in which the unsaved partner is *sanctified* (ἡγίασται, "set apart"). Other uses of this term in the epistle (1:2; 6:11) concern the position of believers in their union with Christ. But here the unsaved partner, by virtue of their union with a believer in marriage, is in a position whereby the holiness of the believing partner can affect their life. In the same way, while *children* without any parental spiritual input *are unclean*, the children in a home with even one believing parent *are holy*. The impact of one believer in a home without any other witness is profound; that single presence sets all other members of the family apart.

Obviously, we must avoid interpreting the terms "sanctified" and "holy" to suggest in any way that spouses and children are eternally saved by being related to or living with believers. The idea that children of believers can by being (infant) baptized be 'saved' [Mare, 230; Orr/Walther, 214; Barrett, 165f; see Charles Hodge, *Systematic Theology*, 3 vols. (Eerdmans, 1989), 3:547-79ff] is utterly foreign to this context. No one is saved by the faith of another. Rather, contact with believers provides exposure to the love and grace of God, leading to faith in Jesus Christ, which the unsaved might otherwise never know.

15 Before finishing the thought which he has begun concerning the influence of a believer on an unbelieving spouse, Paul inserts this statement on the possibility of the unbeliever leaving the marriage.

The meaning of the first phrase is obvious; *if the unbelieving one leaves, let him leave*. Nothing should be 'read into' this. It is no more than a statement of fact; you can't force a spouse to stay! If an unbeliever divorces the believing spouse, so be it. Paul then adds that *the brother or the sister is not under bondage in such cases*. The meaning here is less clear. Some believe Paul means that the believing partner can now remarry (Orr/Walther,

214). This is doubtful; to be *under bondage* (δουλόω, "bound as a slave," BAGD, 206) is not the same as being "bound" (δέω; cf. Rom. 7:2). Remarriage does not seem to be at issue here; rather, the believer simply is not bound to pursue the relationship.

The final phrase, *but God has called us to peace*, is more cryptic. The reference to being *called* (κέκληκεν) points to their conversion to Christ, and the higher standard of life to which they aspire as believers (cf. 1:9; 7:17-24); believers should exhibit composure rather than being confrontational. Paul may be saying that instead of the unbelieving partner leaving, it is God's desire that there be peace in the marriage and it survive, leading to the salvation of the spouse (16). On the other hand, he may be saying that it is God's desire that the unbelieving partner be allowed to leave (and the relationship maintained from a distance) in peace, with the result that this testimony will lead to the salvation of the unbelieving partner (16). Either may be true of this context, and both are certainly true in the wider context. God desires the continuation of the marriage; if that is impossible, then separate without acrimony.

16 Why go to such extremes—maintaining an unequal yoke, or keeping peace even in the dissolution of a marriage? Paul's reasoning reflects his commitment to "do all things for the sake of the gospel" (9:23). *For how do you know, O wife, whether you will save your husband? Or how do you know, O husband, whether you will save your wife?* The rhetorical questions here stress the distinct possibility of success.

For Paul, the possibility of reaching the unsaved takes precedence over any pursuit of the 'ideal marriage.' To desert an unsaved spouse in order to marry a Christian is unthinkable. The marriage bond (regardless of a spouse's spiritual condition) is binding for life (11, 39; cf. Rom. 7:1-3). Furthermore, the context of a marriage relationship provides a unique setting within which an unsaved partner is exposed to the working of the Spirit in a believer's life (cf. 1 Pet. 3:1-2). This is an opportunity not to be missed! To save a life for eternity through efforts in time is never too great a sacrifice.

7:17-24 *Christians should not seek to alter their position in life as a result of conversion because keeping God's commands—not status—is what matters.*

As the 'centrepiece' of Paul's discussion of issues related to marriage, this paragraph relates to what has preceded and what will follow. In both contexts, the theme of not seeking to change one's marital status—whether married, widowed, or single—is evident. As such, this paragraph does not really belong exclusively to the first half of this chapter (and its discussion of the married and formerly-married).

However, it is clear that this paragraph follows directly from the subject of verses 12-16—instruction to Christians married to unbelievers. Paul has told these brothers and sisters to stay with their unsaved spouses, since they may lead them to faith through their example of self-control and contentment. This is a practical reason, but there is an even more fundamental reason why they should not try to change their situation; that is because their relationship with Christ is not affected by nor dependent on any social relationship. Their newfound fellowship with the Lord *is* affected by their obedience to God's commands, but anything else is incidental.

17   The link between this paragraph and the preceding one is the negated conditional conjunction, Εἰ μὴ (lit. "If not," but best rendered as in the NIV, *Nevertheless*). The idea follows from v.15: "If an unbelieving spouse wants to leave, that is their prerogative, and the believer is not bound to pursue the union. Nevertheless..." Verses 17-24, then, affirm that while a marriage between an unbeliever and a believer may end in divorce, it is *never* something which a believer should desire or pursue as a result of coming to Christ.

Rather, *as the Lord has assigned to each one, as God has called each, in this manner let him walk* (περιπατείτω; i.e., live his life; cf. 3:3). The focus again returns to the time of their conversion. What was their status when they first believed? Married to an unbeliever? Married to a believer? Widowed? Whatever their status, this is their "assignment" (ἐμέρισεν; *distributed*/NKJV; *assigned*/NASV, NIV). This term refers to division elsewhere in this letter (1:13; 7:34), and here denotes that specific 'slice of life' in which they were called and are living. Therefore (to apply the principle in the preceding context), if they were saved when married (and their spouse did not convert), they are not to try to get out of the relationship; God has called them to be a witness in it.

Practical Note: This principle needs to be heeded by contemporary Christians. Many are converted while living in bad relationships. It can be tempting to want to remove them from that environment, almost as if their salvation depended on it! While divorce may not be suggested, the pressure on a new believer to join in religious activities may create conflict with the unbelieving spouse, and weaken the marriage. Separation from impure and unethical behavior is important (2 Cor. 6:14-7:1), but that was never meant to promote isolation from the world (see 5:9-10), or (in this context) divorce from an unbelieving spouse. We are to be holy in our actions and relationships (cf. 15:33f); however, this is not achieved by separation from the world (5:9f)!

We are to be holy because that is who we are in Christ, and we are to be holy without leaving the state we were in when saved. What could be a better witness to the life-changing power of Jesus Christ than to remain after being saved in the same setting one had been in before being saved, letting one and all see the effects of Christ on a life?

The final phrase of verse 17 (*And thus I direct* [διατάσσω; "order, command," BAGD, 188] *in all the churches*) indicates that this teaching may have been received less than enthusiastically by the Corinthians. Their pride made them want to go their own way, and in their wisdom they had a tendency to question Paul's instruction. So Paul emphasizes that what he is telling them is standard teaching in all churches, a fact which also signifies that it is the Corinthians, not all other Christians, who are out of line!

18   The first illustration of this principle (remain in the condition in which you were saved; cf. v.20) is drawn from the socio-religious arena. *Was any man called [already] circumcised? Let him not become uncircumcised. Has anyone been called in uncircumcision? Let him not be circumcised.* Circumcision is simply of no concern to a believer (v.19; cf. 12:13). To become uncircumcised was unnecessary for a Jewish convert, and to be circumcised was pointless for a Gentile (as Paul emphasizes elsewhere; cf. Gal. 2; 5:1-6; 6:15; Col. 2:11f).

Historical Note: The practice of "un-circumcising" was not uncommon for Jews who wanted to look like Greeks and avoid abuse or ridicule, or just conform to society. Josephus (*Antiquities* 12.241) tells of Jews who, because of going to a "gymnasium" where exercises were performed naked, hid the circumcision of their genitals—some by an operation [see Fee, 312, n.27; Robert G. Hall, "Epispasm: Circumcision in Reverse," *Bible Review* 8:4 (August 1992), pp.52-57.]

---

19   With abruptness to emphasize the total lack of question which exists on the matter, Paul asserts that in Christ the issue of circumcision is totally superfluous; it is *nothing*. (Since this is so, it is also true by implication that whether one is married or not, or married to a believer or not, is also nothing. It just does not matter.)

What matters is the *keeping of the commandments of God*. Paul's off-hand dismissal of the issue of circumcision here suggests it was not a problem with the Corinthian church. To tell a Jew that circumcision was nothing, then add that one should obey the commandments of God, would seem self-contradictory. Circumcision *was* the commandment of God (Gen. 17:10-14). What they failed to distinguish was the difference between physical circumcision (essential in the covenant nation) and spiritual circumcision (Deut. 10:16; Jer. 4:4; Rom. 2:28f). God's concern was with the latter. They were to be obedient to Him, which once included circumcising all males (Exod. 4:24-26). In the New Testament, spiritual circumcision is revealed as a result of the work of Jesus Christ on the cross (Col. 2:11). What is now called for is "obedience of faith" (Rom. 16:26). The unity of Jews and Gentiles together in the body of Christ renders physical circumcision of no effect (Eph. 2:11-22). But the principle of being obedient to God's commands, whatever they might be, is unchanged.

20   This leads Paul back to his original principle, only here he states it more succinctly than in v.17. *Let each man remain in that condition in which he was called.* Regardless of their "condition" before conversion, they are now one of "the called," not called out of the world, but called to exhibit as living examples to the world the difference knowing Jesus Christ makes in a life.

21   Paul's second illustration comes from the practice of slavery. *Were you called while a slave? Do not worry about it.* To those thus bound, Paul says, in effect, *'Never mind'* (μέλει; BAGD, 500). He adds that *if you are able to become free, rather do that.* This illustration is appropriate in the present setting. Paul has told them to stay in the condition in which they were called, and those "stuck" in marriages they would prefer to get out of might view themselves as 'enslaved' (forgetting their opportunity to save their partner). Not only should they stay as they are, they should stop worrying about changing it. What matters is keeping God's commands.

22   Why shouldn't one who is a slave worry about it after conversion? *For he who was called in the Lord while a slave, is the Lord's freedman;*

likewise he who was called while free, is Christ's slave. In Christ, all have been set free, and all are slaves of Christ. Paul here reduces the question of human conditions to the level of insignificance which it should have in comparison with spiritual reality. The theological reality of what has happened in Christ far outweighs any existing social arrangement, even slavery. Spiritually, a slave is no different than a free man, since both were under the bondage of sin, and both are now delivered from it. They have been "bought with a price" (23), and they are now serving another. The slave now serves the Lord in his service of his earthly master, knowing that his ultimate reward will come from the Lord (Eph. 6:5-8; Col. 3:22-25). In this regard, he is no different from a person who is free; both serve the same master.

The bottom line? Don't worry about your condition. If you were a slave, you're now free in Christ! Conversely, the one who was free is now a slave! So it really doesn't make any difference. Either way, living for Christ—keeping the commandments of God (19)—is what matters.

23   Using the same figure which he drew upon in 6:20, Paul now begins to draw his application from the present illustration for the context of marriage. Because they *were bought with a price*, they no longer belong to the old order. They belong to Christ; He has bought them out of their old slavery to sin, and purchased them as His own slaves.

As such, they are never to *become slaves of men*. This does not simply refer to an economic relationship, although it would seem to follow that a Christian should not put himself willingly under the control of another. But Paul is making an application; since you have been bought out of the old slavery, don't go back to it again! That old way emphasized social status and conditions; the new way disregards them. The old standard emphasized making a name for yourself; the new rule exalts the name of Christ. The former way of life was bound to the wisdom of man; the new way is bound to the commandments of God.

And finally, that old wisdom suggested they should seek to change their condition now that they were saved, but God has a better way. Remain as you are, do not worry about your status, and serve Christ. Others will see this, especially spouses, and who knows? Perhaps they will as a result be saved (7:16).

24   The conclusion follows closely v.20. The differences between that verse and this reflect the added ideas drawn from the slavery image. Paul begins by calling them *brothers* (ἀδελφοί); in Christ, a slave is a spiritual sibling (cf. Philem. 16)! The Church is an egalitarian assembly: Social conditions don't matter; who you are in Christ does. (Communism seeks to imitate this equality by using the title "comrade," but it doesn't work, because while all are 'equal,' some are 'more equal' than others! Not so in the body of Christ!) One married to an unbeliever is no less than one who is celibate. A celibate widower is no more spiritual than one who does not have that gift and thus choses to remarry. After all, each one is a free man, and a slave in Christ.

Paul concludes that *each man* should *remain with God* (μενέτω παρὰ θεῷ) *in that [condition] in which he was called.* Whether they are married, widowed, separated, married to an unbeliever, circumcised, uncircumcised, enslaved, or free, they now belong to God, and what is important is that they remain with Him. All other relationships now take second place. It is in their responsibility as slaves of Christ that they should live, and one feature of His will is that they remain as they are.

Homiletical Ideas

The practical instruction of 7:1-16 is transparent. In a sex-saturated society like Corinth (and western society today), emphasis on physical things is dangerous. All should live in accordance with their gift (7). Those who are married should give themselves to each other sexually so as to prevent any undue pressure on the relationship (1-7). Widows/widowers should remain single unless their passions compel them to remarry (8f). Divorce is never the option of choice for Christian couples, but if it does occur, the former partners must remain single or be reconciled (10f). Those married to unbelievers should remain with them if possible as a 'live-in witness' for Jesus Christ so that they might be saved (12-16). In all these things, the overriding principle is that believers should not be focusing their efforts on changing social status.

In preaching these truths, do not duck the vital social ramifications, but emphasize the need to focus on our standing in Christ, not our status in the world. In verses 17-24, the principle of satisfaction in Christ is laid down. All believers need to learn to heed their heavenly master, not worldly goals. In whatever condition we are, that is where we should strive to serve Christ. And in a sex-driven society, these truths need to be heard.

7:25-40 *Paul encourages unmarried believers to remain as they are, but those who are engaged and desire to get married should feel free to do so.*

This section is Paul's instruction to unmarried members of his audience, continuing the theme that Christians should not seek to alter their position in life. Fee (323f) observes correctly that even Paul is not overly dogmatic in his instruction here, and thus we are wise to be careful not to be overbearing in our intrusion into the personal lives of others. However, for a variety of reasons, Paul suggests that his unmarried readers (including those unengaged, engaged, and widowed), if possible, remain unmarried.

The section as a whole breaks down into two major parts: advice to those never married (25-38), and advice to those previously married (widows; 39-40). Within the first section, the essence of Paul's advice is given (twice), in verses 25-28 and 36-38; in between, he explains in more detail his reasons for advising those who are single against getting married.

25-28   [Paul encourages unmarried believers to remain single to spare them difficulties (although those who do get married are not sinning).]

25   The opening *Now concerning* (Περὶ δὲ) sets this section apart as a distinct unit, while its subject matter clearly ties it to the issue of relationships from the first half of the chapter. The main issue to resolve at the outset involves the meaning of τῶν παρθένων (*virgins*). It is not enough to say this refers to those who are unmarried, for Paul has already used ἀγάμοις (lit. "unmarried") in verse 8. While verses 39-40 are addressed to widows (and thus this section is directed to *all* unmarried believers), παρθένος refers to someone *never* previously married. The issue of betrothal (engagement) is also involved here, since for those not involved in a relationship of any kind the question of these verses would be largely unnecessary. Perhaps it is best to see Paul writing in response to some who were engaged and wondering whether they should go ahead and get married or not; at the same time, his principles would be applicable to all those who had never been married.

Interpretive Note: Some translations force the idea of giving virgin daughters away in marriage on this passage (cf. vv.36-38, especially NASV, but also NIV/NKJV margin readings). This is not necessary, as we shall see, nor is it best, since it certainly is not reflected in Paul's comments in verses 25-35! A second suggestion, that Paul was responding to so-called "spiritual marriages" in which the partners lived together but refrained from sexual relations (cf. NEB on vv. 36-38), can be easily discarded. Paul's instruction in 7:2ff has already made it clear that such a practice is not acceptable.

Paul's admission that *I have no command of the Lord, but I give an opinion...* reflects a more subdued approach which echoes throughout this section (vv.26, 40 [*I think*], 28 [*I am trying*], 32 [*I want you*], 35 [*this I say for your own benefit*], 36 [*let him do what he wishes*], and 40 [*in my opinion*]). Clearly, Paul is garnishing his instruction with a generous amount of grace.

26 Paul's opinion, echoing his theme in vv. 17-24, is that *it is good for a man to remain as he is*. An unmarried believer should remain unmarried.

Translation Note: The NKJV *I suppose therefore...* is too casual; Νομίζω, both here and in v.36, conveys a decisive opinion based on thought and data. In common jargon, at least, *I suppose* communicates doubt as much as assertion. *I think* (NASV/NIV) is preferable.

But Paul prefaces this statement with a reason; it is *in view of the present distress* (contrast ἀνάγκην here, where it has a pejorative sense, with v.37 and 9:16, where it means *necessity* or *compulsion*; cf. ἀνάγκη, BAGD, 52). Paul does not reveal what this 'distress' is. Perhaps he is thinking of the sexual debauchery in Corinth, and the stress it put on marriages, and beyond this, the trials which believers would encounter in the world; in view of these things, rushing into marriage is not desirable. What is interesting is that instead of simply commanding their obedience here, he feels the need to justify or support his advice. In light of this, it is prudent for us to approach this issue without dogmatism. Those who look to this verse for instruction to singles should bear in mind Paul's attitude, and not become a source of distress or compulsion for one facing this difficult and personal decision.

27 Paul now explains what he means by his call for a man to remain as he is, but his precise meaning is far from clear! Is he saying that married believers should not seek divorce, and those who do divorce should not seek remarriage? This is clearly the view of the NIV (*Are you married?... Are you unmarried?*), which is too interpretive for a translation. Favoring this view is the word *bound* (δέδεσαι), Paul's normal way of referring to marriage (v.39; Rom. 7:2). But this view is not without its problems. 1)

The issue of marriage and divorce is not the focus of the present context. 2) Paul's instruction to *not seek to be released* (μὴ ζήτει λύσιν) is not his normal way of referring to divorce (vv. 10, 12f). 3) Even more telling is the fact that Paul's *advice* here is given as an *opinion* (v.25), but if this were instruction on marriage and divorce, it is more than that: It is a command of the Lord (vv.10-11)! There is a better option.

That option is that Paul is here referring to those who are engaged in the first instance, then to all singles in his second question. To paraphrase, he is saying: *Are you bound to (engaged to marry) a woman? Then don't rush out to break it off! Are you free from* (passive of λύω: "loosed;" cf. NKJV) *commitment to a woman? Then don't seek a wife.*

28   This view is immediately qualified by Paul: *But if you should marry, you have not sinned; and if a virgin should marry, she has not sinned.* This is not the begrudging permission of one who is objecting to marriage; after all, Paul came from a Jewish heritage within which it was considered nearly mandatory to be married! Rather, Paul seems to be responding to some dogmatists who asserted strongly that marriage was wrong. His *advice* is that whether or not one gets married is in itself totally outside the question of sin. (The questions of *who* one marries (a believer), and perhaps *when* and *under what circumstances*, might raise moral issues, but the question of whether or not one should get married is not itself such an issue.)

Why does Paul go to all this trouble if either way a person choses to go is acceptable? Because he is concerned for the singles in the Corinthian assembly. They are maturing in a sex-saturated society which, mixed with the ascetic dogmatism of those declaring the merits of celibacy, could lead to confusion and a preoccupation with marriage. Paul wants to defuse the issue, and for them to avoid unnecessary problems. His response is therefore proffered as advice, without any call for strict adherence. He gently warns them that in the present circumstances (v.26), remaining single might well be the less trying way to choose. Those who marry *will have trouble in this life, and I am trying to spare you.*

Practical Note: It is not uncommon for young singles to see marriage as a panacea for all their problems. They come to the altar with insecurities and low self-esteem, hoping to find security and significance. But marriage is not the 'jackpot' in the lottery of life! Unrealistic expectations of 'marriage bliss' often result in disillusionment and divorce. Paul's words, while given in a specific context, could well be heeded in the present day (perhaps modern western society is not so different from Corinth).

29-31   [Paul encourages unmarried believers to remain single because of the imminent arrival of the end of this age.]

29   The opening phrase (*But this I say*, NASV) translates Τοῦτο δέ φημι. While φημι can mean "say," Paul normally uses λέγω to introduce a simple assertion (cf. 6, 8, 12, 35). His use of φημι here probably indicates he is explaining what he has just said, and is better translated *"but this I mean"* (φημί, BAGD, 864, 2. cf. NIV). In other words, to what is Paul referring when he warns about *present distress* (26) and *trouble in this life* (28)?

The answer is that *the time has been shortened* (or "is limited, short;" cf. συστέλλω, BAGD, 795). Paul sees the approaching end of the world in its present form (31b) as a reminder that, for the Christian, all the institutions and emotions and provisions of this world are but transitory; they are not to be viewed as an end in themselves, but as a means to an end. Therefore, the earthly relationship between a man and his wife is not most important, but rather their relationship with the Lord. In fact, *from now on those who have wives should be as though they had none.* This echoes Christ's conditions of discipleship in Luke 14:26. There, as here, the first area which must be submitted to God's control is one's family relationships, including one's *wife.* Paul is not saying that the husband-wife relationship is unimportant (vv.2ff); but rather that we should focus on the things of the world to come. In the remaining time before Christ returns, He is more important than any question of earthly relationships.

30a, b   While those in the world concern themselves with their present happiness, this is not to be a controlling factor for the Christian. After all, those who weep now will laugh when they receive their reward, and those who laugh now will weep then (Luke 6:21-26)! So Paul adds that *those who weep* should be *as though they did not weep; and those who rejoice* should be *as though they did not rejoice*. The faithful believer should follow Christ, whether this means joy or trials (Luke 14:27). Paul knew following Christ would result in suffering (1 Thess. 3:4), both for himself and those he converted (Phil. 1:29f), yet even in his sufferings he rejoiced (Col. 1:24). For Paul *the sufferings of this present time are not worthy to be compared with the glory that is to be revealed to us* (Rom. 8:18; cf. 2 Cor. 4:17).

30c-31a   Paul lastly comes to a discussion of possessions. In His conditions of discipleship, Jesus stated that *no one...who does not give up all his own possessions* could be His disciple (Luke 14:33). Of course, Jesus was not requiring disciples to give away all their possessions! It was their *attitude* toward possessions which mattered. The same is true here.

Paul's meaning in v.30c is that in light of the coming end of the age, Christians *who buy* should treat the material things they purchase *as though they did not possess* them. As Paul makes clear in his later letter, the things which are seen are not real (i.e., they are temporal, passing away with this world), while those things which are not seen are eternal (2 Cor. 4:18). The motivation and attitudes of believers are foreign to the world.

So it is that Christians may *use the world*, all the time knowing that it is passing away. For this reason, they should *not make full use of it*; that is, they are not wrapped up in it, carried along by it. They make use of it, but do not let it use them. They may have possessions in it, but they do not let those possessions possess them.

31b   And why? Because *the form of this world is passing away.* Only a fool would invest his life savings in a company he knew was going bankrupt. So too a Christian is foolish to invest his life in the things of this world. The wise believer recognizes that the things of this world bring distress and trouble, and focuses instead on the things of the world to come in the short time which remains. To be so focused, Paul now explains, is another good reason for those who are single to postpone marriage.

32-35   [Paul encourages unmarried believers to remain single so they can be undivided in their concern about the things of the Lord.]

32a   Paul wants his readers to be *free from concern* (ἀμερίμνους; "without care" (NKJV) is acceptable, but suggests the idea "carefree," not really Paul's point here; cf. Matt 28:15, "out of trouble"). It is not that Paul does not want his readers to have *any* concerns; all will have some, as the following verses show. What Paul does not want his readers to be concerned with is *the things of the world* (33, 34). The thought progression with the previous section is this: When a Christian looks at the world, he should recognize that the relationships, motivations, and possessions which drive it are temporal and meaningless. Any preoccupation with worldly distractions can only mean anxiety for a believer, and Paul wants the Corinthians to avoid these concerns. The issue of whether one is married or not should never detract from the more important issue of one's relationship with Jesus Christ. However, since getting married itself requires attention being paid to worldly matters, Paul suggests—for their own good—that those unmarried remain single, and entirely devoted to the Lord.

32b-33 As evidence that remaining single can keep one free from concern, Paul first points to the male. The *unmarried* man can focus entirely on *the things of the Lord, how he may please the Lord*; the *married* man, however, to be obedient to the Lord, must be *concerned about the things of the world, how he may please his wife* (Eph. 5:25ff)!

Thus, in doing what is right, he has less opportunity to devote himself totally to pleasing the Lord. He will have more worldly concerns to take care of. Paul is not saying that a single man is concerned about the Lord, and a married man is concerned about the world! He is simply noting that a married man has responsibilities which limit his undivided attention to the things of the Lord.

Application: There is an implicit message here to Christian men, particularly those in vocational Christian service, which should not be missed. Some husbands and fathers believe that devotion to the Lord requires they 'deny' their wife and family to spend time in ministry. But scripture is clear that a husband's first priority is his wife, as Paul makes clear here. A husband *needs* to be concerned about the things of the world, about how he may please his wife. This is, by virtue of his choice to get married, his 'divine assignment.' To fail at this task in order to perform other duties, no matter how spiritual, is to abandon one's most important responsibility.

---

34   A minor textual variation in this verse has resulted in major differences in translations. The addition of καὶ (and, also) at the beginning of the verse, coupled with some differing word orders, has resulted in the following renderings:

> *There is a difference between a wife and a virgin. The unmarried woman cares...* (NKJV, following the MajT)
>
> *...and [his interests] are divided. And the woman who is unmarried, and the virgin, is concerned...* (NASV/NIV, following CrT)

Some conclusions:

1) Both readings convey virtually the same meaning.
2) The MajT reading has better continuity and balance between Paul's comments to men and women.
3) The inclusion of καὶ is well attested in CrT sources; the omission of καὶ is attested by a large, but not overwhelming, majority in the textual tradition.
4) Most modern translations and commentators follow the CrT reading.
5) Many commentators on 1 Corinthians (Godet, Lightfoot, and Robertson and Plummer) favor the MajT reading.

Both readings have difficulties, and each has factors in its favor. If the CrT reading is taken, the initial phrase of verse 34 belongs with verses 32-33, and states the obvious conclusion that the married man has his interests divided. This is then followed by a division of the categories of women, the *unmarried woman* (ἡ γυνὴ ἡ ἄγαμος) and the *virgin* (ἡ παρθένος), the latter perhaps a specific reference to those already betrothed. The MajT reading makes verse 34 a unit, pertaining to the woman in the same way verses 32b-33 pertains to a man. The most difficult question concerns the meaning of μεριμνᾷ (*divided*, NASV/NIV; *difference between*, NKJV; the former is the more literal reading; cf. 1:13; 7:17). The MajT reading requires something like, "A wife and a virgin are also divided," with the *division* being between the two roles, just as Paul has distinguished between the unmarried and married man.

Following this introduction, the verse develops in parallel form to the previous comments about a man. Paul points out that an unmarried woman *is concerned about the things of the Lord, that she may be holy both in body and spirit.* On the other hand, *one who is married is concerned about the things of the world, how she may please her husband.* The single woman can concentrate wholly on the Lord, while the married woman shows her godliness by being devoted to her husband (cf. Titus 2:4f; 1 Pet. 3:1-6). One role is not preferable to the other; they just have different tasks. Because of her commitment to her role as a wife, a married woman has responsibilities which limit her undivided attention to the things of the Lord.

Application: There is an implicit message to wives and mothers here which should not be missed. The wife who puts personal aspirations, whether spiritual or not, above pleasing her husband, is not fulfilling her 'divine assignment.' As a married woman, her concern should be first of all to please her husband.

---

35   Paul now summarizes his reasons for all he has said to this point. His instruction is *for* their *benefit*. It is *not to put a restraint upon* them, but *to promote what is seemly* (encourage appropriate behavior for a believer), and permit *undistracted devotion to the Lord*.

Devotion to the Lord is a lifelong pursuit for every believer, marital status notwithstanding. But such devotion requires special tenacity in the midst of the demands of marriage and family. Paul therefore wisely counsels singles to build a strong spiritual foundation *before* getting married. This echoes Solomon's advice in Ecclesiastes 12:1: *Remember also your Creator in the days of your youth* (cf. Ps. 119:9-11).

36-38   [Paul instructs single believers who feel they cannot resist sexual urges to get married, but those who have control he encourages to remain single.]

N.B. See comments pertaining to this section in the discussion of v.25 above.

Translation Note: Translators have struggled with the term γαμίζων (*give a woman in marriage;* MajT has ἐκγαμίζων, *marry, give in marriage*) in verse 38, and how it affects the meaning of παρθένον (virgin).

Four views are reflected in various translations:

1) Paul instructs a father on whether or not to give his virgin daughter in marriage [NASV].
2) Paul instructs a man and his virgin (an engaged couple) on whether or not to get married [NIV, RSV].
3) Paul instructs men on virginity and whether or not to get married (*New Translation* [Morrish, 1890]; *The New Translation* [Tyndale, 1990]).
4) Paul instructs those in celibate "spiritual marriages" on whether or not to consummate their relationship sexually (NEB).

Some translations allow for various interpretations (KJV, NKJV). Of the options above, the second best fits with the text and the context. From verse 25 on, the focus has been on unmarried believers facing the decision of marriage. Nothing in verses 36-37 changes this, but because of the reference to *giving* a virgin in marriage (38), the NASV had to make all three verses refer to a virgin *daughter*. This idea is foreign to the context, and not required by v.38. It furthermore creates an incomprehensible line of reasoning in vv. 36-37 (see Wilson, 115f). The NIV, while adopting the proper context, goes beyond the limits of pure translation and is unnecessarily interpretive (the virgin *he is engaged to*; cf. RSV).

36   Paul's meaning is actually very simple, and reflects his instruction to the unmarried and widows (v.9). *If any man thinks that he is acting unbecomingly toward his virgin, if she should be of full age, and if it must be so, let him do what he wishes, he does not sin; let them marry.* If an engaged couple behaves in such a way that is not proper for singles (the wording is pejorative, cf. ἀσχημονέω, BAGD, 118; this refers only to what is indecent for those who are unmarried; Paul is not discouraging sexual relations within marriage), they should get married. The man is responsible for gauging his own emotions and knowing if he is losing the battle with self-control. This instruction is in keeping with

Paul's emphasis throughout; to deny such a couple marriage would be a spiritual distraction at best, and at worst promote sin. Just as those who are married should not abstain from sexual relations (which would open them up to temptation), so too those who evidence a need for sexual fulfilment should get married.

37 The man *who stands firm in his heart, being under no constraint, but has authority over his own will, and has decided this in his own heart, to keep* (τηρέω, "keep watch over, preserve," BAGD, 815) *his own virgin, he will do well.* The individual who does not feel the need to get married, and who determines to remain single, should by all means do so. No social pressure should be used to promote marriage, just as no ascetic restriction should prohibit it. Perhaps being careful to make sure that no one chooses this pathway without carefully determining that it is in fact the way they should go, Paul gives four clear checks: 1) his heart must be firm in the decision; 2) he must be under no constraint; 3) he must have demonstrated control over his desires; and 4) this must be a decision he has come to on his own.

38 The verb γαμίζων (or ἐκγαμίζων) need not mean to *give* in marriage; it can simply mean to marry. This is the best way to understand it here. Even if the meaning *to give in marriage* is favored, this is still a summary of Paul's teaching; getting married or staying single are both valid options, and Paul's preference is the latter.

39-40 [Paul instructs Christian widows that while they are free to marry any believer, in his opinion they would be happier remaining unmarried.]

39 Precisely why Paul raises this point here is not totally clear, but since this is a letter, and further since he was clearly responding to specific issues within the Corinthian assembly, it need not follow a logical progression. However, as he has just finished stating that previously not married virgins are free to marry, he now adds that the previously married widow *is free to be married to*

whom she wishes. He qualifies *who* she may marry by emphasizing that he must be a believer (*only in the Lord*).

The most important point from this verse in the present moral climate, however, is Paul's clear assertion of the permanence of the marriage bond: *A wife is bound as long as her husband lives.* As Fee succinctly puts it, this "is a final word against divorce and remarriage" (355; cf. Rom. 7:2f). It is only *if her husband is dead* that remarriage is allowed.

40   Paul continues his pastoral encouragement of his audience here, giving his *opinion* that a widow *is happier if she remains as she is* (unmarried). There is no hint of dogmatism here. As in verse 35, this is for their own benefit. But Paul is not beyond claiming some spiritual weight to his words: *I think that I also have the Spirit of God.* Considering the presence of the Spirit of God which he enjoyed, his readers would be wise to heed his advice.

Homiletical Ideas

The nature of the material in this chapter makes it sound more topical than expositional when it is preached. Paul's instruction here is practical and specific, but it has a consistent spiritual principle throughout.

While the second half of this chapter is vital instruction for single Christians, the underlying spiritual theme is that for the Christian, questions of earthly issues like marriage, sex, and celibacy need to be kept in proper perspective. None of these issues can compare with the surpassing importance of maintaining a vibrant and growing relationship with the Lord. It is this, as much as anything else, which Paul wants his readers to understand and apply by "staying as they are" unless a change is unavoidable.

B. QUESTIONS CONCERNING CHRISTIAN LIBERTY ARE DISCUSSED (8:1-11:1)

The issue which connects these four chapters is eating meat offered to idols. However, this matter alone did not engender Paul's somewhat passionate response, which goes beyond a simple question of diet. It is apparent throughout that Paul is not trying to impose restrictions on what they can eat; idols are nothing (8:4-6), things sacrificed to idols are nothing (10:19), and what you eat shouldn't be an issue (8:8; 10:25, 27). However, two things do matter: First, their participation in idol feasts held at pagan temples (8:10; 10:1-22), and second, the resulting effect such activities can have on the conscience of a weaker brother (8:7-13; 10:28-29).

The Corinthians viewed themselves as mighty in their wisdom and knowledge—and were arrogant (8:1). They knew that idols were nothing (since there is only one true God), and that therefore meat offered to idols was nothing, too. Because they knew this, they were free to mock the idols by going to idol temples and joining in at their feasts—in fact, they viewed it as a sign of their spiritual maturity! What could hurt them?! They were impregnable! They thought that baptism and participation in the Lord's Table gave them magical powers against any idol temptations (cf. 10:1-4, 12). Perhaps their written question to Paul read something like this:

> You have taught us to stay away from the feasts at idol temples, but why? Idols are nothing, and food is for the stomach! Our own religious practice is not affected in the least; we have all been baptized, and observe the Lord's Supper regularly. We enjoy these temple feasts, so why shouldn't we join in them?

In this smug, arrogant state, they had fallen into error:

1) They were ignoring Paul's instructions, and openly scorning his apostolic authority (he defends it in ch.9).
2) They were ignoring the needs of newer converts who were struggling to break old idolatrous habits. By attending idol feasts—and possibly even taking new believers along—they seared their consciences and exposed them to grave temptation (8:7-13; 10:28-29).

3) They were ignoring the dangers that were present in idolatry itself. Idols were not real, but the demonic powers behind them *were* (10:20f)! Israel's judgment for similar practices (10:5-11) was God's "Exhibit A" to warn them away from such careless contact—especially as they thought they could withstand anything (10:12)!

This section, then, is instruction on handling our liberty in a way so that we do not endanger ourselves or others spiritually, but instead become stronger in our faith, and effectively reach others for Christ as well.

8:1-13 *Paul exhorts Corinthian believers on the basis of Christian love to forego eating at pagan temples, which may cause a weak brother to go against his conscience, stumble into sin, and be ruined.*

This chapter is Paul's initial exhortation on the question of 'Christian rights' or liberty. He gains the Corinthians' ear by basing his instruction on things which they knew, but had misapplied. This is evident in 1a and 4-6 ("we know," cf. v.8); His correction of their errors is signaled by "but" (1b, 9) and "however" (7).

It should be noted at the outset that the specific action Paul is responding to involved more than just eating meat which had been offered to idols. This is only part of their offense. It is condemned elsewhere in scripture (cf. Rev. 2:14, 20), as well as in the Church Fathers (cf. Didache 6: *Now concerning food, bear what you are able, but in any case keep strictly away from meat sacrificed to idols, for it involves the worship of dead gods.* [Note that this statement endorses an uninformed Christian's thinking, making idols out to be "gods." Paul's statement is that for Christians there is only one God, and idols are nothing; v.4.]).

But Paul is not simply exhorting his readers to abstain from eating food offered to idols. In fact, as he makes clear in chapters 8 (v.8) and 10 (vv.25, 27), where food comes from is not important! The issue Paul specifies here and which fits both chapters is not just *eating* such food, but eating the food *when it is being served at a pagan idol temple* (8:10). It is this which abused the weaker brother's conscience and became a stumbling block, by emboldening him to join in temple banquets when, for him, such an activity signified worship of a false god.

Paul's progression is as follows:
1) Knowledge without love is not a basis for Christian action, because knowledge puffs up, but love builds up (1-3).
2) The knowledge that idols are nothing for the believer who knows the one true God may alone lead one to take the liberty of eating meals at pagan temples (4-6).
3) But some believers don't understand that what a person eats makes no spiritual difference; they still feel they are worshiping an idol when they eat temple meals (7-8).
4) Those with knowledge must be careful to not, by joining in temple meals, prompt weaker believers to go against their conscience (9-11).
5) Since prompting a weaker brother to thus eat, which leads him to spiritual ruin, is a sin both against that brother and against Christ who died for him, the stronger brother should forego taking this liberty (12-13).

1-3   [Knowledge without love is not a basis for Christian behavior, since knowledge puffs up, but love builds up.]

1   With Περὶ δὲ (*Now concerning*), Paul introduces a new discussion. The subject is introduced as εἰδωλοθύτων (*things sacrificed to idols*; cf. BAGD, 221), what the pagans referred to as ἱερόθυτόν ("things devoted to a god;" cf. 10:28). Paul had instructed the Corinthians on matters of pagan idolatry, and states that *we know that we all have knowledge* (γνῶσιν). This knowledge alone was the guide for their actions, but Paul begins his discussion of their participation at idol temple feasts by pointing out that knowledge *alone* is not a good guide for Christian behavior.

The Corinthians knew they had knowledge, but as we have seen repeatedly, their knowledge had been tainted with that of the world (instead of the love of God), and the mixture was volatile and unpredictable. So Paul, while granting that they have knowledge (and, as will be shown, correct knowledge, but knowledge which *all* do not possess), begins by indicating that knowledge alone is not a trustworthy guide for Christian behavior. Why? Because *knowledge makes arrogant* (φυσιόω; lit. blow up, puff up, BAGD, 869; cf. NKJV/NIV). Here the pride of the Corinthians is implicit. No charge is made, but the inference is clear; they had knowledge, and had grown arrogant because they had not tempered it with love.

Love (ἀγάπη; God's—or godly—love) is the one ingredient which transforms knowledge from something which puffs up to something which *edifies* (builds up; οἰκοδομεῖ).

2   This verse harkens back to 3:18, where Paul exhorts the Corinthians to become foolish (in the eyes of the world) that they might be wise (in the things of God). Here, the message is the same. *If anyone supposes that he knows anything* (and considers his knowledge a virtue in itself), he is evidencing that *he has not yet known as he ought to know*. He does not yet possess real knowledge. Knowledge that puffs up is not that which should characterize the believer.

3   The kind of knowledge Christians need, particularly when making decisions concerning behavior, is knowledge which is guided by love for God. One who *loves God* will deny self in order to help a weaker brother (as Paul exhibits in v.13). In his first epistle, the Apostle John would later write: *Beloved, let us love one another, for love is from God; and every one who loves is born of God and knows God. The one who does not love does not know God, for God is love* (4:7, 8). Paul is, in effect, exhorting on the Corinthians to get to know God, who *is* love, better. This will lead to love being shown for weaker brothers.

The final clause of verse 3 may play on the same idea as Gal. 4:9, that to know God equals to be known by God. If we love God in a personal way, whereby our lives are open to Him, our behavior will be guided by love.

4-6 [The content of the Corinthians' knowledge was that idols are nothing to those who know God the Father and the Lord Jesus Christ.]

In these verses Paul alters slightly the subject he introduced in verse 1. There, he wrote *concerning things sacrificed to idols*. Here, he writes: *Therefore concerning the eating* (τῆς βρώσεως) *of things sacrificed to idols*. The issue of eating is added to the first statement, which was used to introduce the inadequacy of knowledge alone to determine correct Christian behavior. This completed, he now moves on to discuss the subject at hand. What they know concerns not just food offered to idols, but the eating of that food. But there is no hint that their knowledge is in any way wrong; nor is there any prohibition on eating food sacrificed to idols. It is not their knowledge which is flawed, but the fact that they are acting on the basis of their knowledge *without love*. Hence, the message of these verses is not to be viewed as a veiled attack on eating meat offered to idols. Paul is simply endorsing their knowledge, after which he scores them for the callous way they were allowing their freedom in Christ to hurt those who were less enlightened, by leading them into activities they were spiritually too weak to handle.

4 Περὶ...οὖν (*Therefore concerning*) picks up the discussion following the interlude on knowledge and love in vv.1b-3. The repeated *we know* (cf. v.1) may indicate that vv. 1b-3 were not originally planned by Paul, but added 'on the spur of the moment' to prepare his readers to see beyond what they knew to how they were acting.

What the Corinthians (and Paul; *we*) knew was that *there is no such thing as an idol in the world, and that there is no God but one*. That is, there was no reality to any of the gods of the Greek pantheon; at best, they were carvings or paintings of men. There was only one God. In declaring that the Greek gods were only figments of Greek imagination, they were right; however, they were overlooking the fact that there are real forces behind those gods (cf. 10:19ff).

5-6   Not only does Paul reiterate what they know, he defends it! *Even if there are so-called gods* (λεγόμενοι θεοì), and *whether* these "gods" are *in heaven or on earth*, it does not matter. At this point, following on from verse 4, we might expect Paul to say that such gods are not real, that they simply do not exist. But he does not. He has another tack; his point is not that such gods do not exist—since they do, at least in the minds of their worshippers, and certainly in the demonic realm as well. In fact, he asserts that *indeed there are many gods and many lords*. His contrast is between the *many gods and many lords* of the pagans, and the *one God... and one Lord* of Christians. In this way Paul retains the contrast between false idols and the true God, but at the same time prepares the way for his exhortation to use this knowledge in a proper way.

First, he builds the idea of community into the equation. The important thing is *not* that idols are nothing, but that God is *one*. All believers are under the same God; with Christians, it's 'all for One and One for all'! This attitude will be important for them to remember in the context of the weaker brother.

Secondly, Paul injects the idea of responsibility into the equation. *God* is the Father, *from whom are all things, and we for Him. Jesus Christ* is the Lord *by whom are all things, and we through Him.* Believers are part of both God's physical creation and spiritual re-creation. Our behavior is not to be associated with idols which can do nothing, but with our creator/redeemer God, who is powerful and jealous (cf. Deut. 32:21).

7-13   [Paul exhorts the Corinthians to abstain from eating meals at idol temples in deference to those with weak consciences.]

The reason why the Corinthians should refrain from eating at idol temples is now spelled out. Paul focuses on those individuals in the church who are "weaker," not having the knowledge or strength claimed by others. Of course, Paul's argument rests on the foundation he has already laid, the need for love guiding knowledge, the unity of believers under one God, and our responsibility to determine behavior based on allegiance to Him.

With this in mind, Paul states that Corinthian believers should not eat at idol temples because:

1) while they know idols are nothing, not everyone knows this (7);
2) there is no spiritual profit in eating, nor any harm in not eating, so there is no incentive or necessity to do so (8);
3) by eating at idol temples, they may prompt a weak brother to do the same, and fall into sin (9-11);
4) this amounts to sinning against a brother, and against Christ, which should be avoided at all costs (12-13).

7   While the knowledge which Paul has described is well-known in the Corinthian church, *not all men have this knowledge*. Perhaps Paul had taught these things to some in the church who now considered themselves mature; he distinguishes between the "we" of verse 1 (those who have this knowledge) and the "not all" of verse 7 (indicating some who do not have this knowledge). It may be that while all have a "knowledge" of the meaninglessness of idols, not all are strong enough in their Christian walk to handle that knowledge yet (the rest of v.7 would suggest this understanding). Those with knowledge must recognize the needs of these 'weaker brothers.'

Textual Note: MajT reads συνειδήσει (dat. sing. from συνείδησις; "for some, *with consciousness* of the idol" [NKJV]; BAGD, 786, cf. 2.), while CrT reads συνηθεία ("but some, *being accustomed* to the idol" [NASV]; BAGD, 789). The two terms sound similar enough that an error based on itacism, a scribal error based on faulty hearing, can be surmised. But which one is the original? Both have internal support. Regardless, weaker Corinthian believers were those who had been accustomed to idol worship, and thus had a moral consciousness of the veneration their peers associated with the eating of idol food. They couldn't eat the food without feeling as though they were somehow paying homage to other "gods." For them, such a practice, while technically acceptable, was a slap in the face of Jesus Christ who died for them.

The result is that these Christians *eat food as if it were sacrificed to an idol*, and as a result *their conscience being weak is defiled*. Conscience (συνείδησις) refers to their moral awareness of the significance of eating idol food at the temple. They may have known cognitively that idols were nothing, but in their hearts the old practices still lingered. Old feelings of worshiping an idol by joining in such feasts would return, and their new union with Jesus Christ would be defiled (μολύνω, BAGD, 526f; used only here in Paul's writings, it means to stain, soil, make impure; cf. Rev. 3:4).

8   Obviously, thus offending a weak believer should be avoided if at all possible. Here, there is no reason for the activity. This is because *food will not commend us to God; we are neither the worse if we do not eat, not the better if we do eat.* That is, since it is true that eating this food is no advantage and not eating it is no disadvantage, why eat it? Why lead a brother to defile his conscience over something that doesn't matter?

9   The onus for self-denial falls on the stronger brother. He should *take care* (βλέπετε, imperative from βλέπω, "to see;" here we might translate, "Watch out!"); by exercising his *liberty* (ἐξουσία, BAGD, 277f; cf. 6:12), he could *become a stumbling block* (πρόσκομμα; BAGD, 716; something that hinders or trips up spiritually) *to the weak*.

10 Paul now identifies specifically that which leads the weaker brother to stumble: It is seeing those *who have knowledge, dining in an idol's temple*. The problem is not that the person will be offended; Paul never makes food—nor allows other believers to make it—an issue in Christian behavior. Food simply does not matter. But people do!

The problem is that when the weak Christian sees his more mature brother joining in idol temple feasts, *his conscience* will *be strengthened to eat things sacrificed to idols*. He may decide to go ahead and eat with his stronger companion, even though his heart still feels the tug of the idol during the meal. The same affect which the observation of the Lord's Table had for believers (remembrance of Christ's death) this eating would then have for the weak brother (remembrance of idol worship). This was not something he needed to be reminded of!

11 The result of the more informed believer acting on the basis of his knowledge (without love) is that *he who is weak is ruined* (ἀπόλλυμι; BAGD, 95, 2.). The seriousness of this action is heightened by the reminder that this is a *brother for whose sake Christ died.* The fact that we might destroy one for whom Christ died anticipates the grave offence which Paul spells out in v.12.

Theological Note: Some commentators stumble into bad soteriology as a result of this passage. Fee (387) writes: *In saying that the brother "is destroyed" Paul most likely is referring to eternal loss...*; Conzelmann (*1 Corinthians*, Hermeneia Series [Philadelphia, 1975]), 149, n.38, writes: *[Paul] of course presupposes the idea that the Christian, too, can lose his salvation.* The implication is that a former idolater who believes in Jesus, then falls back into the grips of his old idolatry, is condemned to hell. This is theological nonsense; if this sin causes God to renege on His gift of salvation, what about murder, rape, gossip, thievery, divisiveness—or any other sin? This sentences believers to a lifetime of insecurity, wondering if some sin they have committed may have resulted in a loss of their salvation. It creates a "padded cell" mentality, where the church becomes detached from and irrelevant to the world. But the weak brother is not *damned* because of his sin; he is *damaged* (wounded, v.12). His spiritual life may even disappear as he reverts back into idolatrous ways; he may even die physically as a result of such sin (cf. 10:9; 11:30). But eternal life is secure for the believer, because it is based on the finished work of Christ, not the ongoing works of the believer. Christ died for all sins—including those committed by the believer. Such failing may lead to temporal judgment and a loss of rewards at the Judgment Seat of Christ (4:5), but it does not affect the believer's eternal standing as a child of God.

---

12 By bringing weak brothers to idol temple feasts, the more secure believer was *sinning against* them by *wounding their conscience when it is weak.* Furthermore, because Christ died for that weak brother, he commits *sin against Christ!* The term for "wound" (τύπτω, BAGD, 830) is informative here. It refers to striking or beating someone, causing their wounds by our direct action. As such it brings to mind Isa. 53:5, and our part in the death of Christ. How awful to consider that after recognizing our sins are the reason for Christ's wounds, wounds which led to our spiritual healing, we should go out and wound a faltering brother through our actions! Not only is the contrast between our actions and Christ's highlighted (He was 'wounded' to heal the weaker brother, and then we wound them!), but our character is like that of an unbeliever! We have been healed, and should now reflect that in our relationships with others. To batter a brother's conscience when it is weak is to do the Destroyer's work for him!

13 The end (διόπερ, *Therefore,* "for this very reason," used in the New Testament only by Paul, and only in 1 Cor.; cf. 10:14; 14:13 [MajT]) is expressed by Paul in the form of a conditional first-person commitment which he wants the Corinthians to adopt. Because of the danger of causing such terrible destruction in a fellow believer's life, Paul makes it clear that he will do whatever it takes to avoid causing a brother to stumble: *if food causes my brother to stumble, I will never eat meat again, that I might not cause my brother to stumble.* He widens the issue to "food" in general (although "meat" is singled out), declaring that if eating anything might lead a brother to stumble, he will never eat it again! He may be using hyperbole to emphasize his point, but his commitment to guard the spiritual lives of others is clear. Absolutely nothing should cause us to engage in activities which could result in a weaker brother falling into sin (cf. Rom. 14:13-15).

Homiletical Ideas

This chapter conveys a message which is needed in many congregations where *liberty* on the one hand, or *legalism* on the other, rules in decisions of Christian behavior, instead of *love*. In conservative churches this passage is misused by legalistic Christians to force everyone to defer to their scruples. Anything they find offensive should be avoided by all others! Of course, this is not Paul's message; in areas of personal preference, he is clear that Christians should live together in harmony as much as possible (cf. Rom. 14:1-12). The question here is: *What motivation should guide Christian behavior in the local church?*

In preaching this passage the main idea to be emphasized is that Christian behavior is to be dictated by love for one another. Instead of finding fault in believers who engage in behavior that offends *me*, we should instead examine ourselves, to see if anything we are doing might cause a brother to fall. Will other believers look at our life and be motivated to higher standards of godliness and greater commitment to Christ, or will they be led into areas of conduct where there is danger of sin and spiritual ruin? As surely as if we had fallen ourselves, we will give answer for these actions.

9:1-27 *Paul's example of self-denial illustrates the attitude toward Christian 'rights' which results in spiritual rewards.*

1-14   [Paul demonstrates that his position as an apostle entitles him to financial support.]

In these verses, Paul 'kills two birds with one stone.' First and foremost, he provides an illustration in himself of the right attitude towards 'rights' or 'liberty' which the Corinthians claimed for themselves, culminating in his example of voluntary self-denial in vv.15-18 (which illustrates his exhortation of 8:13 in action). Secondly, he defends his apostleship against some in Corinth who had been questioning it.

The most notable literary feature of this section is the number rhetorical questions (16). Paul effectively uses this tool to force his readers (and detractors) to admit his position and rights; when they have done so and are ready to support him, he 'pulls the rug out from under them' by declaring that he will forego his rights for the sake of the gospel. The obvious inference is, will they in a similar way forego their "rights" for the sake of weaker brothers?

1-2   Paul sets the stage for all that follows with these two verses. Without warning, we encounter four rhetorical questions, all requiring the answer "Yes" (as signified by the negative οὐ/οὐκ/ οὐχὶ). First of all, Paul is *free* (ἐλεύθερος, BAGD, 250; cf. 9:19); he is not bound by rules or traditions; he does not act in order to please (or not offend) others. His decision in 8:13 was not required, but voluntary.

This fact is emphasized by his second question (these two questions are reversed in MajT; the order is not critical); Paul is *an apostle!* Certainly he has the authority to do as he pleases, if anyone does!

The evidence that he is an apostle is reflected in the remaining two questions. *Have I not seen Jesus our Lord?* He had, on the Damascus Road (15:8); the qualification of being an eyewitness of the resurrected Christ is reflected in the identification of the other apostles, too (15:7). [Other qualifications for apostolic office include miraculous signs (2 Cor. 12:12), pioneer evangelism and church planting (9:16-18; cf. Rom. 15:15-21), special divine insight (in Paul's case, insight into the *mystery*; 2:7-10; Eph. 3:1-13), and commissioning by the Lord (15:8-11; cf. Gal. 1:16).] *Are you not my work in the Lord?* They are—a testimony to his apostolic role (cf. NIV), evidence that he was doing effective missionary work (cf. 4:15).

In verse 2, Paul affirms his claim to apostleship, especially in the eyes of the Corinthians. *If to others I am not an apostle, at least I am to you; for you are the seal of my apostleship in the Lord.* The reference to "others" may refer to some who had joined the Corinthian congregation after his ministry, who doubted his apostleship, or it may be purely hypothetical. Regardless, the church in Corinth could not escape his claim to apostleship;

they themselves were the "proof" of it! As long as they existed, denying his office was ludicrous. So it is that in the opening two verses Paul firmly establishes his position as apostle.

3   Paul commences his *defense* (ἀπολογία; "apology;" cf. BAGD, 96) *to those who examine* or sit in judgment of him (ἀνακρίνουσίν; those who are asking questions, cf. 10:25, 27). Both are legal terms (cf. 4:3-4; cf. 2 Tim. 4:16). Paul views himself as in court, being judged by some in Corinth. His defence is presented in the form of a string of (12) rhetorical questions.

He is defending not only his apostleship (which vv.1-2 have affirmed), but his rights as an apostle, and (in this context) of the authority of what he taught. After all, was it *really* true, as he has written, that they should give up their rights for the sake of weaker brothers? Paul must show that, as an apostle, he has certain rights, then demonstrate that he does the right thing in denying himself those rights.

4-6   In these verses, Paul three times repeats the phrase *Do we not have the right...?* (μὴ οὐκ ἔχομεν ἐξουσίαν). The parallel is hard to miss with the position of the Corinthians in chapter 8. They had knowledge (8:1) and as a result they had rights (or liberties; ἐξουσία; 8:9). Paul has told them to forego their rights, and pledged the denial of his own privileges (13). But some are sceptical. Would he? And, in fact, does he? Come to think of it, what *are* an apostle's rights?

The first right which Paul claims echoes the context of eating from chapter 8; it is *a right to eat and drink*. But the addition of "drink" carries him into the area of sustenance. The question is, does Paul (and Barnabas; "we;" cf. v.6) have the right to be supported (so they can eat and drink)? Of course, the answer is "Yes."

The second right claimed is the freedom to be married (5). *Do we not have a right to take along a believing wife...?* Assuming Paul was either never married or a widower, he still had the *right* to be married (even though he is clear this is not something he is pursuing; cf. 7:8f, 28, 36-39). Other church leaders clearly had this right, including *the rest of the apostles*, Jesus' earthly *brothers* (cf. Matt.13:55; this is a clear indication that Jesus' siblings, who rejected Him during his ministry (Matt. 13:57; John 7:3, 5), later believed; cf. Acts 1:14), *and Cephas* (Peter; cf. Matt. 8:14). But beyond the right to get married, this again seems to be pointing to the issue of support. The question is, do Paul and Barnabas have the right to be supported so they can take a wife with them in their apostolic travels? Again, the answer is "Yes."

Application: The practice of clergy celibacy is once and for all put to rest here! Beyond this, the implication of Paul's appeal to the behavior of other church leaders (they took their wives along on ministry trips!) is a good suggestion for ministers today. Separation puts marriages under stress, and ministry (especially itinerant) can contribute to this. Suggestion for pastors: When possible, take your wife along! The marriages of church leaders might be stronger (and the incidents of infidelity fewer) if this were a normal practice.

That Paul's first two "rights" involve being financially supported is made clear in verse 6. He asks: *Do only Barnabas and I not have a right to refrain from working?* Shouldn't they be supported like other apostles, and not have to work a 'second job'? Paul's practice was to work (cf. Acts 18:3; 1 Cor. 4:12; 1 Thess. 2:9), but he is emphasizing that he has a *right* to not do so.

In summary, Paul has the right to be supported, to be able to eat and drink, have a wife and take her along on ministry trips, and be able to live without holding down an outside job. These rights are self-evident for one of the apostles, which he is. But Paul now goes on to illustrate his point, first in an argument from common sense (7), then in a scriptural sermonette (8-12).

7   Paul's right to financial remuneration from the Corinthians is now supported by illustrations drawn from three common first century

settings. *Who at any time serves as a soldier at his own expense? Who plants a vineyard, and does not eat the fruit of it? Or who tends a flock and does not use the milk of the flock?* All three questions demand a negative answer: "No one!" So whereas in verses 4-6, Paul's rhetorical questions are *affirming* his right to support, here they are *denying* that such support should be withheld.

8   While his right to financial support is self-evident, Paul appeals to a higher authority. Though apostolic position and common sense clearly demonstrated his right, he now points out that what he is saying is not just his own opinion or good human logic, but is based on God's Law (cf. 1:19, 31; 2:9; 3:19, 20; 6:16; and 7:10 for other examples of Paul appealing to divine revelation). The rhetorical question, *I am not speaking these things according to human judgment, am I?* requires the response "No!" (cf. Μὴ). On the other hand, the question, *Or does not the Law also say these things?* calls for a response of "Yes!" (οὐχὶ/MajT; οὐ/CrT). But since they may not know this, Paul demonstrates it from Scripture.

9   Paul appeals to *the Law of Moses* (*For it is written*) in Deuteronomy 25:4 (*"You shall not muzzle the ox while he is threshing."*). Paul cites this verse in 1 Timothy 5:18 as a Scriptural basis for financially supporting fulltime vocational ministers. It should be remembered that the 'Bible' for first-century Christians was the Old Testament, and the Law was the standard upon which it was built; it was the authoritative guide for life.

Textual Note: The word translated *muzzle* is debated. The MajT has φιμώσεις (φιμόω), the CrT κημώσεις (κημόω). There is no difference in meaning. Evidence for the MajT is strong: It agrees with the LXX reading, and Paul uses φιμόω in 1 Tim. 5:18. Four of the five major manuscripts upon which the CrT reading is based agree with the MajT (p⁴⁶, ℵ, A, and C), and the quality of the fifth manuscript, B, is in doubt. Defence of the CrT reading here is presumptive and groundless (cf. Fee, 398, n.6).

The meaning is clear with either term: *You shall not muzzle the ox while he is threshing.* The quote is proverbial in Deuteronomy, and Paul points out that *God is not* primarily *concerned about oxen* in giving it.

10   With yet another rhetorical question, Paul asserts that God *is* *speaking,* and the Law *was written, for our sake.* And why was it for our sake? Because *the plowman ought to plow in hope, and the thresher [to thresh] in hope of sharing [the crops].* Those who perform the labor have a right to expect rewards from their work.

11-12a   Paul now returns to his own situation, using a farming analogy. *If we sowed spiritual things in you, is it too much if we should reap material things from you?* The argument is this: Paul and Barnabas had planted a spiritual crop among the Corinthians (cf. 3:6); therefore, they had a right to reap a material harvest from them. The logical equation is this: The spiritual things sowed by Paul and Barnabas will reap a spiritual harvest, from which all in Corinth will benefit. The material things sowed by those in Corinth will reap a material harvest, from which all, including Paul and Barnabas, should benefit (Fee, 409).

The opening phrase of v.12 belongs with v.11. Paul refers again to *rights* (ἐξουσίας; 8:9; 9:4-6; cf. v.18). Since other ministers (perhaps Apollos [cf. 3:6], or Peter, or others who were reaping the spiritual harvest Paul had planted; as 4:15 and 9:2 show, the Corinthians had no shortage of spiritual mentors!) were supported by the Corinthians (they *share the right over you*), Paul and Barnabas had a *greater* right to it (*...do we not more?*). The fact they did not ask for such support led the Corinthians to disregard their right to it.

12b   Anticipating his explanation on why he refrained from taking support (vv.15-23), Paul states that he and Barnabas *did not use this right.* They have declined the right to support, and instead *endure all things,* because they are determined to *cause no hindrance to the gospel of Christ.* In other words, Paul has decided to forego his rights for the sake of a higher goal. It is this attitude which he desires his readers to adopt in regard to weaker brothers. To deny oneself the *use* of a right does not mean the right no longer exists; it exhibits the quality of self-denial which Christ made a condition of discipleship (cf. Luke 9:23; 14:27).

13   Paul seals his argument with an illustration drawn from Jewish religious practice, as well as from the Corinthian context; indeed, his reasoning comes from the very idol temples where they had been joining in feasts! His opening *Do you not know...* (Οὐκ οἴδατε) implies this is something which they *do* know (3:16; 5:6; 6:2, 3, 9, 15, 16, 19; 9:24). *Those who perform sacred services eat the food of the temple, and those who attend regularly to the altar have their share with the altar.* In fact, it was this knowledge which led them to join in temple feasts. They were participating in something which, to any casual observer (and to the weak consciences of younger believers) looked like a blanket endorsement of idolatry and those who led in the worship of idols. After all, they were eating the food of the temple just like the priests and patrons who worshipped there. They were then able to proudly demonstrate their knowledge to others, that 'there is no such thing as an idol in the world' (8:4), coming across as 'super-spiritual' by taking part in something evil!

Paul's point here is, while reminding them of the issue at hand, to demonstrate their knowledge that what he is saying is true—that he has a right to material support from them. They cannot deny it; their own action, borne out of an arrogant show of knowledge, demonstrates it!

14   The practice of providing material support to those who devote themselves vocationally to the proclamation of the gospel, reflected in the provision given to temple workers, is now cemented into place by an appeal to the words of the Lord Himself. While Jesus' instructions to the twelve recorded in Matt.10:10 support Paul's conclusion here, his close association with Luke throughout his ministry (cf. Luke's references to *we* and *us* in Acts 16:10-17; 20:5-21:18; 27:1ff; 28:16; and Paul's

references to Luke in Col. 4:14; Philem. 24; 2 Tim. 4:11) makes it more likely that his reference is to the Lord's sending of the seventy in Luke 10:4, 7-8. The message was simple; *those who proclaim the gospel* are *to get their living from the gospel.*

Paul's logical argument is complete. He began with an appeal to social norms (4-7), then to the scriptures (Law; 8-12), then to sacred norms (13), and finally to the Savior (14). All the evidence agrees: Those who proclaim the gospel (and that means Paul!) have a right to get their living from their gospel work.

Homiletical Ideas: It is unfortunate that the subject of this passage is often avoided, or if addressed, used wrongly. On the one hand, the attitude of some Christians that what they do with their money is no business of the preacher (nothing could be further from the truth!) has caused pastors to avoid offending those with fat wallets and thin skins! On the other hand, under-compensated pastors may use this passage as an opportunity to present themselves as sacrificial saints, or subtly appeal for a higher salary.

But Paul's whole argument is going to emphasize that he has given up these rights, and endures all things, for the sake of the gospel! While the principle of providing material support for those who preach the Word is sound, it should be presented in the context of an even higher goal: the proclamation of the gospel. If both minister and congregation attend to their own responsibilities and keep the focus on the gospel, the fiscal desires of the former will not be so great, and the burden of the latter will be more gladly borne. The message here is subservient to the over-riding theme of 8:1-11:1, that we should all be prepared to deny our own 'rights' for the sake of the gospel, and others in the Body of Christ.

The question answered in 8:1-13 is: *What motivation should guide Christian behavior in the local church?* Answer: Love for the brethren. The question answered in 9:1-14 is: *What should be our primary motivation in the local church?* Paul's answer is simple: That in all things we may cause no hindrance to the gospel. With this in mind, Paul now exhibits and explains his own example of this higher commitment.

15-18   [Paul voluntarily declines financial support in order to gain a reward for going beyond his duty.]

15   Picking up from his brief statement in v.12b, Paul states that, despite his right to make a living from his ministry, *I have used none of these things*. He has never asked for their support, and he quickly adds, *I am not writing these things that it may be done so in my case*. Some in Corinth may have taken his comments as an implicit appeal for such support, but this is the furthest thing from his mind! He does not waver. To have his right of financial support in some way hinder the gospel would be a fate worse than death! He most definitely does not want their money!

Neither does he want their sympathy! For him to take a stipend for his spiritual duties would *make* his *boast an empty one*. What does Paul mean by this? For Paul, his boasting was always and only in what God had done. No one could boast before God, since God was the One who did everything for us (1:26-29). However, boasting was possible, if it was *in the Lord* (1:30-31). Paul's boast here is in what the Lord has done through him, namely, the proclamation of the gospel and the establishment churches, all *without taking any financial support*. It is this final element of his ministry in which he boasted. It was this feature of his mission which he viewed as preventing any *hindrance to the gospel of Christ* (v.12b). If he received financial support his boast would be made empty (κενώσει; "deprive me of my reason for boasting;" cf. κενόω, BAGD, 428; cf. 1:17).

16   For Paul, to *preach the gospel* was *nothing to boast of* on its own. He was *under compulsion* to preach. The Greek term is ἐπίκειται (ἐπίκειμαι, BAGD, 294), meaning "to lie upon," which applies to duties imposed or incumbent on someone (1 Clement 40:5: "...upon the Levites the proper ministries *have been imposed*.").

Paul did not preach the gospel because it was a good option, or because he wanted to; he was taken hold of by God in his conversion, transferred from the domain of darkness to the kingdom of Jesus Christ (Col. 1:13), and he cannot help but speak! This is God's 'calling' on his life (Gal. 1:15-16), and to fail to preach would be to disobey God! Hence his concluding confession: *Woe is me if I do not preach the gospel!*

Interpretational Note: There is much 'fuzzy thinking' concerning the "call" or "will" of God today, and this verse is ripe for misuse. Paul is *not* referring to some mystical inner voice which told him: "You've got to be a preacher!" Pastors sometimes justify their ministry or add weight to their words by appealing to God's divine call on their life. This is not Paul's meaning. He has nothing to boast about in his preaching because this is what God saved him to do. It's his basic job-description.

---

17   If Paul did preach *voluntarily*, he could expect *a reward* (financial support). But this is not his case. He is under compulsion. Therefore, the second of the two conditions applies to him. His preaching is *against my will* (not that he fights against it, but that it was not his idea). He is a steward (cf. 4:1f), of whom it is required that he be found trustworthy. He was no hired hand; he was a slave of the Lord (Rom. 1:1; Gal. 1:10; Phil. 1:1)! To him had been entrusted the mysteries of God (2:6-9; 4:1-2; cf. Eph. 3:2-12), and he is compelled, not implored, to preach.

18   If there is no financial remuneration for Paul, *what then is* his *reward* (pay)? Here, we must understand Paul's view of reward. His reward is to do something for Christ over and above what is required. To do this gives him something to boast about in the Lord; he is doing something of our own volition! Since his preaching is under compulsion, a result of God's job description on his life, Paul's reward is to *offer the gospel without charge, so as not to make full use of my right in the gospel.* For Paul, for whom

foolishness is wisdom (3:18) and weakness is strength (1:27), his reward is to receive no reward (ἀδάπανον; *free of charge;* only here in the New Testament).

Application: Too often we view ministry for the Lord as a 'burden' which we bear for Him! Contrast this with the attitude of Paul, who was constrained to preach the gospel, and viewed this not as a favor, but a duty. To gain some small merit from his Savior and Lord, he insisted on preaching the gospel for nothing! His ministry was a model of Jesus' words in Matt. 10:8: *Freely you received, freely give.* Paul had done nothing to receive the gift of salvation; he would seek no gain from preaching it to others. Salvation is free; he would not charge 'postage and handling'! May we always reflect such devotion to service, to go above and beyond the call of duty!

19-23   [Paul voluntarily gives up personal rights in order to win more to the gospel.]

19   Because he preaches the gospel without pay, Paul is *free from* [responsibility to] *all men,* but he has paradoxically used this freedom to make himself *a slave to all,* with the goal *that I might win the more.* He owed allegiance to no supporting group, and thus was free to become a servant of all for the sake of the gospel. The term for *win* is κερδήσω (vv. 19-22; cf. κερδαίνω, BAGD, 429), which means "to gain" (cf. Mark 8:36), and in Jas. 4:13 is translated "make a profit." Paul gave up personal temporal freedom to gain eternal freedom from sin for *the more.* His was a temporal investment, with an eternal reward!

While verses 15-18 explained why Paul gave up his right to support, these verses (19-23) tell why Paul also gives up his *personal* rights. The implication is that if Paul gives up his personal rights for the sake of the unsaved, how much more should the Corinthian Christians give up their rights for their weaker brethren?! Exactly what it means for Paul to be *a slave to all* is now spelled out.

20   For Paul, to be 'a slave to all' means showing deference to the quirks and customs of others. *To the Jews*, he *became as a Jew*. He made himself a slave to their customs, their tastes, their likes, etc., so that he *might win* some of them for the kingdom.

To those who are under the Law (again referring to Jews, emphasizing their legal-religious requirements), although he was *not under the Law*, he lived *as under the Law*, in order that he *might win those who are under the Law*.

21   On the other hand, *to those who are without law* (outside the purview of the Law; Gentiles), he became *as without law*. He participated in their customs, joined in their activities, etc. But his qualification here is more involved. While he may live as one who is outside the (Jewish) Law, he is never *without the law of God but under the law of Christ*. The believer is not under Old Testament law, but *is* now under a new code—the law of Christ. One tenet of this law is love for one another, a principle which the Corinthians needed to heed toward weaker brothers! Paul became like Gentiles with the motivation of love, *that I might win those who are without law*.

22   The final illustration of Paul's 'slavery to all' for the sake of the gospel is especially important for the Corinthians to note. *To the weak*, Paul *became weak*, in order to *win the weak*. This is both a reference to their conversion (cf. 1:26-31) and a reminder of the issue at hand. Their insensitive behavior with *weaker* brothers was scandalous, resulting in spiritual ruin. Paul's example was to be weak with the weak (2:1-5), so that he might gain some more for the kingdom. His summary is inclusive: *I have become all things to all men, that I may by all means save some.*

23   His guiding principle? The first half of this verse is clear; whatever Paul does, he does *for the sake of the gospel*. Here he harkens back to verse 18; his reward is in preaching the gospel without charge. This denial of rights for the sake of the gospel is illustrated in vv.19-22, and restated here.

But what does he mean by the final clause: *that I may become a fellow partaker of it* ("share in its blessings," NIV; "be a partaker of it with you," NKJV)? It is necessary to avoid a theological minefield here; some commentators rashly make eternal salvation itself a result of works. Fee (432) writes: "he...must persevere in the gospel to share in its promises"). This interpretation makes Paul's meaning something like, "I deny myself and preach the gospel so that I might be saved"! But if self-denial and works are necessary for salvation, then who is Paul's gospel going to save (cf. 1:21)? The application of the Calvinist tenet of 'perseverance of the saints' as a requirement for salvation instead of an affirmation of the eternal security of believers is theologically unsound and unwarranted in this passage.

Understanding the connotation of συγκοινωνὸς (*fellow partaker*) is critical here. This term denotes those in a relationship like that of business partners (BAGD, 774), who *own shares* in a venture, and reap the rewards (or loss) of their investment. The NIV translation (*share*) is poor (there is no reason to render the noun as a verb!), and confuses the idea here with that in 9:13, where *share* (συμμερίζονται) simply means to have a part of something. Here the stakes are higher: Being a 'fellow partaker' of the gospel meant much more than simply believing it and knowing you were going to heaven. It meant being a 'full partner' in the blessings of the gospel, as Paul's other uses of this term show.

In Rom. 11:17, Gentile believers are 'full partners' in the privileges once restricted to Jews (cf. συμμέτοχα in Eph. 3:6). In Phil. 1:7, Paul thanks God for those believers who were 'full partners' with him in his suffering and preaching ministry. Paul's use of the verb συγκοινωνέω (participate in, be connected with; BAGD, 774) reflects this meaning. The believer is not to "*participate* in the unfruitful deeds of darkness" (Eph. 5:11); while association with those who do such things is not wrong (1 Cor. 5:9, 10), being 'full partners' with them is (cf. συμμέτοχοι, Eph. 5:7; cf. also 2 Cor. 6:14ff)! In Phil. 4:14f, Paul commends his readers for sharing in his ministry, as evidenced by their financial support (15). They were 'full partners.' John's uses (cf. Rev. 1:9; 18:4) also reflect this understanding.

What is the meaning then in this verse? Paul is not doubting his salvation, slaving to reach others in the hope that he will do enough to be saved himself! This notion is absurd. He is 'investing' himself totally in the gospel so he can be a 'full partner' in the blessings which come from winning the lost for the Savior. His goal is to gain a reward!

The key here is again in v.18. There Paul asked: *What then is my reward?* He is seeking a reward, and that reward is enhanced by him preaching the gospel without charge, without any hindrance. This *is* his reward. The gospel by which he has already been eternally saved is also the source of another 'prize'. Those who give themselves totally to proclaiming it gain a share in its blessings to others. Anyone who has led another person to Christ knows something of this unspeakable joy, the feeling of wonder in realizing that we have had a part in the spread of the gospel. It was for this that Paul gave up his personal rights—all for the sake of the gospel, and all to gain a reward. That reward is to have a share in the blessings which result from proclaiming the gospel. It is the blessings of the gospel that Paul desires to be a *fellow partaker* of. And it is that prize which he trains himself spiritually to win.

24-27   [Paul voluntarily trains himself like an athlete in order to gain an imperishable prize.]

24   Having introduced the idea of a reward for service in verses 18 and 23, Paul now borrows from the field of athletics to exhibit the rigour and dedication with which he pursues his goal. He begins with a self-evident statement: *Do you not know that those who run in a race all run, but only one receives the prize?* Of course, Paul did not need to tell the Corinthians this. The Isthmian Games (forerunner to our modern Olympic Games) were held at Corinth. They knew that every race had one winner! Paul's

question forces them to focus on the winner. As they consider the one victorious runner, Paul adds (to all of them) *Run in such a way that you may win.* For the Christian life, his counsel is: "Live your life in such a way that you will be a winner when you come to the end of it" (cf. 2 Tim. 4:6-8).

25   How can one do this? As *everyone who competes in the games exercises self-control,* so believers must exercise self-control (cf. ἐγκρατεύομαι, BAGD, 216; cf. 7:9) *in all things.* This suggests willful self-denial of desires in any area which interferes with proper Christian behavior. The stakes are very high. While a runner works hard *to receive a perishable* (φθαρτός; BAGD, 857; subject to decay) *wreath,* the believer seeks one which is *imperishable* (ἄφθαρτος, BAGD, 125; cf. Matt. 6:19-21), that will last forever.

The way to live life, then, is by exercising self-control in all things. The reward for doing this is praise (4:5) that will not pass away, or fade with the years, or be forgotten in a season. It will resound through eternity.

26   Because of these facts (*Therefore*; τοίνυν, BAGD, 821), the believer should follow Paul's example and *run in such a way, as not without aim* (with the prize in mind, not aimlessly). The inference is that it is possible for a Christian to live his life so devoid of any thought about the finish line that he never considers the reward to be gained—or lost. The picture is an absurd one—a competitor running aimlessly about the course! The question for every believer is: Where is your focus? For Paul, his focus is on the prize, and every step of the race is run with that goal in mind.

The metaphor of boxing has a similar lesson. A boxer who is *beating the air* is on his way to the canvas! A successful boxer knows his target, and makes contact! So too Paul is not just going through the motions; he is focused on his goal, and working towards it.

27   Continuing the boxing metaphor, Paul points out the need for training: *I buffet my body and make it my slave.* This is like saying,

"I beat myself black and blue!" (Findlay, 856) Paul takes blows so he can cope with those that his opponent may throw at him. This relates back to his exercise of self-control (25). Everything is done with the goal of winning the prize. But why does he drive himself so?

The conclusion is drawn suddenly and succinctly. Paul considers the horrible thought that, *after* having *preached to others* (leading them to salvation and nurturing them in their faith), after running much of the race so well, after `boxing' so effectively, he might *be disqualified* ("become unqualified") for the prize. This may refer to being taken out of the race for the prize through divine discipline (Lowery, 525; cf. 5:5; 10:6-10; 11:30-32). MacArthur suggests it means being "disqualified from being effective witnesses" (215f; in other references to this context, his meaning is not so clear; cf. *The Gospel According to Jesus* [Zondervan, 1988], p.182). It surely represents a loss of rewards when the believer stands before Jesus Christ.

Theological Note: Once again we encounter a passage which some misconstrue to be referring to eternal salvation. Barrett writes: "Paul clearly envisages the possibility that, notwithstanding his work as a preacher, he may himself fall from grace and be rejected. . . . His conversion, his baptism, his call to apostleship, his service in the Gospel, do not guarantee his eternal salvation" (218; cf. also Fee, 440, and Findlay, 857, who are less forthright, but adopt the same view). But such an interpretation is light-years removed from Paul's understanding of the gospel (cf. 1:21; Acts 16:31; Rom. 4:4-5; Eph. 2:8-9; etc.)! Instead, as Orr/Walther suggest, Paul was "thinking of heavenly honor . . . something in addition to being saved, something to be granted to those who perform service beyond the requirements" (243). To be *disqualified* (ἀδόκιμος) has the connotation of being depraved (Rom. 1:28; 2 Tim. 3:8) and worthless (Titus 1:16; Heb. 6:8), but is most closely paralleled with its usage here in 2 Cor. 13:5-7.

If it is possible for the Apostle Paul to fail in gaining rewards, so too all the Corinthians, and all believers! Eternal life is free, but rewards for service require diligence and perseverance. In particular, rewards for proclaiming the gospel are sought by Paul, and he knows that to gain the prize, he must be diligent to the end.

For his readers, their petty actions in going to idol temples as an expression of their freedom and 'rights' has now been exposed in all its ugliness. They, like Paul, must deny themselves those rights which impede the growth and health of the body, lest they too be found, after their lives are over, unqualified for a prize.

Homiletical Ideas: This passage is just one of a myriad throughout the New Testament which teach the doctrine of rewards. This area is neglected by expositors. Perhaps this is sometimes a result of vigilance in preaching the gospel. However, too often it reflects the idea that working for rewards is 'mercenary' and thus a base motivation for Christian service. Such a disparaging of rewards provides, in the words of R.T. Kendall, "a theological loophole which the self-righteous aspect of our nature rather hastily welcomes" (*When God Says "Well Done!"* [Christian Focus Publications, 1993], p. 8). But biblical writers speak often, and clearly, about rewards, and invite commitment and service with a goal of reaping them. (For helpful studies on this area of doctrine and its distinction from the doctrine of salvation, see the above-mentioned book by Kendall; Zane C. Hodges, *The Gospel Under Siege*, 2nd ed., [Dallas: Redención Viva], 1992; and Joseph C. Dillow, *Final Destiny: The Future Reign of the Servant Kings* [Grace Theology Press, 2013].)

In these paragraphs (9:15-27), Paul exhibits three actions which lead to rewards. First, he denies himself his rights, even rights supported by scripture. Self-denial is a foreign concept to many Christians in modern western society, but it is an action which leads to reward.

Secondly, Paul makes himself a slave to all, adopting the customs and behavior of his audience, so that he can win as many as possible to Christ. How far removed this is from the attitude of many Christians! Instead of seeking to force the unsaved to meet us on our terms, we must meet them where they are. To do so will reap a harvest for heaven, and result in us gaining rewards.

Finally, Paul sacrificially trains himself and focuses his efforts on the final reward ceremony. His goal is not earthly praise, for it is temporal. The plaudits of the world may bring merit now, but they will fade before the judgment seat of Christ. Would that believers begin to look beyond the confines of what is seen to the 'real world' of what is yet unseen (2 Cor. 4:17-18). This is where the real rewards await, and it is for these that we should all be working.

Make it a habit to include the motivation of rewards in sermons, and the rewards in the Body of Christ will be great.

10:1-13 *Israel's example of self-indulgence illustrates the attitude toward Christian 'rights' which results in judgment instead of rewards.*

The connection between Paul's instruction here and his personal example in chapter 9 is logical. Paul's position as an apostle gave him certain rights, which he voluntarily denied himself in order to effectively minister for Christ and receive a reward for his service. Like the knowledgeable Corinthians, he was privileged. Unlike them, he refused to use his privilege at the expense of others. After all, a privileged position was no guarantee of spiritual reward—even for an apostle (9:27)!

That point is central to Paul's argument. The Corinthians needed to be convinced that their knowledge, no matter how great, would not preserve them from spiritual ruin. But what if some were prone to disregard Paul's example? Paul therefore reaches back into Israelite history, into the 'Bible' of the early church, to exhibit that spiritual benefits and blessings do not guarantee spiritual rewards. In fact, those so blessed may even face God's severe judgment.

1-5 [The spiritual privileges of Israel, which correspond to Christian sacraments, did not result in spiritual rewards, but judgment.]

1 This verse is understood best when it follows directly on from 9:27. Paul submits his body to the rigors of self-denial so that he will not be unqualified for a reward. The prospect of an apostle being refused a reward would have been startling! It raised an obvious question in the minds of the Corinthians as well: If an apostle could be unqualified, could we as well? Paul's answer is, "Yes! In fact, it is a huge danger for those who are specially blessed. *For I do not want you to be unaware, brethren...*"

Paul introduces his instruction drawn from the history of the Israelites, referred to as *our fathers* (οἱ πατέρες ἡμῶν). In this epistle, references to 'fathers' are both literal (5:1) and figurative (4:15). Here Paul links the Corinthians to the Israelites as their 'spiritual ancestors.' There is a continuity: What happened to the Israelites also applies to them. No more fitting parallel with the Corinthians can be imagined. The Israelites were blessed, but stubborn; despite their blessings, they failed in the area of idolatry and were judged by God.

Paul begins by describing the spiritual blessings of the Israelites. First, they *were all under the cloud, and all passed through the sea.* That is, all the Israelites (whether obedient, sinful, destined to enter the land or to die in the wilderness) were under the cloud of God's guidance and passed through the Red Sea of God's deliverance during the Exodus from Egypt (Exod. 13, 14). Paul has not picked these two incidents at random.

2 Rather, he immediately explains (cf. "καί," BAGD, 393, I.3.) his intention by adding that *all were baptized into Moses in the cloud and in the sea.* Paul wants his readers to see a parallel in their affairs with the experience of God's people in a previous generation. The birth of the nation of Israel was associated

with a "baptism into Moses" (a national relationship with God defined by the Law), and exhibited in the Red Sea deliverance. The beginning of the Christian life is associated with a "baptism into Christ" (cf. Rom. 6:3; Gal. 3:27; this is Spirit baptism, not water baptism (contra Fee, 444); cf. 1 Cor. 12:13), exhibited outwardly in water baptism. Paul's reference may include both the conversion and dedication aspects of baptism, each of which results in spiritual blessing. Indeed, there was a Hellenistic-magical view of the sacraments in Corinth (including both baptism and the Lord's Supper) which taught that these rites secured them from any possible spiritual harm. This may even have emboldened them to attend idol feasts. Paul is clearly illustrating the similarity of the Corinthians' spiritual blessings and those enjoyed by the Israelites. Both had experienced a 'baptism.'

Theological Note: We must resist the temptation to construct any theological conclusions based on a cryptic reference like this. For instance, Paul is surely not seeking to contribute to the debate on modes of baptism by referring to a cloud (which 'sprinkles' rain) and the sea (in which one is immersed; Hodge, 172); in fact, the cloud did not rain and the nation was not immersed in the sea! Again, any attempt to relate a certain kind of baptism to spiritual birth is forced. It is best to read this as Paul's way of preparing his readers to respond to the case of judgment-despite-spiritual-blessing which was Israel's experience in the wilderness, and leave theological considerations to those passages which clearly address them.

3-4   Another blessing experienced by Israel and highlighted by Paul is that *all ate the same spiritual food, and all drank the same spiritual drink.* This refers to the early days of the Exodus, in the wilderness provision of manna and water (Exod. 16, 17). The food and drink were 'spiritual' not in that they had any mystical value (Barrett, 222; cf. Fee, 447, n.31), but that they had a supernatural origin (Robertson-Plummer, 200), and signified the spiritual link between the nation and the God who provided for their needs. Again, Paul has chosen his events with the intention of reminding the Corinthians of their own spiritual blessings, as reflected in the bread and the cup of the Lord's Supper.

Some confusion is elicited by the explanatory phrase which follows: *for they were drinking from a spiritual rock which followed them; and the rock was Christ*. In what way was the rock "spiritual," in what way did it "follow them," and in what way was it Christ? It is tempting to solve all these difficulties by making "rock" here a figurative reference to the pre-existent Christ providing for the nation's needs in the wilderness (Grosheide, 220ff). However, in the context of Paul's reference to historical events, we should seek a literal meaning. The reference must be to the actual rock which flowed forth with water in the wilderness (Exod. 17; Num. 20, 21).

In this case, the rock was spiritual in that, like the manna and water, it had a supernatural origin and was God's provision for His people. Because a water-producing rock is mentioned in different places (Rephidim, Ex. 17:1; Kadesh, Num. 20:1), a rabbinic legend held that the rock actually followed the nation during the wilderness wandering (Robertson/Plummer, 201; Fee, 447f). In response to this idea, Paul now explains that while the Israelites did get water from the rock twice, it was not the physical rock which moved, but Christ who was with them all the way. Two grammatical factors suggest this. First, the actual presence of Christ in the wilderness is indicated by Paul's use of ἦν ("the rock *was* Christ"). Second, the particle δὲ has a disjunctive quality, connecting two clauses with some contrast between them (BAGD, 171); we might translate, "*but* the rock was Christ"). Paul is thus saying: "The Israelites drank from a rock God provided for them, and that rock of provision followed them—not a physical rock, as some have inferred, but Christ Himself." In this way, Paul emphasizes the similarity between the spiritual provision of Israelites' in the wilderness, and the Christians in Corinth. Both have their source in Christ, only the Israelites saw it in the form of a rock. Christ was just as present at the rock in the wilderness as He is present at the Lord's Supper in Corinth.

Interpretive Note: The typological significance of the link between the rock in the wilderness and Christ is open to conjecture here. Does this relationship have anything to do with the events of Num. 20? After telling Moses to strike the rock in Exod. 17:6, God instructs him on the second occasion simply to speak to the rock (Num. 20:8). When Moses strikes the rock twice instead (11), he is immediately judged by God (12). Obviously, Moses was guilty of disobeying God's directions, but why were they given, and why was the judgment so harsh? Perhaps it is because the first striking of the rock was intended to prefigure the wounds Christ bore on the cross. (The Hebrew verb describing Moses' striking of the rock in Exod. 17:6 and Num. 20:11 is also used to prophetically describe Christ's death in Isa.53:4 [הֻכָּה]. As the author of *Hebrews* affirms, Christ suffered for sins 'once for all' [cf. 7:27; 9:12, 28; 10:10ff].) God's instructions on the second occasion might indicate that the provisions of the rock come not through re-crucifixion, but through an expression of faith in the rock once smitten (cf. Heb. 6:6). The implicit lesson from Moses' experience, then, might be to never forget the once-for-all sufficiency of the death of Christ!

Paul's explanation of Israelite spiritual blessings is complete. The Old Testament nation had visible agencies which conveyed to them the benefits of Christ, corresponding to the New Testament ordinances of baptism and the Lord's Supper. Three factors are notable:

1) The *whole nation* received these benefits of God (just as *all* believers have received the same benefits of salvation).

2) These benefits were of a spiritual character, signifying a relationship with God.

3) These benefits came from Christ (as do all the benefits of Christian experience).

Paul has established that the Israelites experienced the same kind of benefits of a relationship with God that the Corinthian Christians do. He now moves to confront their wrong belief that such blessings are any guarantee of spiritual protection and favor before God.

5   With the strong adversative particle Ἀλλ' (*Nevertheless*), Paul emphatically introduces his key point; while *all* (πάντες; 5x in vv.1-4) the Israelites received God's blessings, yet *with most of them* (ἐν τοῖς πλείοσιν αὐτῶν) *God was not well-pleased*. What an understatement! In fact, with only two (Joshua and Caleb) was God pleased enough to allow them to enter the Promised Land (Num. 14:30-32)! The rest *were laid low in the wilderness.* Paul is dramatically making his point to the Corinthians: Let no one think they are immune from a loss of rewards; even with the blessings of grace and spiritual gifts, the possibility of loss exists. Just as the graves of an entire generation of Israelites were scattered about the desert ("laid low;" cf. καταστρώννυμι, BAGD, 419; Fee, 450), receiving death instead of the prize (9:24) of entering the Promised Land, so too the Corinthian believers were jeopardizing their future reward through their idolatrous liaisons.

6-10   [The Corinthian believers should stop arrogantly joining in idol feasts, which are evil, because the Israelites acted in this way and were judged as a result.]

Having established a link between the blessings of the Israelites and the Corinthian believers, Paul now sets about establishing a parallel between the sins of the wandering nation and the wayward church.

6   He begins by stating that *these things* (the judgment-despite-spiritual-blessing of the Israelites) *happened as examples* (τύποι) *for us.* In the wilderness wandering there is a pattern to be

discerned, a moral lesson to heed. The Corinthian believers need to learn from the past, lest they repeat it! God was pleased to bless His people, but He was not pleased with the response of most of them!

The lesson for the Corinthians from the wilderness event is that they *should not crave evil things, as* the Israelites *also craved.* This craving reveals the motivation behind all the actions in vv.7-10, and is often viewed as Paul's general exhortation, with specific admonitions to follow (Barrett, 224; Fee, 453). His instruction would thus be: "Don't crave evil things, like the Israelites did; for example, some of them were idolaters...some of them acted immorally...etc." However, this craving is also reflected in the record of Israel's 'greed' in the wilderness (Num. 11:4, 34), and there may be an implicit reference to it here (Ellicott, 178). Certainly the idea of craving past heathen pleasures fits well in the Corinthian context, and the repetition of μηδὲ (and not, nor) in vv.7-10 supports this view. In either case, Paul is exhorting his readers to resist the lure of evil things, the temptation of which led to judgment on Israel.

7   Paul is primarily concerned with the Corinthians' arrogant attendance at idol feasts, and highlights this problem with two specific citations. They are *not* to *be idolaters, as some of* the Israelites *were; as it is written: "The people sat down to eat and drink, and stood up to play."* The historical event Paul recalls is the episode of the golden calf rebellion at the foot of Mt. Sinai (Exod. 32). However, his scriptural citation is *not* from the initial worship of the calf idol as a god (Exod. 32:4), but rather *the feast* which took place on the following day (Exod. 32:5-6). These festivities aroused God's fierce anger (7-10). It was the revelry and enjoyment of idols which identified the nation as idolaters, a point the Corinthians must not miss! Merrymaking and celebration in idol temples did not reflect their strength in Christ, but an endorsement of idols! Paul dispels the idea that joining in idol feasts is morally neutral. It is tantamount to idolatry.

Application: One might question whether Paul has contradicted himself, instructing the Corinthians not to avoid association *with the immoral people of this world* (5:10), but now indicting them as idolaters for joining in the temple feasts. Those intent on abusing their freedom might seek to weaken Paul's message in this way. But no weakness is present, nor in Paul's character. He *does* desire believers to be *in* the world, *infecting others* with the message of Christ, but he *does not* want them to be *of* the world, *infected by* the immoral society in which they live. Paul here clearly defines when the line between infecting others and being infected is crossed. Joining in idol feasts is endorsement and participation in idolatry, and wrong.

8   The second illustration of idolatry is drawn from the end of the 40-year wilderness wandering, while the nation was camped at Shittim (Num. 25) preparing to cross the Jordan. Moabite women (evidently following Balaam's advice; cf. Num. 31:15f) lured Israelite men into sexual immorality and worship of Baal of Peor, which included eating a meal (Num. 25:1-3), arousing God's fierce anger (Num. 25:4). The idolatry of Corinth was closely tied with harlotry, a point not missed by Paul. Thus he exhorts: *Nor let us act immorally* (πορνεύω, BAGD, 693; practice prostitution, commit sexual immorality), *as some of them did*. Sexual license was synonymous with Corinth, and joining in feasts at temples known for sexual forms of worship was no different than the action of the Israelites. The result for Israel was catastrophic; *twenty-three thousand fell in one day!* The Corinthians were courting disaster.

Textual Note: The difference between the number who died here (23,000) and in Num. 25:9 (24,000) has prompted numerous suggestions for harmonization or explanation. These include Paul being confused and having a lapse in memory (Orr/Walther, 246), both numbers being round estimates (the actual number being somewhere in between; Hodge, 178), or 23,000 being the number killed *in one day*, while 24,000 was the final total (Mare, 249; MacArthur, 223). The best solution may be a combination of the latter two suggestions, but any certainty is impossible (Fee, 456).

9   The final two *evil things* (v.6) which the Israelites did, and which the Corinthians needed to avoid, highlight the arrogance which led them to dabble in idolatry. Paul first warns the Corinthians not to *try* (ἐκπειράζωμεν) *the Lord* (better: *Christ*; see Textual Note below), *as some of* the Israelites *did*. In Num. 21:4-9, the Israelites complain about their conditions in the wilderness. Although it was their own sinful action which resulted in their 40-year 'death march' in Sinai, they blame God: "Why have you brought us up out of Egypt to die in the wilderness? For there is no food and no water, and we loathe this miserable food [manna]." God responded to this affront by sending lethal serpents among the people, and many died.

What does it mean to *try* (NASV) or *test* (NIV) the Lord? The verbs in this verse (ἐκπειράζω and πειράζω; cf. v.13, where the verb and its cognate noun πειρασμὸς, *temptation*, appear), indicate a trial in which the intention is hostile (DNTT, 3:809). In Numbers 21, this describes the refusal of the Israelites to trust God and His word, instead 'pushing Him' to prove His power on their terms.

This is the very thing the Corinthians were in danger of doing. Some Christians "put the Lord to the test" (BAGD, 243; cf. Matt. 4:7; Luke 4:12; 10:25) by brazenly going to idol temples on the premise that He was the only true God, and thus they had nothing to fear (8:4-6). They even viewed themselves as protected by their participation in the sacraments. They arrogantly thought they were proving God's strength by doing evil, but they were only testing His patience. Continued arrogance would lead to destruction.

Translation Note: Although the NASV and NIV read *the Lord* in verse 9, external evidence (including both MajT and CrT) supports *Christ* (τὸν Χριστόν; see NKJV). As the Israelites tried the Lord, the Corinthians tried Christ.

10   Paul concludes his reference to specific sins by warning the Corinthians against arrogantly ignoring instruction which comes through God's messenger. He exhorts them not to *grumble, as some of [the Israelites] did, and were destroyed by the destroyer.* The recalls Num. 16:41-50, when the Israelites grumbled against Moses and Aaron following the harsh judgment on Korah (who had himself challenged Moses' leadership). As a result of this grumbling, 14,700 (Num. 16:49) died.

     Paul is warning those who might be disposed to grumble against him (and cause insurrection) because of his severe rebukes and warnings in the letter. He is God's messenger. Rather than grumble about his strict instructions, they should obey.

11-13   [The purpose of Paul's reminder of Israel's failure was to warn arrogant Corinthian believers to be watchful and trust God in facing temptation.]

11   Paul signals a 'wrapping up' of this discussion with the repetition of ταῦτα δὲ (*Now these things*; cf. v.6), adding πάντα in the MajT ("*all* these things") indicating that he is referring to his entire 'historical review' in vv.1-10. This is his summary statement, his purpose for writing.

     As he stated in verse 6, he reaffirms here that the events of Israelite history *happened to them as an example*; furthermore, *they were written for our instruction.* Whatever instructive value the accounts of the Israelite's wilderness failings had for the nation, Paul sees their ultimate benefit as being for Christians—those *upon whom the ends of the ages have come.* All previous ages looked forward to the coming Savior, and now, awaiting His second coming, we profit from their experiences. The final stage upon which the lessons of the ages find their fulfilment is in the new age ushered in by Christ.

12   *Therefore* (Ὥστε), since spiritual blessing does not guarantee spiritual reward, *let him who thinks* (ὁ δοκῶν) *he stands* (he views himself as being strong spiritually, and may be prone to become careless) *take heed lest he fall.* The Corinthians had a habit of thinking (δοκέω; BAGD, 201, 1.b.) they were something they weren't (cf. 3:18; 8:2; 14:37). Paul has demonstrated in the Israelites that it is those who *think* they are strong (like the Corinthians did) who are likely to fall (as the Israelites did). They should "go to school" on the experiences of Israel in the wilderness, lest they too reap judgment instead of rewards.

Interpretive Note: Paul's concluding warning for Christians in Corinth to "take heed lest [they] fall" is sometimes wrongly applied to eternal salvation. For example, Fee (459) writes: "This can only mean that the Corinthians, too, as Israel, may fail of the eschatological prize, in this case eternal salvation. Their way of placing themselves in this jeopardy is through their idolatry..." At the outset, it must be admitted that any 'eternal salvation' which can be lost as a result of human failing was never 'eternal' in the first place! Whatever 'salvation' was possessed was temporal and provisional at best! But all the evidence points to Paul warning against a moral fall which will result in judgment, *not* a loss of salvation. This paragraph follows a discussion clearly dealing with the issue of rewards for service (9:15-27). Paul's exhortations in this section, including all the Old Testament illustrations, involve temporal, not eternal judgment. Indeed, the same term translated "fall" (πίπτω) in verse 12 appears in verse 8 describing physical death. Finally, the rest of Paul's concluding admonition is to resist temptation, from which a faithful God will provide a way of escape. This is not a threat from a vengeful God, but the urging of a faithful deliverer. Paul is warning believers to beware lest they fall—not out of the family of God, but out of fellowship with Him; not losing the promise of eternal life, but losing the potential for future rewards; not reaping eternal death, but temporal punishment—possibly even physical death (cf. 11:30).

13 For those chastened by Paul's rigid refusal to bend in the area of attendance at idol feasts and despairing of resisting their urges, he now informs them that the situation is far from hopeless, and that help is available. The first encouraging point is that *No temptation* (πειρασμὸς; the implication is to evil; cf. BAGD, 640f) *has overtaken you but such as is common to man.* A good rendering here is, "You have been involved in no trials except those which are part of the human situation" (Barclay). This is not to say, however, that man can bear them alone!

It is therefore an even greater comfort to know that *God is faithful, who will not allow you to be tempted beyond what you are able.* This is not to say that we will never face a temptation that will overcome us; the enticements the Corinthians faced were "common to man" (including Israel), yet had caused many to fall. Rather, the promise is that our faithful God *with the temptation will provide the way of escape also.* Again, we must avoid saying more than Paul does. He does not mean that God will always give us a way out of every trial we face when we want out! Rather, His purpose is *that you may be able to endure* (cf. ὑποφέρω, BAGD, 848; "bear up under") *it.* The trials/temptations which Satan sends our way are designed by him for our destruction, but allowed by God for our strengthening (Jas.1:2-4). And in this process, God is on our side, always ready to help as we depend on Him. Our duty is to avoid putting ourselves in any position where we will be unduly exposed to temptation. Of course, this includes feasts at idol temples. It is a renewed appeal to flee from such associations which Paul presents in v.14ff.

Homiletical Ideas: It is not uncommon for those in countries with religious freedom to give God thanks for the liberty they enjoy. Similarly, when those in affluent economies see images of starving in third-world countries, they thank God for the abundance they enjoy. In free western societies today, Christians enjoy a higher standard of living and a wealth of spiritual resources beyond the wildest dreams of those in previous generations. Yet these blessings have often not produced the kind of commitment exhibited by Paul in 9:15-27! Living in a spiritually needy society, the church is often immature (spoiled) spiritually, isolated socially, and invisible morally. The alarms are sounding, but a lethargic Church is unable to respond.

This described believers in Corinth, and it also describes believers today. Instead of viewing freedom and affluence as an opportunity to deny self and give more for Christ, many become self-indulgent, consuming in ever-increasing amounts. Ultimately, their abundance of blessing brings no joy (they hoard instead of giving), and becomes a spiritual distraction resulting in judgment.

The Corinthians thought their participation in the sacraments would secure for them spiritual blessings and reward. In fact, their practice was leading them to judgment (11:17-34)! Many believers today treat church affiliation the same way. Their orthodox doctrine, biblical teaching, outstanding pastor, and other such things are the 'security blanket' to which they cling, expecting to be rewarded for their association with such a group. These may be spiritual blessings, but they guarantee no reward.

The theme of these verses is: *Spiritual blessings do not guarantee spiritual rewards*. Blessings are often a source of temptation, and can become an addiction from which we need God's help to escape. Here then is an exceedingly practical message for Christians today. Let us not be falsely lured into thinking we are spiritually healthy by our doctrine or church affiliation. Let us not think that our spiritual blessings insure spiritual rewards. And let us depend on God to deliver us from the temptation to focus on our blessings, instead of the God who gives them.

10:14-22 *Paul exhorts the Corinthians to heed the example of the Israelites in the wilderness and not join in idolatrous fellowship with demons in idol feasts, which is incompatible with fellowship with the Lord, and incurs His jealous anger.*

In 10:14-11:1, Paul applies principles of Christian liberty first to the question of participation in idol temple feasts (14-22), then to some related areas (buying meat in the market, or eating meat in unbelievers' homes; 23-11:1). The first section is instruction for their specific situation; the second section guards against any incorrect applications being drawn from this instruction (a problem which occurred following Paul's earlier letter to them; 5:9f).

14   Paul is now ready to draw conclusions from the example of Old Testament Israel for the Corinthians' practice of joining in idol temple feasts. His instruction follows directly from the events in verses 1-13. Israel had spiritual blessings, yet was judged because of idolatry (evidenced by participation in idol feasts). Let those in Corinth who think they stand beware (βλεπέτω; 12)! The temptation to join such feasts can be overcome with God's help (13), but they must act. With a strong inferential conjunction (*Therefore*; διόπερ; cf. 8:13; 14:13; "for this very reason," BAGD, 199), Paul exhorts believers (*my beloved*) to *flee from idolatry*. An arrogant Corinthian might object that "we know that there is no such thing as an idol in the world (cf. 8:4), so what is there to be afraid of?" But they missed the point of the Old Testament illustrations. Joining in idol festivities constituted more than innocent contact with an idolatrous society. Corinthian Christians rightly did not avoid interacting with the unsaved (cf. 5:10), but accepting their invitation to meals held in idol temples went beyond the bounds of 'friendship evangelism' (cf. Wilson, 149)! That was tantamount to idolatry, which is not something neutral, but something to be feared, and to flee from.

15   The Corinthians thought of themselves as wise (4:10), so Paul will put their wisdom to the test. *I speak as to wise* (φρονίμοις; sensible) *men; you judge* (κρίνατε, "decide for yourselves;" BAGD,

451; cf. 11:13) *what I say* (φημι; "what I mean by what I say;" cf. BAGD, 856, and v.19 below). Paul is not looking for support, as if he needs them to affirm that his teaching is correct! His words are tinged with sarcasm: "You are so intelligent! Try to discern the meaning of what I have said!" The implication is that even though he does not subscribe to their claim of being wise, what he is telling them is something they should know.

16   Using logic and rhetorical questions, Paul makes his meaning clear: Attending idol feasts arouses God's anger. It involves fellowship with demons which is inimical to a believer's relationship with the Lord, and provokes Him to jealousy (16-22).

Drawing from the Lord's Supper, the observance which they valued highly (see above, 10:3-4), Paul highlights a self-evident truth. *Is not the cup of blessing which we bless a sharing in the blood of Christ? Is not the bread which we break a sharing in the body of Christ?* Both questions require a positive answer (οὐχὶ). The meal they observed reflected their *sharing* (κοινωνία; fellowship) in the body and blood of Christ. This κοινωνία relationship reflects both communion with the Lord (cf. 1:9) and the fellowship between believers partaking of the meal together (BAGD, 439). The Lord's Supper reminds believers that they share in the provisions and benefits of the New Covenant (Fee, 466ff). Paul's purpose is not simply to instruct the Corinthians concerning the Lord's Supper; it is to prepare them for his instruction concerning idol feasts in vv.19ff. His message here is simple: "Note how your participation in the Lord's Supper ties you to all others partaking in the meal, as well as to the Lord whom the elements represent."

17   To emphasize the horizontal fellowship, Paul draws an analogy from the bread. This may explain why the cup is mentioned first, instead of second as elsewhere in the New Testament (cf. 11:24-29); since Paul is not describing an actual observance of the supper, the order is not important (cf. v.21). *Since there is one bread, we who are many are one body; for we all partake of the one*

bread. Jesus said of the bread, "This is My body, which is for you" (11:24); Paul here points out that the bread which symbolizes Christ's body also signifies that all who join in eating it are united together as members of His Body (cf.12:12ff). The 'feast of the Lord' identifies those who share in it as the Lord's people, part of the redeemed community. They are all one in Christ (cf. Gal. 3:28). Since the Lord's Supper meal in His 'temple' (3:16f) shows those who join in it to be followers of Him, so too the meal in an idol's temple shows that those who join in it are followers of it. This, of course, is idolatry.

18   With abruptness designed to finalize his argument, Paul again refers to Old Testament Israel: *Look at the nation Israel; are not* (οὐχὶ) *those who eat the sacrifices sharers in the altar?*

Translation/Theological Note: The translation *the nation Israel* (NASV) or *the people of Israel* (NIV) does not literally render the Greek τὸν Ἰσραὴλ κατὰ σάρκα ("Israel according to the flesh;" cf. NKJV). These terms can denote the nation of Israel (cf. Rom. 9:3), but may here implicitly point to a distinction between earthly and spiritual people of God (Rom. 2:28f; 9:8; Gal. 4:23, 29; 6:16; BAGD, 743f; Hodge, 191).

The earthly nation of Israel had been instructed by God (cf. Deut. 12:17f; 14:22-29) to bring the so-called "second tithe" to provide for an annual feast, held in the central sanctuary. On this occasion the sacrifices were given, then eaten by the people. The offerings could only be eaten in the place of God's choosing, in His presence. In this way the people would rejoice and celebrate together their relationship with the Lord. In referring back to this practice, Paul shows that *those who eat the sacrifices* also fellowship in the worship offering of the food (*sharers in the altar*). Just as the Israelites indicated their worship of Yahweh through their participation in the feast, the Corinthians were indicating their worship of idols when they joined in temple feasts.

19   Paul's evidence is complete. Those who join in temple meals are also joining in worship of the gods the temple represents. This is reflected both in Christian practice (16-17) and in Israel's history (18). Therefore, by implication, Christians in Corinth should not participate in idol temple meals.

But some might still wonder why such meals are forbidden, since Paul has already said that *there is no such thing as an idol in the world* (8:4ff). So now, Paul clarifies why it is that idolatry is something which must be avoided. *What do I mean* (φημι; cf. v.15) *then?* Is Paul changing his previous statement? No. He does not mean *that an idol is anything*, nor that *a thing sacrificed to idols is anything*. Idols are not real gods, nor is the food offered to idols inherently evil.

20   Rather, he is exposing the fact *that the things which the Gentiles sacrifice, they sacrifice to demons, and not to God*. In this allusion to the Song of Moses (cf. Deut. 32:17), Paul is not merely saying that pagans do not sacrifice to God, but that they sacrifice to an entity which is no-god (Fee, 472). Just as the Israelites made God jealous by joining in such worship (Deut. 32:21), the Corinthians did as well. Idols are not 'beings,' nor do they have power, but the demons behind them are and do!

It is obvious therefore why they must not join in idol feasts. Paul does *not want* them *to become sharers* (κοινωνοὺς) *in demons.* Israel enjoyed a meal of worship and celebration to Yahweh of the sacrifices they brought. So too believers joining in a pagan idol feast were joining in worship and celebration of demons! But they joined together at the Lord's Table, worshiping Jesus Christ and remembering His great sacrifice. To participate in a similar setting where demons were being worshipped was incompatible with their faith and must not occur under any circumstances.

21   Paul now strengthens his prohibition from the soft *I do not want* (οὐ θέλω; v.20) to the blunt: *You cannot* (οὐ δύνασθε). It is

impossible to *drink the cup of the Lord and the cup of demons*, or to *partake of the table of the Lord and the table of demons*. That is, no believer can at the same time enjoy fellowship with the Lord and fellowship with demons. It is inconceivable.

22   With two rhetorical questions, Paul brings his exhortation to a climax. To join in idol feasts is to *provoke the Lord to jealousy*, as the Israelites learned (Deut. 32:21)—the results of their idolatrous acts have already been noted (vv.7-8). Do the Corinthians want to try the Lord's patience? *We are not stronger than He, are we?* Paul here 'steps aside' to reveal that those who challenge his teaching are in fact confronting not him, but Christ Himself! Those who want to please Him, and win the prize (9:24-27) must never be party to such activity; those who do leave themselves open to God's harsh judgment.

Homiletical Note: What is a modern parallel to Corinthian Christians eating at idol temple feasts? There are many suggestions, often held to so strongly that they cause divisions! It is ironic that a letter which confronts divisions can become a source of them! To avoid this, focus on three things which are always true. 1) An *idol* is something that comes between a believer and God; anything we have or do is either a tool (for His use) or an idol (that distracts us from Him; cf. Col. 3:5). 2) Satan and his minions (demons) are behind all 'idolatry;' distractions which deter spiritual devotion and growth are his doing. 3) Fellowship with the distractions of this world is incompatible with fellowship with Christ. The believer who desires to grow must flee from all idolatry; those who do not do so arouse God's jealous anger and wrath upon themselves.

10:23-11:1 *Paul exhorts Corinthian believers to be free from concern about meat offered to idols, but to always regulate freedom by what is good and edifying for others, and what is glorifying to God.*

This paragraph summarizes Paul's principles concerning freedom in Christ—particularly in areas related to the main issue of participating in idol temple feasts. Here Paul addresses the question of meat which *may have been* offered to idols, and which is either sold in the market or served in an unbeliever's house. He first repeats one previously mentioned slogan (cf. 6:12; 10:23), then—in effect—combines two others—'food is for the stomach and the stomach for food' (6:13), and 'there is no such thing as an idol in the world' (8:4)—to affirm that eating meat offered to an idol is a non-issue, but restraining principles must be applied to every situation. As in ch.8, concern for others (here for both the saved and unsaved) is a major consideration, and to this is added the parallel motivation of bringing glory to God.

10:23-30 [Paul instructs believers to disregard the issue of meat offered to idols when buying or eating out, but to abstain from eating if someone else makes an issue of it, so as not to offend but to edify.]

23 Paul begins with an abrupt reference to the same slogan he mentioned in 6:12. *All things are lawful, but not all things are profitable.* In the previous instance, that which enslaved a believer was unprofitable. Here, Paul focuses on another issue: *All things are lawful, but not all things edify* (οἰκοδομεῖ; not all things are profitable to others). Believers should restrict the exercise of their freedom not only when their actions tear down a brother (8:7-13), but when they fail to build them up.

24 It is this principle which must govern every aspect of Christian practice. Proper behavior is determined by what is constructive for others. Actions which build up others are those which are motivated by love (8:3), and love "does not seek its own" (13:5). Paul explains what it means to be edifying here: *Let no one seek his own [good], but that of his neighbor* (τοῦ ἑτέρου; of another; cf. Rom. 15:1-2; Phil. 2:3-4). The ultimate expression of love is laying down one's life (giving up the right to life) for another (John 15:13; Rom. 5:6-8). It is this self-denying love which identifies those who are obedient followers of Jesus Christ (John 13:35).

25   Paul is now ready, with the proper restraint on freedom in place, to affirm the Corinthians in their liberty. There is no mention of concern for weaker brothers here, since the issue of eating at idol temple feasts is settled. Rather, bearing in mind the need to build up others, Paul instructs them to *Eat anything that is sold* (πωλούμενον; "offered for sale;" BAGD, 731) *in the meat market* (μάκελλον, BAGD, 487; only here in the New Testament; "slaughter-house"), *without asking questions for conscience' sake* (διὰ τὴν συνείδησιν). Some believers were evidently divided over the issue of possibly eating meat offered to idols. Perhaps they had been swayed by Jewish converts who still followed traditional restrictions on such food. Paul, once a champion of such legalistic restraints (cf. Phil. 3:5-6), now makes a clean break from them (Barrett, 240; cf. 7:18f, where circumcision is treated similarly). He indicates that meat is *not* an issue of conscience, so they are not to make it one. Those making meat an issue are just over-emphasizing their own preferences. Some actions lie outside the bounds of right or wrong; in these areas, one is free, provided the practice is edifying to others (and glorifying to God; v.31).

26   The moral neutrality of food was established by Christ when the disciples questioned Him after he rebuked the Pharisees for stressing ceremonial washing, but ignoring the need to be spiritually clean (Mark 7:1-23). It is not that which is taken into the body (stomach) which defiles a man, but that which is inside (the heart) and comes out (Mark 7:18-23; cf. Jer. 17:9). But Paul goes beyond this here, stating that any meat sold is *good* to eat, since (*for*) *the earth is the Lord's, and all it contains.* God created meat, and everything created by God is good (1 Tim. 4:4), therefore any meat is good to eat. In addition to this, it may be observed that since Paul has just admonished his readers to only do those things which edify, he also considers eating meat without questioning its previous use as an action which builds up. Unlike eating meat at an idol temple, the setting of which might motivate a recent convert to fall back into old ways, buying and eating meat from the market without concern about its source

would exhibit to all that meaningless legalistic restrictions are done away in Christ.

27 That which is not an issue at the butcher is also not an issue in an unbeliever's home. *If one of the unbelievers invites you* over for a meal, *and you wish to go, eat anything that is set before you, without asking questions for conscience sake.*

28-29a Is there ever a time when a believer should restrict this freedom to eat of meat, regardless of its connection with idol worship? Paul states that there is. In what amounts to a parenthetical statement (cf. RSV), Paul provides an illustrative instance when exercising freedom is not good for another person (24). *But if anyone should say to you, "This is meat sacrificed to idols," do not eat it.* The question here is: Who is the "anyone" who reveals that the meat has been offered to idols? Is it a believer, or an unbeliever? The answer depends in part on the resolution of a textual problem.

Textual Note: CrT and MajT differ on the word translated *meat sacrificed to idols*. CrT reads ἱερόθυτόν (something devoted or sacrificed to a divinity; BAGD, 372), a pagan reference for a temple-offering (Orr/Walther, 254), and would lead to the conclusion that Paul here has in mind an unsaved dinner-guest. MajT reads εἰδωλόθυτόν, the same term used in chapter 8 and 10:19, a pejorative reference to something offered to idols. If this is the word Paul used, he probably had in mind here another Christian guest at the same meal (Lowery, 528). Both views have merit. In favor of the second interpretation, it is possible that both a strong and a weak believer were invited to the home of an unbeliever, and the situation described arose. A weaker brother might have his conscience offended by eating such food (v.29; cf. 8:7, 12). It is also possible that this 'weaker brother' may have used the old pagan term to refer to the idol meat. But this view is not without its difficulties (Fee, 484, n.42). Why would Paul instruct Christians to disregard the issue of where meat came from in verses 25 and 27, then support a believer who makes an issue of it here? Furthermore, how would the weak believer know the source of the meat? Paul surely would not approve of someone snooping about, making inquiries of his host or in the kitchen (Barrett, 242). A believer spying out the liberty of a brother (cf. Gal. 2:4) would never receive Paul's endorsement (cf. Rom. 14:1-4)! In favor of this second guest being unsaved is the context in general. Whatever similarities exist between the situation here and offending a weaker brother in 8:7-13, there are contrasts as well. Paul's concern here is not with offending another believer (for whom the source of meat is not an issue; 25-27), but an *unbeliever* (vv.32f).

The situation seems to be this: An unbeliever informs a believer sitting next to him that the meat being served has been offered to idols. When this happens, the believer should limit his freedom, first of all *for the sake of the one who informed you*, and secondly *for conscience' sake*. Not the believer's conscience, for—as Paul has taught—the source of meat was not a matter of conscience (25, 27); hence he explains, *I mean not your own conscience, but the other man's*.

Textual Note: MajT repeats the quote from v.26 (Ps. 24:1) at the end of verse 28: *for "The earth is the Lord's, and all its fullness"* (NKJV). There is also a third possible reading in the early papyrus text P[46] (ca. 200) which omits not only this phrase, but the preceding reference to *one who informed you and conscience* as well. If the quote is original, Paul is pointing out that the fact that the earth is the Lord's promotes both freedom and restraint. All things may be eaten because they are from the Lord, but since they *are* from Him, let not your eating of them ever bring dishonor to His name.

How does a believer eating meat offered to idols affect an unbeliever's conscience? It is necessary here to understand συνείδησις (conscience, moral consciousness; BAGD, 786; cf. Fee, 485) as it applies to an unbeliever. The problem is not with the unbeliever being tempted to sin, but with his expectation of Christian behavior. His view of what is right and wrong may be confused, but he is sincere in wanting the believer to know the connection of the meat to idols. Since the believer is under no compulsion to express his freedom, he should not disregard the unbeliever's expectations. The goal, as always, is to *please all men in all things* (v.33). Paul did all things, including denying himself, for the sake of the gospel, that he might save some (9:19-23). He urges his fellow-believers to do the same.

29b-30 Paul now returns to his defense of the believer's freedom which was interrupted in verse 28, affirming it with two rhetorical questions. The general rule to eat whatever is served, asking no questions for conscience' sake, should be followed, *for why is my freedom judged by another's conscience?* That is, do not let your conscience be burdened by the restrictions of others, and— excepting the kind of situation described in verses 28-29a— do not let your conscience be burdened by the expectations or limitations of others.

If I partake with thankfulness, why am I slandered (βλασφημέω; defamed; BAGD, 142) *concerning that for which I give thanks?* It may be that while some Corinthian believers were callously attending feasts at idol temples (to whom Paul directs his comments in 8:1-10:22), others were legalistic and were attacking Paul for his teaching on the freedom of believers. Paul instructed those who misused their freedom to avoid tacitly endorsing idolatry. He now instructs those who piously avoided anything 'polluted' by contact with idols (and slandered those who did not do so) to stop judging others. The earth is the Lord's, and all it contains (26); He gives thanks to the Lord for that which he eats. His freedom is not determined by others; *for everything created by God is good, and nothing is to be rejected, if it is received with gratitude; for it is sanctified by means of the word of God and prayer* (1 Tim.4:4-5).

10:31-11:1 [The principles of Christian liberty are summed up in the ideals of doing everything to the glory of God, offending no one, pleasing all, and imitating Christ.]

31   Paul has affirmed that there are both rights and restrictions in the area of Christian freedom. An overemphasis in either direction results in problems. Specific examples have been cited, and instruction given, and no doubt much more could be said. But Paul is ready to sum up his basic argument. The earth is the Lord's, and all it contains (26), and the believer acknowledges this in giving thanks (30); therefore (οὖν; *then*), *whether...you eat or drink or whatever you do, do all to the glory of God*. The freedom a believer experiences as he gains knowledge of spiritual things must be applied in life with a desire to bring glory (δόξα; praise, honor; BAGD, 204) to God. This principle, which should guide one in eating meat, applies in every area of life.

32   Paul's second command is: *Give no offense either to Jews or to Greeks or to the church of God*. The first half of this admonition is directed toward unbelievers; Paul states that whatever we do, we should seek to not offend (ἀπρόσκοπος; damage in any way; BAGD, 102) anyone. Nothing should be done which might cause another to trip and fall (DNTT, 2:705-707). This echoes Paul's instruction in 9:19-23 and 10:24. We are to seek the good of our neighbor, especially that they might be saved. What a tragedy that what God has created can be used by believers to deter unbelievers from responding to the gospel!

       The last phrase, *or to the church of God*, recognizes that some in Corinth were actually becoming a stumbling block to the weak (8:9), impeding the spiritual growth of others by offending their tender conscience. Paul's purpose here is not so much to raise that issue again, as to insure that no hindrance will be placed in the spread of the gospel.

33   This is clear from his personal testimonial which follows. The Corinthian believers are to avoid giving offense to all, Paul

writes, *just as I also please all men in all things, not seeking my own profit, but the profit of the many, that they may be saved*. To avoid causing offense involves positive action—seeking their good (24). Paul strove to please all men (ἀρέσκω; BAGD, 105), not that he said only those things which they wanted to hear (cf. Gal. 1:10; 2 Thess. 2:4), but that he sought the best of others over his own pleasure or profit. He had his rights as an apostle (9:1-14), but voluntarily restricted his exercise of them that as many as possible might be saved (9:19-23). The idea of *profit* (συμφέρον, MajT; σύμφορον, CrT; cf. BAGD, 780) is not necessarily linked to material gain, but certainly fits it well here. Paul had denied himself the right to financial support so that he might win as many as possible to Christ; others should follow his example. In so doing, they will also be following the example of Christ (Rom. 15:1, 3).

11:1   The greatest challenge for Paul, and all believers, is ultimately to follow Christ. To this end, Paul calls his readers to "*Be imitators of me, just as I also am of Christ.*" While this verse (with v.2) is clearly transitional (Orr/Walther, 256), it sums up what has gone before, while verse 2 anticipates the discussion which follows. In 4:16, Paul exhorted the Corinthians to *be imitators of me* (μιμηταί μου γίνεσθε, as here) in his example of unity and humility. Here again he exhorts them to "use me as your model" (cf. μιμητής; BAGD, 522), with the added appeal to his own example of using Christ as a model for his life. In the same way that (καθὼς; *just as* (4:17; 12:11), *as* (10:6), or perhaps *since* (5:7); cf. BAGD, 391) Paul seeks to mimic Christ's life in his own, the Corinthians should copy him. Paul is not haughty or self-righteous here; he does not present himself as a perfect replica of the Lord (cf. 1 Tim.1:15; Paul did not exalt himself). Even though he had a clear conscience, he knew the Lord was his final judge (4:4f). If they will follow his example—and Christ's—any problems related to freedom will be dissolved.

Homiletical Ideas:

In 8:1-11:1, Paul provides a number of guidelines to enable a mature believer to know when and how to regulate his exercise of freedom. The primary thing to avoid is any tacit endorsement of evil—as the Corinthian Christians were doing by participating in idol temple feasts. Demonic forces empower and direct this world's systems, and the believer must expose this (Eph. 5:11). But beyond this, even when something is morally neutral, there are reasons for believers to restrict their own freedom. For example, a mature believer will be concerned for the needs of others (8:7-13), aware of how behavior affects his testimony to unbelievers (9:15-23), and will do everything with the goal of winning the prize of a reward at the Judgment Seat of Christ (9:24-27). Actions guided by knowledge alone lead to pride, arrogance, and an internal weakening of the body of Christ; actions motivated by love lead to unity and a building up of the body of Christ.

The tendency in preaching these passages is for the pastor-teacher to decree those areas which are immoral and thus absolutely to be avoided (those corresponding to the Corinthians joining in idol temple feasts), and those which are morally neutral, limited only by application of the above principles. This tendency must be avoided. 'Gray areas' are fertile ground for legalism and divisiveness. It is good for a teacher to understand these issues (and know where he stands and why; cf. Rom. 14:5), but he must avoid superimposing his own views on scripture. 'Liberal' Christians have a tendency to remove all restrictions; 'legalistic' Christians may impose restrictions by raising the specter of offended brethren. Fee notes that *in most contemporary settings the "offended" are not unbelievers or new Christians, but those who tend to confuse their own regulations with the eternal will of God* (491).

In the spirit of promoting unity in the body, Paul's fundamental goal throughout this letter, we should *de-emphasize* differences, and *emphasize* instead the ideas summarized in 10:31-11:1. Let us glorify God, offend no one, seek the profit of others—especially their salvation, and imitate Christ. If we do these things, we will avoid sin and promote the unity and edification of all.

C. QUESTIONS CONCERNING PUBLIC WORSHIP ARE DISCUSSED (11:2-34)

This chapter continues Paul's discussion of issues raised by the church at Corinth which commenced in chapter seven. Following his discussion of marriage (and divorce, and the related issue of celibacy for the never-married; ch.7), Paul took up the question of Christian liberty, the balancing of rights and responsibility in the Christian life (8:1-11:1). This discussion was a lengthy one, not only because the issue is difficult, but because he used it as a springboard to affirm his apostleship (and his example as an apostle), and because the matter so evidently displayed the heart problem of the Corinthian assembly, pride.

Paul now addresses the subject of corporate worship, focusing on two areas in which difficulties had arisen. The first concerned the role of women in the church (and how that role was exhibited; vv3-16); the second concerned the observance of the Lord's Supper (vv17-34).

Some commentators include this chapter in one section along with 8:1-11:1, since the issues here are clearly Questions Concerning Christian Liberty (Lowery, 528): Paul discusses restrictions on the liberty of women in the worship of the church, and the misuse of liberty in connection with the Lord's Table which resulted in it becoming a source of judgment instead of blessing. The distinction between these two sections is that the issues of liberty discussed here (head-coverings for women and the abuse of the Lord's Table) involve the public worship of Christians, while the question of joining in idol temple feasts did not. Even so the two are related in that these problems in the public worship of the church almost surely resulted from their contact with the pagan worship in Corinth.

Again, the title we have given this chapter (Questions Concerning Public Worship) could apply to the following chapters dealing with the misuse of tongues as well (cf. esp. 14:26-36). All three issues relate to abuse within the assembly (Fee, 491). Other general categories, like unity in the body and the role of women in the church, also connect these chapters. (Lowery, 528, entitles 8:1-11:1 "Christian Liberty in Relation to Pagan Worship," and 11:2-14:40 "Christian Liberty in Relation to Christian Worship.")

For sake of clarity, however, 11:2-34 will be treated as a separate unit. The issues discussed are sufficiently distinct from that which precedes to warrant a special category, and the section following concerning spiritual gifts and the abuse of tongues is set apart by *Now concerning* (Περὶ δὲ, 12:1), clearly a matter for separate consideration.

11:2-16 *Paul instructs Corinthian women to exhibit their submission to male authority in the public worship of the church by having their head covered when ministering in the assembly.*

2   [Paul praises the Corinthians for their general following of his example and teaching.]

Paul begins this section with an unexpected endorsement of the Corinthians' actions: *Now I praise* (Ἐπαινῶ) *you.* This indicates 'recognition with approval' (BAGD, 281; cf. 4:5), something Paul expresses rarely in this epistle! In fact, Paul's only other uses of the verb in this letter are to expose actions for which he *cannot* praise them (11:17, 22)! Here Paul praises them *because you remember me in everything, and hold firmly to the traditions, just as I delivered them to you.* The term translated *traditions* (παράδοσις, "things handed down;" BAGD, 615f) can be misleading; it refers not to some long-held teaching or customary practice, but to the things Paul had taught them (cf. 2 Thess. 2:15; 3:6).

This verse provides a 'hinge' between Paul's final exhortations on Christian liberty in the previous chapters, and his instruction on matters of public worship which follow. 11:1-2 might be loosely paraphrased as follows: *Use me as your model and follow my example, in the same way that I follow the example of Christ. And in relation to this, let me commend you for the way you have borne in mind the things I taught you. (Of course, sometimes you get my message confused—like in 5:9-13, or you wrongly apply it—like in 8:1-11. And I believe you need to be straightened out in one area here too.)*

Looking ahead, Paul's praise here sets the stage for his rebuke in vv.17ff. His statement "you remember me" is notable. He praises them for their remembrance (μιμνῄσκομαι; BAGD, 522) of his teaching, but will not praise them for abusing that which Jesus said for them to do "in remembrance of Me" (24, 26).

3-16   [Paul instructs the Corinthians that a woman should wear a head-covering when she is ministering in the assembly to show her submission to the man.]

We now encounter one of the thorniest sections of scripture in contemporary biblical studies. The exegesis of this passage is debated, largely because of the religious feminist movement (Fee, 492f). The desire to be 'theologically correct' (with the latest theological trend) is a powerful force in biblical studies; the student seeking to discern the true meaning of this text must ignore this.

Paul's moves his argument forward in three steps. This is an outline of his thought-progression:

1. A woman should wear a head-covering while ministering in the assembly to show her submission to the authority of the man (3-6).
2. A woman should wear a head-covering because of God's order of creation, not because she is in any way inferior to the man (7-12).
3. A woman should not pray without her head covered because, just as her long hair was a social norm, so too having a head-covering was the norm in the church (13-16).

3   Paul introduces his discussion by laying down a theological basis for his following instruction. *But* (δὲ) *I want you to understand* sounds more like a mild corrective than harsh invective. Paul will deal harshly with them later (vv.17-34), but here indicates there is one area in which he cannot praise them (see vv.4-5 below). What he wants them to understand is *that Christ is the head of every man, and the man is the head of a woman, and God is the head of Christ.*

Interpretive Note: The question of the meaning of *head* (κεφαλὴ) dominates the study of this verse, and must be determined in order to understand the significance of the whole section. Used figuratively, κεφαλὴ usually denotes superior rank (BAGD, 430), and indicates one having 'authority over' another. This sense is common in Paul's writings (Eph. 1:22; 5:23f; Col. 2:10). There is no reason (except to avoid the idea of male authority, which is 'theologically *in*correct') to look for any other meaning. But this has not prevented scholars from making search. As a result, some optional meanings have sprung up.

Most popular among these is the idea of 'source' (Barrett, 248f; Fee, 502f). The arguments in favor of this are few and weak. Virtually every commentary adopting this meaning appeals to Herodotus' *History* 4.91 or *Orphic Fragments* 21a (Lowery, 529; Barrett, 248f), yet both these documents date from over four centuries *before* Paul wrote! An exhaustive survey of the use of κεφαλὴ demonstrates conclusively that the idea of 'source' has no basis in Greek literature (see Grudem, "The Meaning of Κεφαλὴ ('Head'): A Response to Recent Studies" (*TrinJ* 11 NS, 1990), pp. 3-72). Evangelical feminists are at pains to establish 'source' as the meaning of κεφαλὴ here, but their own words are the only support. For example, some suggest Paul's reference to creation and the origin of man and woman in verses 7-12 supports understanding κεφαλὴ as 'source.' This might be the case had Paul used κεφαλὴ to describe man being the "source" of woman in creation, but he does not. Rather, the fact that woman originated from (8) and was created for the man (9) is further reason why the woman should cover her head. For Fee (503) to write that 'source' is "almost certainly" the only meaning the Corinthians would have grasped reveals more of his feminist views than it does the meaning of the text (cf. Fee, 493, n.8!). Other suggestions for the meaning of κεφαλὴ, like 'pre-eminence' (cf. Richard S. Cervin, "Does *Kephale* Mean 'Source' or 'Authority' in Greek Literature? A Rebuttal" (*TrinJ* 10 NS, 1989), pp. 85-112), also lack foundation. In short, the *only* acceptable meaning of "head" is superior rank or authority over (cf. Findlay, 871; Orr/Walther, 262).

N.B. Some evangelical feminists admit that the New Testament teaches male authority, but call it a result of the fall. To them, male leadership in the home and church is a reflection of sin's presence, not God's plan. Genesis 3:16 is viewed as *descriptive*, not *prescriptive*. This view cannot be sustained, since Paul bases male responsibility on God's *pre-fall* creation order (vv.8-9; 1 Tim. 2:13).

Paul's reference to *the man* (ὁ ἀνήρ) and *a woman* (γυναικὸς) probably refers to a husband and wife (Grosheide, 249; Orr/Walther, 262). The authority of the husband in the home has implications for male authority in the Christian assembly (cf. 1 Tim. 3:4-5), and the wife's supportive role in the home has implications for female actions in the assembly as well. It is to this issue which Paul now turns.

4   Although his instruction is directed mainly toward women, Paul first addresses men. *Every man who has something on his head while praying or prophesying, disgraces* (dishonors, humiliates, shames; καταισχύνω; BAGD, 410f) *his head*. After three metaphorical uses of κεφαλὴ in the previous sentence, Paul begins this verse with a cryptic reference to a man's literal head. The phrase (κατὰ κεφαλῆς ἔχων; lit. "having down the head") is an idiom for having a garment of some kind on one's head. This meaning is clear from the contrast with ἀκατακαλύπτῳ (an *uncovered* or *unveiled* head) in verse 5. The second use of κεφαλὴ (*head*) can convey both literal and figurative nuances (Barrett, 250); whatever the reason (perhaps tradition), for a man to pray or prophesy in the assembly with his head covered brought shame on himself, but especially dishonored Jesus Christ, his spiritual head (3).

Translation Note: The NIV marginal reading relates this instruction to hair length, men *with long hair* and women with *no hair* (5) or *short hair* (6). This borrows from verses 14-15, but does not reflect Paul's meaning (cf. esp. v.6b).

5-6   In contrast to the man (*But*), *every woman who has her head uncovered while praying or prophesying, disgraces her head.* The wording is identical to the instruction given the man, except that the woman brings shame on her head if it is *uncovered* (ἀκατακαλύπτῳ). Head coverings were customary for women in Paul's day (Lowery, 529). While this covering might be called a "veil," it probably amounted to the upper fold of a garment or a shawl pulled over the head. Just as a man, by being covered, brought shame on himself and his "head" (Christ), a woman, being uncovered, brought shame on herself and her "head." In the assembly, a woman without her head covered dishonored her husband—and by extension, all other men in the assembly.

Why might a woman desire to pray or prophesy without a head covering? Perhaps in the climate of liberty prevalent in the church at Corinth (cf. "All things are lawful for me," 6:12), women were discarding that which customarily distinguished them from men (Fee, 510). Beyond this there almost certainly was insubordination, a desire to be free from any sex-related restrictions (Lowery, 529). It is ironic that this passage is used by feminists to establish their agenda of gender-neutral roles in the home and the church!

Paul wants women to know that these actions do not represent deliverance, but dishonor. The woman who does this *is one and the same with her whose head is shaved* (ξυράω). *For if a woman does not cover her head* (κατακαλύπτω; veil herself; BAGD, 411), *let her also have her hair cut off* (κείρω, BAGD, 427; cf. Acts 18:18); *but if it is disgraceful for a woman to have her hair cut off or her head shaved, let her cover her head.* A shaved head was a sign of dishonor for a woman, and hair cut short like a man's may have been a cultural indicator of lesbianism—a sure source of shame for a woman (cf. Fee, 511, n.81)! Paul's message is simple; women should not discard the symbol of sexual distinction and subordination when praying or prophesying. To do so may express a kind of independence (cf. v11 below), but not the

Christian liberty which results in the fulfilment of ministry and a future reward (9:19-25). Instead, it brings shame and disgrace.

7   While contemporary custom made head coverings the issue, the basis for observing this custom in the assembly—the core matter of the man as the spiritual authority—was rooted in creation. Paul in verses 7-9 explains the reason (γὰρ) for the distinction in head coverings between men and women. He first states that *a man ought not to have his head covered, since he is the image and glory of God; but the woman is the glory of man.* The contrast between a man and woman is not that man alone is the image of God, since both male and female share this quality (Gen.1:27). But a man is the glory (δόξα) of God, while a woman is the glory of man. Paul's meaning at least is that a man in some way brings glory to God, while a woman brings glory to man. How this relates to head coverings may be clarified by considering the final reference to glory in this section; namely, that a woman's hair "is a glory to her" (v.15).

For a woman to have her head uncovered would have been seen as her bringing glory to herself; to cover her "glory" (her hair) would keep the focus on her spiritual "head" (the man). In so doing, she would also glorify God, who set the authority structure in place. Likewise, a man who covered his head would bring glory to himself, instead of keeping the focus on his spiritual head, Christ. In both cases, the goal is to prevent distraction away from our spiritual head.

Beyond this, a woman—as the glory of man—who prays or prophesies in the assembly without her head covered, glorifies man instead of God (Barrett, 254).

Practical Note: Whatever head-covering customs a culture may have, the principle in these verses is applicable. God created man and woman as part of an order which the Church should reflect. In the assembly, women should not detract from the authority designated for the man; neither a man or a woman should detract from the authority due Christ. *Anything* (not just woman's hair—this was an issue in Corinth) which distracts from the worship of Jesus Christ and the authority structure of the Body in the meeting of the church is to be avoided. In Corinth, sexual temptation was rife and passions ran hot; it was absolutely necessary that women avoid drawing attention to themselves.

8 Why is woman described as the glory of man, not of God? Because (γὰρ) *man does not originate from woman, but woman from man.* The point is *not* that God made man out of Himself, then made woman out of man (MacArthur, 258), because *both sexes* were formed from pre-existent material (Gen. 2:7, 22). Rather, this is a simple statement of order; man came first, then the woman.

Theological Note: Paul is not here trying to explain the meaning of head; this passage is not concerned with that fundamental issue, but instead is concerned only with explaining why woman is the glory of man. Evangelical feminists, in their effort to avoid any distinction in authority or function between men and women, exhibit contorted exegesis in this passage (e.g., Fee, 512-24).

9 The order of creation is significant because it reflects who was created for whom; *for indeed man was not created for the woman's sake, but woman for the man's sake.* He is the one for whom she was created; she is "a helper suitable for him" (Gen. 2:20). In the home and the church, the man is to be the leader, the woman his helper. This does not imply any distinction in value. A woman is not inferior to men (and what man would want to try to prove that thesis?). But the tasks given to each are different, and neither is more difficult than the other. God designed men and women so that they function best when they fill that role for which they were created.

10   Paul now brings his argument to a conclusion, and in doing so provides an additional reason for compliance. *Therefore, the woman ought to have [a symbol of] authority on her head, because of the angels.* When Paul says "authority" here, he is talking about a woman's head covering, which exhibits—or symbolizes—her acceptance of the authority of her spiritual head. She covers her own head—veiling her own glory—to bring glory instead to him. This much has already been made clear in context.

Paul then mentions, almost as an afterthought, the angels. Perhaps the Corinthians had an interest in angels; Paul has already mentioned them twice in this letter (4:9; 6:3). While his meaning is not certain, angels are revealed as diligent observers of the church, from which they learn of God's amazing grace (cf. Eph. 3:8-10; 1 Pet. 1:10-12). Because angels are observing, women in the church—who will one day judge the angels for their obedience to the heavenly authorities (6:3)—should exhibit their submission to divinely established authority on earth.

11   While the Corinthian women should wear a head covering to exhibit their recognition of man's authority, Paul hastens to add that such authority is not to be confused with superiority. For men and women *in the Lord* there is a kind of co-dependency; *man is not independent of woman*, nor is *woman independent of man*.

Translation Note: CrT and MajT invert the order of the phrases in this verse. CrT has woman-man-man-woman, while MajT reads man-woman-woman-man. Although the meaning is not drastically affected, the MajT order fits Paul's overall flow better.

What distinct situation lies behind this admonition is unknown. Perhaps, in addition to the divisions relating to spiritual leaders (1:12), there were some who had divided over gender issues. Perhaps there was a party advocating women as spiritual leaders in the church; on the other hand, some may have adopted a position that men had greater spiritual value than women. As Paul in the next chapter has to remind them that those with different spiritual gifts all need each other, so too here he reminds them that both men and women are equally important in the body of Christ.

12 Creation and reproduction come together to provide an illustration of this necessary cooperation. In creation, *woman came from man*; in reproduction, *man comes through woman*. Each has a role to play in their existence physically, and each likewise has a role to play in the spiritual body of Christ. Lest any should be prone to emphasize one aspect over another, Paul adds that *all things are from God.* Let no one judge the value of a brother or sister in Christ on the basis of their gender; in Christ all are of the highest value, bought with a price—the precious blood of Christ. Working together, and complementing each other by performing the task and filling the role divinely prepared for us, the body of Christ will continue to reproduce and grow from one generation to another.

13 Paul now invites the Corinthians to consider an analogy from nature. He has argued for the women in the church at Corinth to wear head coverings because of the shame they would bring on the men if they did not, and because creation confirms the man's role of authority. These arguments have won his case morally, but like a skilled lawyer, he concludes his comments with an appeal based on something self-evident and simple. His goal is no longer to win an argument, but to win their obedience. As in 10:15, Paul invites his readers to come to a conclusion: *Judge for yourselves: is it proper for a woman to pray to God [with head] uncovered?* To be proper (πρέπον) has nothing to do with moral right or wrong; rather, it concerns that which is appropriate or suitable behavior.

14-15 Paul turns the spotlight on creation—not at its beginning, but in the present. He wants us to look at 'the way things are naturally viewed' (cf. φύσις; BAGD, 869, 3.). *Does not even nature itself teach you that if a man has long hair, it is a dishonor to him, but if a woman has long hair, it is a glory to her?* In effect, Paul says, "Look in the mirror! Are men or women enhanced in the natural order of things by having long hair?" While there are exceptions (perhaps Absalom; 2 Sam. 14:25f), long hair is generally a symbol of beauty for a woman, not a man. Why is this the case? Because (ὅτι) *her hair is given to her for a covering* (περιβολαίου). This covering in the arena of nature suggests a parallel in the arena of the church, when a woman is praying or prophesying. If it is appropriate in nature for a woman to have a covering, so too in the church.

16   *If,* after all this reasoning and explanation, *one is inclined to be contentious,* then they should understand they are out of step with apostolic authority and accepted church practice: *we have no other practice, nor have the churches of God.* It goes without saying that many in the church at Corinth were contentious (φιλόνεικος); on this issue, Paul's decision is clear. While women have an essential role in the function of the church, the responsibility for spiritual leadership has been given to men; therefore, when leading in prayer or prophecy in the assembly, they should reflect this. In Corinth, and in the other churches of God in that historical setting, this called for women to wear head coverings.

Homiletical Ideas: The issue of head coverings does not come up in many churches today; although the practice continues, there are other ways for women to show respect for the spiritual leadership of men in the local church. The issue which grates in modern society, of course, is the idea of male authority at all. The church is following society's mores in this regard today, to its detriment.

Because of the storm surrounding this topic, there is a need for both clarity and grace when addressing it. It is vital to emphasize the responsibility of men to be spiritual leaders in the church; this is the effect of God's creation order. The absence of male leadership has created the vacuum which women have been filling. William Merrill's hymn *Rise Up, O Men of God* reflects this need for male leadership:

> *Rise up, O men of God!*
> *The Church for you doth wait:*
> *His strength shall make your spirit strong,*
> *Her service make you great.*

One's view concerning the role of women in the local church will not ultimately come from this passage alone. Whatever those conclusions, this passage affirms one point, based on the order of creation: Women should respect the authority of men in the church assembly. How this is done, and to what extent it is carried out, are further issues. This passage affirms the importance of women in the life of the church, both in their participation, and in their respect for the leadership of men.

11:17-34 *Paul instructs the Corinthians to exhibit the unity of the Body of Christ when they observe the Lord's Supper together, or face divine judgment.*

No regular observance in the Church carries the depth of significance, or sustains its existence, like the Lord's Supper. If the confusion over the role of women in the public worship of the church was a cause for concern, the abuse of the Lord's Table was a cause for outrage. The gospel was encapsulated for Paul in the words "Christ crucified" (1:23; 2:2); it was this simple message the Corinthians had neglected, confusing it with their human wisdom. Here is yet another reason for their forgetfulness: they have ceased to remember the Lord's death in the ceremony of the Lord's Supper (11:20f). They regularly partook of the bread and the cup; in fact, for them it was a sign of spiritual blessing and provision (cf. 10:3, 4). But while they observed the meal, they had lost its meaning. Each time they partook of the bread and the cup, they should have been reminded of their salvation, and the awful price that had to be paid for their sin. They should have focused on "Christ crucified," and been humbled and united around the memory of His unspeakable gift. Instead, they had become smug and segregated. That commemoration of the Lord's death, the event which united Christians in the Body of Christ, had become a time of discrimination and division. This defect in their public worship is now exposed and dealt with by Paul.

17-22   [Paul condemns the Corinthians for making the Lord's Supper a place where poor Christians were discriminated against, thus dividing the Body.]

17   Paul's discussion of head coverings was a gentle response to a problem needing clarification. From the outset here, however, it is clear that the gloves are off. *But in giving this instruction, I do not praise you*; the contrast to Paul's words in 11:2 is stark. They need to correct their shameful behavior in connection with the observance of the Lord's Supper! He cannot praise them at all here, because when they *come together*, it is *not for the better* (τὸ κρεῖσσον, cf. 7:9, 38) *but for the worse* ("more harm than good;" NIV).

18   Why is this so? Because (γὰρ) *in the first place* (since there is no "second place," this is probably here for emphasis; Orr/Walther, 266), *when you come together as a church, I hear that divisions exist among you.* Divisions (σχίσματα; 1:10) were a problem in the church at Corinth, but unlike the factions addressed at the beginning of the letter, these divisions are based on members' economic standing (21). Where Paul heard about these divisions is unknown, but he adds that *in part, I believe it.* Perhaps his source was less reliable than usual (Grosheide, 266), or perhaps he is just tactfully attempting to avoid alienating the rich who were guilty (Fee, 537). On the other hand, considering the fractious nature of the Corinthian church, this may also reflect a bit of sarcasm. A policeman viewing the scene of a brawl, with debris scattered about, might sarcastically say: "I heard there was a fight, and to some degree I believe it!" Paul knows they have

divisions, and he wants them to know he believes what he has heard. Clearly he accepts the truth of the report, or he wouldn't have dealt with it here!

19   Are divisions all bad? No. Paul adds that *there must also be factions among you, in order that those who are approved may become evident among you.* "Factions" (αἱρέσεις; "heresies") refers to a sect or religious group. This word is used of Sadducees (Acts 5:17), Pharisees (Acts 15:5), and Christians (Acts 24:5), often with a negative connotation (Acts 24:14; 28:22; Gal. 5:20). Here it is an implicit warning to those who are wronging their brothers in Christ.

When there are factions, those who are approved ("tried and true, genuine;" cf. δόκιμος; BAGD, 203) become evident (φανερός; BAGD, 852). The quality of work for the Lord will be "proved" (δοκιμάζω) by fire at the Judgment Seat of Christ (3:13), at which time the true merit of our service will be revealed. But before that time, we are to examine (put to the test; δοκιμάζω) ourselves (11:28), making sure that we are not guilty of causing division in the Body of Christ. Those who do foster such schisms in the church are not "approved," and face present and future judgment (3:15, 16-17; 11:29-30).

20   Returning to the issue at hand, Paul levels his charge against them: *When you meet together* [for your communal meal]*, it is not to eat the Lord's Supper.*

Interpretational Note: In the early church, the observance of the Lord's Supper took place as part of a meal (cf. Acts 2:46; 20:11; Jude 12; Fee, 531f). This meal, called a love feast, was the perfect setting for the Lord's Supper, exhibiting the oneness of believers in fellowship before it was commemorated in ceremony. All were in the Body of Christ by the blood of Christ, and as one they would partake of the bread and the cup.

Paul's indictment is brief but devastating: they have ceased to eat the Lord's Supper!

21   Not that they have ceased to partake of the elements, but that by their actions they have been denying the very unity of the body which the Lord's Supper proclaims. This is the case because when they come together *each one takes his own supper first*. The contrast is one of emphasis; the *Lord's* Supper declared their unity; their *own* supper declared their individuality. Each one was taking his own supper (BAGD, 708), and while some of the poor went *hungry*, others were *drunk*. This kind of thoughtless and callous behavior was proof enough: they were not really observing the Lord's Supper. They were coming to eat their own meals, not the Lord's.

Historical Note: It is probable that the Corinthians' participation in idol temple feasts contributed to their misbehavior at their own love feasts. The raucous celebrations in pagan temples were designed to arouse and feed the *fleshly* lusts of the "worshippers." Although some in Corinth had considered attending such feasts a sign of spiritual strength, there certainly was no *spiritual* content there! By emphasizing the fleshly over the spiritual in their love feast, they changed a celebration of selflessness into a demonstration of selfishness (Lowery, 531). In so doing, they again reflected that they were not spiritual, but carnal (2:15; 3:3).

---

22   Paul's consternation is obvious: *What! Do you not have houses in which to eat and drink?* It is not simply the fact that some gorged themselves which bothers Paul; it is that they are doing this when they come together for their celebration of the Lord's Supper! This goes to the heart of Paul's argument; their view of the church of God, the body of Christ, is skewed. Their actions display it.

Or do you despise the church of God, and shame those who have nothing? Where was their awareness of the unity of the body?

Had they forgotten that they were once spiritually poor, having nothing? How could they proclaim the Lord's compassionate death for them and show no compassion to their brothers? Paul is exasperated with them: *What shall I say to you? Shall I praise you? In this I will not praise you.* Paul is upset, not because the Corinthians are profaning a holy rite, but because they are fragmenting a holy society (Orr/Walther, 269).

23-26 [The reason Paul condemns the Corinthians' divisive actions at the Lord's Supper is that the purpose of the Supper was to remember and proclaim Christ's death (which united them all together in the Body of Christ) until He comes.]

23a With the opening *For* (γὰρ), Paul signals he is going to explain why the Corinthian's divisive actions in connection with the Lord's Supper are so heinous. In order to do this, he must rehearse the purpose of the Lord's Supper as laid down by the Lord Jesus himself. This is information he had *received from the Lord*, either by direct revelation from Christ (cf. Gal. 1:12, 15-17; 2 Cor. 12:2-4) or indirectly through other Christians (see I. Howard Marshall, *Last Supper and Lord's Supper* (Grand Rapids: Eerdmans, 1980), pp. 32-33) and *also delivered to* them.

23b-25 While the precise wording of the original accounts of the Lord's Supper vary in each New Testament appearance (Matt. 26:26-28; Mark 14:22-24; Luke 22:17-20), the primary elements are the same, and the essential theological content is not seriously affected (Marshall, 56; Fee, 546f). With the addition of the historical setting (*in the night in which He was betrayed*), Paul states that Jesus *took bread, and when He had given thanks, He broke it, and said, "(Take, eat* [MajT]); *This is My body, which is* (*broken* [MajT]) *for you; do this in remembrance of Me." In the same way [He took] the cup also, after supper, saying, "This cup is the new covenant in My blood; do this, as often as you drink [it], in remembrance of Me."* The most significant difference between the Gospels and Paul's account of Jesus' words is his repeated reference to *in remembrance of Me* (found only in Luke, and only following the distribution of the bread). This highlights the first purpose of the Lord's Supper which Paul wants to communicate: It was to *remember*.

This then is the first reason Paul condemns the Corinthian's divisive actions. They have failed to *remember*...the price that was paid for their salvation; to *remember* that because that price had been paid with Christ's blood, they were no longer under the old covenant of law, but the new covenant of grace! To *remember* that nothing they did had saved them, and therefore everyone had the same standing before God. Any divisiveness was therefore absurd.

26   But there was a further reason why divisive actions in connection with the Lord's Supper were especially repugnant. This is because *as often as you eat this bread and drink this cup, you proclaim the Lord's death*. The love feast provided an apt setting for the observance of the Lord's Supper because it demonstrated the unity of believers and proclaimed the effect the Lord's death had on sinful men. But because they failed to remember Christ in their coming together, and thought only of themselves, they also were failing to proclaim the uniting effect of the Lord's death. Truly, in the purpose and effect of their gathering, they had ceased to eat the Lord's Supper (20).

Paul's closing phrase, *until He comes*, was a not-so-subtle reminder that not only did the Lord's Supper look back to His death, it looked forward to His coming. That original supper had been for the disciples an anticipation of the coming banquet in the kingdom, and every observance of it pointed forward as well. But their actions in no way resembled the spirit of that future celebration. They exalted themselves instead of Christ. They must know that to do this would result in God's judgment.

27-32   [The result of failing to exhibit the unity of the Body in the observance of the Lord's Supper will be divine judgment designed to restore oneness.]

27 Paul's announcement of the divine 'verdict' is immediate. *Therefore whoever eats the bread or drinks the cup of the Lord in an unworthy manner, shall be guilty of the body and the blood of the Lord.* To eat or drink *in an unworthy manner* (ἀναξίως; unworthily, carelessly; BAGD, 58) was to eat without regard for the unity of the body, as evidenced by their treatment of the poor and selfish.

To be *guilty* (ἔνοχος, BAGD,267f) indicates that those who fail to proclaim Christ through their words and actions at the Lord's Supper have sinned against the Lord, and are liable for the body and blood of Christ. Just as His accusers on earth had crucified Him and killed His body, so too they are now dividing and destroying His Body. Paul has already indicated that those who destroy the Church will be destroyed by God (3:17). That severe judgment is now imminent.

28 To avoid this, Paul advises: *But let a man examine himself, and so let him eat of the bread and drink of the cup.* Paul is not suggesting Christians should be wary of participating in the Lord's Table. Personal holiness is a prerequisite to fellowship with the Lord, but this does not mean that the observance of the Lord's Supper should be a time of anxious self-examination. After all, it is a reminder of the sacrificial death of our Lord which has redeemed us, and His soon return to reign! Paul's desire is for believers to examine (δοκιμαζέτω; cf. δόκιμοι, v.19) themselves to see that they are approved by God in what they do. If they continue to carelessly and unworthily come to the Table, they will be guilty before God and subject to His judgment.

29 This is because *he who eats and drinks, eats and drinks judgment to himself.* The Lord's Supper is an event with an explicit purpose: To proclaim the Lord's death, and the salvation and unity it brings. To join in the Supper, and then dishonor the Lord and His death by mistreating other believers, is passing judgment (see κρίμα, BAGD, 450f) on himself. He brings this judgment

on himself *if he does not judge the body rightly*. This may mean that one who fails to discern the significance of the death of Christ, and as a result confess his sin, will face judgment. But it probably means more.

In this context, the abuse of the poorer members was a sin against the *body* of Christ (cf. 10:17; 12:12, 20, 27). Those who fail to recognize (*judge*; cf. διακρίνω, BAGD, 185) the unity of the body incriminate themselves through their divisive actions. This is a harsh indictment of those who abuse others in the body of Christ (see 8:12 for one example). Until restitution is made, their presence at the Lord's Table is not appropriate, and invites divine judgment.

Translational Note: The MajT reading (reflected in the NKJV) is: "For he who eats and drinks *in an unworthy manner* eats and drinks judgment to himself, not discerning the *Lord's* body" (words in italics omitted in CrT). Although this gives a different slant to Paul's instruction, the meaning is not changed.

---

30   As a direct result of such mistreatment of the brethren (*For this reason*), Paul declares that *many among you are weak and sick, and a number sleep*. The results of sin in life are real, and can be devastating. Already this is evident in Corinth. Some are sick, and some have died (κοιμῶνται ἱκανοί; cf. 7:39; 15:6, 18, 20, 51). Such extreme temporal judgment was not new in the early church (Acts 5:1-11), and there is no reason to doubt its presence today.

31-32 But such judgment is not necessary; *if we judged ourselves rightly, we should not be judged*. This has the tone of exhortation. "Let's start judging ourselves, so that the Lord won't have to!" The goal in either case is the same. If *we are judged, we are disciplined* (cf. παιδεύω, BAGD, 603f; to bring up, train, instruct, correct, give guidance) *by the Lord in order that we may not be condemned* (κατακριθῶμεν) *along with the world*.

> **Interpretive Note:** Paul's statement that the Lord disciplines believers *in order that we may not be condemned along with the world* has caused some to wrongly conclude that failure to respond to God's discipline may result in a loss of eternal life. Fee (566) writes, "The purpose of such discipline is 'so that we will not be condemned with the world,' when brought to final judgment being implied." Findlay (883f) suggests that the sinning man in 5:5 "is the extreme case of such 'chastening' unto salvation." This misses the point entirely. Paul never makes behavior at the Lord's Table a condition for salvation! Rather, he says that believers who are 'child-trained' by the Lord are guided away from behavior that leads to judgment—the kind of judgment that afflicts those in the world. This is reflected in the treatment of the incestuous man in 5:5; his discipline had nothing to do with his eternal salvation, but to his joy and fellowship as an active part of the body of Christ. Sin always results in death (Rom. 6:23; Jas.1:15b). Those in the world are enslaved in sin and under a death sentence. Those who are saved are called to life more abundant (John 10:10). Ignoring the chastening of the Lord, however, may result in believers experiencing God's *temporal* judgment, even to the point of physical death.

33-34   [The solution to the problem of discrimination against poor Christians at the Lord's Supper is for rich Christians to share everything in the common meal, and save their own feasts for the privacy of their homes.]

33   Paul's conclusion to a practical problem is very practical. *So then* ("Ὥστε; cf. v27; "in view of all that has been said"), *my brethren, when you come together to eat, wait for one another.* This is a direct answer to the issue raised in verse 21. Instead of some gorging themselves, while others go hungry, each should wait till all have come, all should share what they have, and all should eat together. Perhaps the custom of a church 'potluck' dinner reflects what Paul had in mind. By doing this they will reflect the unity of the body (they 'judge the body rightly;' v.29), and avert the judgment of God.

34 *If anyone is hungry* (cf. πεινάω; BAGD, 640) is directed not at those who had been hungry at the table, but those who are wealthy and gorged themselves in front of the poor. If anyone wants to eat such a feast, Paul says, *let him eat at home, so that you may not come together for judgment.* Paul's goal is that the body of Christ might truly proclaim the Lord's death until He comes (26). What better way for them to do this than, amid the materialism of Corinth, for rich and poor Christians to unite in mutual love for a meal. The rich need to show uncommon (for Corinthian society) concern for the poor, just as the strong needed to show concern for the weak (chapter 8). God had shown mercy toward each of them in their salvation, and they must now reflect it in their relationships with each other.

Paul does not go beyond calling for civility and unity in the love feast, though no doubt he would have encouraged the rich to share of their wealth with the poor. Perhaps this was another matter that needed attention. While we are not privy to them, Paul closes by affirming that *the remaining matters I shall arrange when I come.*

Homiletical Ideas: The significance of the Lord's Supper is mistaken or overlooked in most churches today. For many believers, it is a weekly or monthly religious ritual, and other than providing a few moments of guilt or pious introspection, it has little significance. Paul exposes the significance of the Lord's Supper in his instructions to the Corinthians on their behavior at their love feasts. Although regular love feasts *per se* are no longer practiced in the church, the principles Paul gives apply to every believer who partakes of the Lord's Supper. Any division between the 'haves' and 'have nots'—or people of different races, ages, educational levels, or social status, all reflect the lack of unity and worship which afflicted the church at Corinth.

Paul's remedy can be applied in the contemporary setting. The Lord's Supper is a reminder that everything we have and are is from the Lord—given freely for us. To take these elements is to admit our absolute dependence on Him. To exalt ourselves, or put down another, to harbour malice, or to ignore the need of others, is to forget the significance of the Lord's Supper. In so doing we show that we are neither remembering His death or prepared for His return!

Paul's instruction, while directed primarily to the rich, has a common application to all. Show respect for one another. Don't ever behave in a way that will injure a brother. By putting the health of the body of Christ first, you may well preserve your own!

Paul here gives us "A Lasting Lesson from the Last Supper"—emphasizing the significance of Jesus' words, and the events they pointed to, the night He was betrayed. It is important to clarify the meaning of being *guilty of the body and the blood of the Lord* (27), what self-examination entails (28), and to highlight the practical unity of the body. Forgiveness, restoration, and genuine *koinonia* is needed in the church. Many Christians today, like the Corinthians, have taken communion for years—but have not been *really* observing the Lord's Supper (20f). This passage is a wake-up call for the local church to experience true communion as Christ's body. Certainly this is Paul's wish.

D. QUESTIONS CONCERNING SPIRITUAL GIFTS ARE DISCUSSED (12:1-14:40)

While these chapters are viewed as separate from the preceding context, there is a connection. The core issue—the abuse of tongues in public worship—is not addressed until chapter 14. The discussion of spiritual gifts in chapter 12 (especially the diversity of gifts in the unity of the body) prepares the way for his instruction. Since the body is a diversity in unity, all things should be done for the good of the whole. In this regard, love (chapter 13) is not something to desire instead of (or in contrast to) gifts, but is rather the ingredient without which spiritual gifts can never be adequately exercised. This understanding leads to Paul's call for the Corinthians to pursue actions which result in edification and order when they are gathered together.

In relation to the wider context, two connections are apparent. First, chapter 11 is concerned with public worship, as is this section; even chapters 8-10 deal with public worship—in idol temples! The public worship of the church and the behavior of believers in the assembly was a primary concern for Paul.

The second connection is a repeated theme in Paul's responses to questions raised in the Corinthians' letter to him (7:1). Over and over he emphasizes the need to be non-judgmental, to show love and understanding, and to deny self. In regard to marriage (chapter 7), he made recommendations, but (except for divorce and remarriage) allowed for differences. In chapters 8-10, he uses his own example of self-denial to promote concern and love for weaker brothers. In the section on head-coverings (11:2-16), he instructs women not to dress in an offensive way in their social context. In relation to the Lord's Supper (11:17-34), they need to care for those who are poorer—sharing, and thus building up the body.

This theme of doing all things to glorify God and build up the body is evident in 12:1-14:40 as well. There are many gifts, and no one gift should be made a benchmark of spirituality. Rather, they should exercise their gifts—whatever they are—with love, since gifts are given to build up the body, and this will never happen without love. Finally, since the

Corinthian practice of uninterpreted tongues edifies no one, they should forego this activity in the assembly.

To summarize, Paul encourages the Corinthians to appreciate and accept the diversity of gifts (instead of emphasizing one), to exercise any and all gifts with love, and—on the basis of this principle—to exercise only those gifts in the assembly which edify all.

These chapters progress from a general discussion of spiritual gifts to specific guidelines for the exercise of those gifts in the assembly. The following is a working outline:

1. Diverse spiritual gifts are given by the Spirit in order to build up the body of believers (12:1-11).
   a. Spiritual gifts show their origin by whether or not they exalt Jesus as Lord (1-3).
   b. Spiritual gifts, though exhibited in diversity, are unified in their source in the triune God through the Spirit (4-11).

2. The diversity of gifts in the unity of the body of Christ is pictured by the human body (12:12-31).
   a. The diversity of believers in one united Church results from all being baptized by the Spirit into Christ's body (12-14).
   b. The human body reflects a diversity of members but a mutuality of dependence (12:15-26).
   c. The body of Christ has a diversity of membership (gifts) but a mutuality of dependence (12:27-31).

3. Love is essential to the exercise of spiritual gifts because of its superior character and permanence (13:1-13).
   a. Love is essential to the exercise of spiritual gifts (13:1-3).
   b. Love is superior because of its selfless characteristics (13:4-7).
   c. Love is superior because of its permanence (13:8-13).

4. The gift of prophecy is preferred over the gift of tongues because it edifies the church and convicts unbelievers, while tongues do not (14:1-25).
   a. The gift of prophecy is preferred over tongues because it edifies the church, while tongues do not (1-19).

b. The gift of prophecy is preferred over tongues because it convicts unbelievers, while tongues do not (20-25).

5. The public meeting of the church should be conducted in an orderly manner in order to edify the whole body (26-40).

12:1-3 *Spiritual gifts show their origin by whether or not they exalt Jesus as Lord (1-3).*

1   The opening Περὶ δὲ (*Now concerning*) signals that Paul is addressing a new topic. The issue here is τῶν πνευματικῶν ("spirituals;" BAGD, 685, 2.b.), which refers to "spiritual gifts" (cf. 14:1) or "spiritual persons" (cf. 14:37). While there are arguments for both readings (Fee, 575f), *it seems impossible to find objective ground for a decision between the two possibilities* (Barrett, 278). When the dust of this debate settles, the difference is really minor. Some of the Corinthian believers thought they were "spiritual"—and based this assessment on their exercise of certain "spiritual gifts"—in particular, speaking in tongues. So whichever interpretation one assigns to τῶν πνευματικῶν, in this context, Paul is concerned *both* with those who think they are spiritual, and with spiritual gifts.

Regardless of their actions, he clearly regards them as regenerate (ἀδελφοί, *brethren*). Their present behavior, however, is not acceptable. So, as he began in 10:1 (*I do not want you to be ignorant*), he draws to their attention something which they have forgotten, information which they need to apprehend anew in order to avoid wrong actions.

2   Paul reminds them of their pre-conversion experience (*when you were pagans*). "Pagans" (ἔθνη, tr. *Gentiles*, NKJV) describes their previous spiritual condition. Before they were saved, they had no citizenship in God's future kingdom; instead, they were instead *led astray to the dumb idols*. As they once followed idols, they should now follow the Spirit—if they are truly *spiritual* men! But in light of Paul's comments concerning the demonic power behind idols (10:20f), and in the context of the abuse of tongues in the assembly, a further idea is implied. *Dumb idols*, which do not impart spiritual

knowledge like the Spirit (2:11-13), depend on the demonic utterances of devotees to speak for them! Whether intelligible or not, this "inspired speech" once led them to idol worship. Supernatural tongues are no guarantee of the Spirit's leading!

3   So what *is* valid evidence? The *intelligible* content of such speech. While we rightly emphasize the evidential value of a person's *actions*, Scripture often emphasizes the *words* we speak (cf. Matt. 12:31-37; 15:18; Luke 6:43-45; Eph. 4:29; Jas.3:1-12; see Phil. 1:15-18, where proper preaching, even from selfish motives, leads Paul to rejoice). Paul's conclusion (διὸ, *Therefore*) follows from his previous reminder: *No one speaking by the Spirit of God says, "Jesus is accursed," and no one can say, "Jesus is Lord," except by the Holy Spirit.* It is hard to imagine that anyone would have said this (intelligibly) in the assembly, but it may be that some were saying this in tongues, thus showing the demonic source of their speech (cf. TDNT, 1:414). In the wider context of the Corinthians' misuse of tongues, this is a likely scenario. Such language would have been expected in their previous lives as idol worshippers, but it reveals a glaring error in their present experience! On the contrary, if they spoke of the Lordship of Jesus Christ, this would be sure evidence that what they said was from the Holy Spirit, not demons.

Another option is that this is a hypothetical situation which Paul envisioned *could* happen in the context of a misuse of the gift of tongues. It is also possible that Paul is making a clear distinction between what is pagan and what is spiritual. Regardless of which scenario is right (and thus being careful not to read too much into this), Paul's central instruction is clear. The best evidence that a 'spiritual gift' is from God (and that the one using the gift is spiritual) is that both it, and they, exalt Jesus as Lord.

12:4-11 *Spiritual gifts, though exhibited in diversity, are unified in their source (in the triune God) and their purpose (for the common good).*

4-6   [Unity in diversity is exhibited as an inherent characteristic of the gift-giving God.]

Theological Note: While no single biblical text clearly teaches the doctrine of the Trinity (1 John 5:7-8 [only in KJV/NKJV; see margin in latter] is not original; even the MajT excludes it), passages like this have the same effect. See 2 Cor. 13:14 and Eph. 4:4-6. These three verses show the unity in diversity of the Godhead. The divine persons and effects are distinct, but all together are the Godhead.

4   As it is the Spirit through whom the gifts are given, and since gifts are the general topic under discussion, Paul begins with the Spirit. There are *varieties* (διαίρεσις; BAGD, 182) *of gifts* (χάρισμα; BAGD, 887), *but the same Spirit* (who gives them). Whatever the meaning of τῶν πνευματικῶν in v1, Paul is now concerned with *spiritual gifts*. In this one phrase, Paul states his central point for the remainder of this chapter. It will be illustrated, explained, and applied, but it will not be changed.

5   The variety of gifts from the one Spirit is reflected in the *varieties of ministries* for believers—all serving *the same Lord*. There should be no 'unemployment' in the body of Christ; for the Christian, the innumerable fields of service give absolute job security. There are countless places and ways for a believer to minister in this life.

6   There are also *varieties of effects* (ἐνέργημα; used only here and in v.10 in the NT), *but the same God who works all things in all*. God (the Father) is the ultimate cause of all that is done for Him in body of Christ.

7-11   [The diverse gifts are given by the Spirit for the common good of all.]

7   Paul's initial statement says it all: The spiritual capacity given *to each one* in the Body of Christ is a *manifestation of the Spirit*. Every believer has been so blessed by the Spirit. These gifts (v.4) are not given to enhance the status of those gifted (regardless of the gift), but *for the common good*. No gift fulfils its purpose unless it is used for the building up the body as a whole. This need for love for others, rather than self, in the exercise of spiritual gifts will

be emphasized in 13:1-3; any gift, no matter how great, without love, is of no effect. This single purpose must be a constant check on any understanding of the meaning and function of all the diverse gifts.

8   The gifts in verses 8-10 are not a complete list. Indeed, the lists in verses 28 and 29-30 leave out some gifts and add others. Neither is this list a "ranking" of gifts, since the order is inverted in other lists. Many possible divisions are suggested (see Martin, *The Spirit and the Congregation*, pp.11f), but *Paul's concern here is to offer a considerable list so that they will stop being singular in their own emphasis* (Fee, 585). In their emphasis on tongues, they ignored the diversity of gifts. Ironically, in their insistence on *uniformity* of practice (all speaking in tongues as a sign of being spiritual) they were destroying the *unity* (and the strength) of the body.

Nine gifts are listed. Paul begins with two that would be particularly desirable to the Corinthians. Neither is found in any other gift list (unless *knowledge* in 13:8 is equated with *word of knowledge* here).

The *word of wisdom* (λόγος σοφίας) immediately reminds us of the Corinthians lust for worldly wisdom. This, in fact, was the basis of their divisions (1:17-3:4; 3:18-20)! They were enamored with wise words; what they needed was speech characterized by wisdom from God. Some think the 'word of wisdom' was supernatural insight into doctrinal or practical truth, but it is just as likely to have been an ability to recognize the wisdom of the "foolish" gospel of Christ crucified, and proclaim it instead of the worldly wisdom so prevalent in Corinth. If so, Paul may have demonstrated this insightful gift when he presented the gospel to the Athenians (Acts 17).

The *word of knowledge* (λόγος γνώσεως) would also appeal to the Corinthians. Even Paul has noted their knowledge (1:5), but unfortunately, their knowledge had done little for them but make them arrogant (8:1)! The exact meaning of the 'word of knowledge' is unclear. Like the 'word of wisdom,' it may have been supernatural godly knowledge. Some have characterized this as a 'gift of preaching' or teaching, or special insight into the meaning of Scripture. Whatever this gift is, it has nothing to do with modern religious hucksters who pretend to 'receive' information about some secret physical need of an audience-member!

9-10   The gift of *faith* is also sensationalized in the church today, but this misses the mark. A person with extraordinary faith is one who demonstrates uncommon trust in God, and does great things by virtue of that faith (cf. 13:2). Such a person might be known for their dedication to prayer.

Healing and *the effecting of miracles* may be related to faith, although this is not certain. Supernatural healing was part of Paul's ministry (Acts 19:11f; 20:9f), and marked him as an apostle (cf. Rom. 15:19; 2 Cor. 12:12). The demonstration of these gifts in his life as proof of his office may signal that they were given by God for the apostolic age only. It is however clear that Paul envisions these gifts, with all the others, as being present in their congregation.

Prophecy (προφητεία) refers to both fore-telling the future and forth-telling any message from God. The idea of ecstatic speech (Barrett, 286) is foreign to prophecy; rather, prophecy is an intelligible message which builds up, motivates to action, and consoles the assembly (14:3). Paul's prophetic words in 1 Thess. 4:13-18, for example, were provided to bring comfort in the face of their grief over dying brethren.

Distinguishing of spirits (διακρίσεις πνευμάτων) is a supernatural ability to discern whether a person is speaking truthfully or not. But what was it a person with this gift was to discern? If this is the ability to discern doctrinal truth, it refers only to the foundational period of the church (when the completed scriptures were not available), and even then only sometimes, since Paul commends the Bereans for *examining the scriptures daily to see whether these things were so* (cf. Acts 17:11). Perhaps this was an enablement to discern the truth of a prophetic utterance (cf. 14:29). A third possibility is that this relates to the discerning of spirits in 1 John 4:1-3; if so, it is more an ability to evaluate a person than his message, to perceive whether he is a true prophet or a demonic deceiver (12:2f; cf. 2 Cor. 11:12-15).

The gifts of *kinds of tongues* (γένη γλωσσῶν) and *interpretation of tongues* (ἑρμηνεία γλωσσῶν) are inseparable, as 14:27f makes clear. The *nature* of these tongues has been debated. Modern Pentecostals and Charismatics often understand these tongues as 'ecstatic' or unintelligible speech. Such speech was not uncommon in first-century pagan religions (Lowery, 537f), and it was present in Corinth (cf. 12:2-3). Paul distances himself (and his readers) from such a practice, however, so it is hard to imagine him identifying it now (or anything similar to it) as a gift of the Spirit! The evidence *against* the gift of tongues referring to ecstatic speech is great. Nowhere in the New Testament does γλῶσσα refer to ecstatic speech, and a few years later, when Paul's travelling companion Luke penned his *Acts of the Apostles*, he did not have this understanding (cf. Acts 2:4-12, where γλῶσσα clearly refers to known languages, unlearned by those who were speaking them). The only conclusion consistent with the use of γλωσσα throughout the New Testament is that the gift of tongues is a special spiritual ability to speak in a known language, unlearned by the speaker. The gift of interpretation, then, was the corresponding spiritual ability to interpret a known language, unlearned by the interpreter.

Application: The desire for a common and easily verifiable spiritual experience has caused an increase in the practice of ecstatic speech in the church. This focus has resulted in a lack of attention to true spiritual gifts, and a loss of spiritual depth in the church. Ironically, the presence of 'ecstatic speech' among almost all members of some groups exposes it as a counterfeit. The spiritual gifts listed by Paul are clearly not common; rather, they are apportioned by God for the common good of the assembly. As Paul makes clear in verses 14-20, any predominance or preference of one gift is not of God, but man. Enthusiasm and excitement are laudable, but not at the expense of truth. The visible attributes of spirituality are not most important; the invisible working of the Spirit is, and the results of His work on believers and the church will be great.

11   Paul now returns to his overriding thesis; even though there are all these gifts, there is only one source, *one and the same Spirit,* who *works* (ἐνεργέω; cf. v.6, where it is God who *works* all things) *all these things, distributing* (διαιροῦν; this is the cognate verb to the noun translated *varieties* in vv.4-6) *to each one individually just as He wills.* The distribution of gifts is under God's sovereign control; hence, the Corinthians should not be pursuing or specially valuing any one gift. This point should be heeded by all in the body of Christ today as well.

12:12-14   *The diversity of believers in one united Church results from all being baptized by the Spirit into Christ's body (12-14).*

12   Having established that gifts of the Spirit exalt Jesus as Lord, and that there are many different gifts, Paul now turns to the diversity of gifts within the unity that is the body of Christ. He points to a physical body as an illustration of this diversity-in-unity, a metaphor which he will in the verses following develop in order to indicate a number of areas in which the Corinthian 'body' needs to shape up. His initial point here is simple: a physical *body is one and yet has many members* (μέλος; cf. BAGD, 502f; refers to limbs or other parts of the body), *and all the members of the body, though they are many, are* still only *one body*; in the same way, *so also in Christ* (i.e., the body of Christ).

13   The opening καὶ γὰρ ("for also") here and in verse 14 indicates that Paul is explaining and restating his 'diversity in unity' theme from v.12 in these two verses. Verse 13 is answering the question, "Why (or how) is it that though different, we are all united in one

body?" The answer is that, just as the gifts, though different, are all united by their one common source, so too all Christians are united by their common experience at the moment of salvation. At that point each one is *baptized by/with/in* (ἐν) *the one* Holy Spirit *into* the *one body* of Christ. The function of the Holy Spirit in this baptism is debated, but the grammar leads to only one conclusion: Just as one is baptized in water, so too the Holy Spirit is the element or medium in which the believer has been immersed into the body of Christ. Because all have this common beginning, there is no distinction based on race (*Jews or Gentiles*) or social standing (*slaves or free*). All have likewise been *made to drink of one Spirit*, referring to the indwelling of the Holy Spirit which also occurs at conversion.

Theological Note: Misuse of this reference to baptism in (of) the Holy Spirit has resulted in theological and practical aberrations in the church. The phrase occurs six times in the New Testament: Five precede and point to Pentecost (Matt. 3:11; Mark 1:8; Luke 3:16; John 1:33; Acts 1:5), one follows and points back to Pentecost (Acts 11:16), and here. This occurrence alone indicates that *water* baptism is not in view. The additional fact that Paul's reference to them being *made to drink of one Spirit* is clearly not literal, but spiritual, confirms this. The subject, then, is *Spirit baptism*. This passage alone identifies when it occurs, and what it produces. Believers are, at the moment of faith, immersed in the Spirit, and they drink of (take into themselves) the Spirit. This is not a reference to a second work of grace at some point following salvation; it is a description of the Spirit's work in a believer at the point of salvation.

Practical Note: The indwelling Spirit is given at the point of salvation, and without the Spirit, no one is truly regenerate (Rom. 8:9). But there is a further figure to be heeded in having been made *to drink* of the Spirit. In Eph. 5:18, Paul instructs believers to *not get* *drunk with wine...but be filled with the Spirit.* The indwelling Spirit is an interminable and uninterrupted source of spiritual life and growth; that which we drink of at the point of salvation is also that which we continue to drink of in our daily lives. We begin by being immersed in and indwelt by the Spirit; we grow by being filled with the Spirit (Gal. 3:2-3). Finally, Eph. 5:19f indicates that the result of this continued filling of the Spirit is functional unity in the body. There is a crying need within the Church of Jesus Christ today for the unifying work of the Spirit to cease being made a source of division! Divisiveness—the Corinthian problem—is never a result of the Spirit's work! Instead of making a position on the Holy Spirit a basis for 'selective unity' with those who agree with me, let's pray for the Spirit to have His way in our lives, and lives of other believers, so that our unity in diversity will display the Spirit to all who observe us.

14 The oneness of the body of Christ has been shown clearly (v.13). The emphasis now returns to the diversity which exists in this unity. While *the body* is a unity, it *is not one member, but many.* This is clear from the parallel between the physical and spiritual bodies—as Paul now elaborates. At the same time, he draws some applications of this truth for the Corinthian church.

12:15-20 *The diversity of members in a functional physical body exhibits the need and importance of each gift placed in the spiritual Body by God.*

15-16 To extract further instruction from his 'physical body-spiritual body' parallel, Paul now gives voice to various members of the physical body. His purpose is to show the fallacy of emphasizing one member (gift), and devaluing others. The gift of tongues had captivated the Corinthians, leading them to emphasize it over other gifts. In Paul's imaginary dialogue, the *hand* and *eye* are more desirable 'members' than the *foot* and *ear.* Paul's point is clear: Just because one function of the body is valued less than another does not mean that it is not part of the body! The diversity of parts is essential to the normal functioning of the body.

17   Using two rhetorical questions, Paul drives home this point. If the body was only one member (one gift), it would be dysfunctional. *If the whole body were an eye, where would the hearing be?* (There would be none.) Again (suggesting that it is not just supposedly superior gifts, but any gift which is emphasized to the exclusion of others), *if the whole were hearing, where would the sense of smell be?* (There would be none.) All members (gifts) are needed, or some function of the body will be missing.

18   And this is the way God has planned it. Unlike the aberration of verse 17, God has constructed the body with each member. Just as the physical body shows the hand of a magnificent designer who put each part in its desired place and with its desired function, so too in the spiritual body that Divine Designer has His hand. As in verse 11 (and v.24), the diversity of functions in the body is the result of God's (i.e., the Spirit's) will and work.

19   Paul reiterates the fact that one member does not make for a functional body (cf. v.17), but now goes even further; not only is such a body dysfunctional, it is a grotesque monstrosity! It is like one big eye, or ear, or foot, or –considering the preoccupation of the Corinthians—a giant tongue! Hollywood has created many such freaks, from aliens to imaginary creatures. In movies, these may be enthralling; in the church, such a specter is appalling! The point is this: If we are a *body*, we need a healthy diversity of gifts.

20   This is Paul's conclusion. With a decisive *But now* (νῦν δὲ; also v.18), he reiterates what he has said before (vv.12, 14): In the body of Christ, as illustrated by the physical body, there are many members (functional gifts).

12:21-26 *The mutual dependence of diverse members of the physical body exhibits the need for mutual concern for each other in the spiritual Body.*

21   As in verse 15, Paul introduces a new application of the body metaphor by giving voice to members of the body. In verse 15 the issue was the need for a diversity of members in order to

have a functioning body; here the emphasis is on the fact that within the body, there are no 'independent' members. All are co-dependent; all have need of the others.

As evidenced throughout this letter, some in Corinth, for various reasons, thought of themselves as 'a cut above' the rest of the body (1:26-31; 3:18; 4:5,6-8; 5:1-2,6; 8:1-3,7,10; 10:12; 11:20-22). This was also true in the context of spiritual gifts. Just as the 'wise' despised the 'foolish' (at least until this letter arrived; cf. 3:18), the strong had no regard for the weak (8:10-11), and the 'haves' had no need for the 'have nots' (11:21f), so too here the self-proclaimed 'spiritual' look down on those deemed less spiritual. This attitude is implicit in the higher-lower contrast between members: *eye* to the *hand*, and *head* to the *foot*. No 'high' member (with a more spectacular or desirable gift) can say to a 'low' member (who lacks such gifts), *"I have no need of you."* In the wider context, with the disproportionate emphasis placed on tongues, it was likely the gift which was viewed by some in Corinth as that which marked one as *spiritual*.

22 With a strong adversative (ἀλλὰ; *On the contrary*), Paul makes clear that not only is the attitude found in verse 21 not true, it is the furthest thing from the truth! The opposite is actually the case! This is emphasized by πολλῷ μᾶλλον (*much more/rather*), which may modify the whole phrase (*it is much truer*; NAS/NKJ), or the necessity of seemingly weaker members (they are *indispensable*; NIV). The seemingly *weaker members* (cf. 2:3; 4:10; 8:7-12; 9:22) are not unneeded, but necessary. All believers, no matter how insignificant their gift may seem (like an internal organ), are important to the proper functioning of the body.

23-24a To further evidence his point, Paul refers cryptically to the sexual organs, using the pejorative adjectives ἄτιμος (*less honorable*; BAGD, 119) and ἀσχήμων (*unseemly*; BAGD, 119). Whether Paul sees these as the same as those he referred to as "weaker" (v.22) is not clear, but the same principle is evidenced. Those members deemed lesser in some way are honored, so that those that are unpresentable become presentable (*have more abundant seemliness*; i.e., they are given the honor of covering). By treating these members of our body this way, while not providing such covering to those parts which have no need of it (like the face), we show that all parts are mutually dependent on and important to each other.

24b   For the third time (vv.11, 18; cf. also vv. 4-6 and 28), Paul highlights the divine composition of the body (physical and spiritual; although both fit the continuing analogy, the eventual application to the spiritual body is clear). God has *composed* (συγκεράννυμι; mix together, blend, unite; BAGD, 781) the body so that those in need (whether because of weakness or because deemed less honorable) receive that which they require. In Gen. 3:21, we read that God made the first suitable garments to cover Adam and Eve after they became aware of their nakedness (their less honorable parts), thus giving honor to those members which lacked. This attribute continues to be part of God's working both now (1:25, 26-29; cf. Rom. 8:26; 2 Cor. 12:9-10; Phil. 4:13) and in the future (15:43; cf. Matt. 5:3; Jas. 2:5; 2 Cor. 13:4).

25   God has so composed the spiritual body—as co-dependent members in one united organism—*so that* (ἵνα) that which the body was designed to be (a functional unity) will be realized, through the action of all its members. Therefore, *there should be no division in the body*, since no one member is above any other, nor independent of any other. All *should have the same care for one another.*

26   What does this mean precisely and positively? It means that, first, when *one member suffers, all the members suffer with it.* The truth of this is self-evident, even when the suffering member is of less honor (stubbing one's toe has a distressing effect on the whole body!) On the other hand, when *one member is honored, all the members rejoice with it.* It is impossible for one part of our body to be uplifted without the rest of us sharing in the joy.

The desire of the Corinthians to be "spiritual" led them to pursue certain spectacular gifts, which in turn led them to look down on those who did not have those gifts, which in effect denied the unity-diversity of the body as intended by God. Instead of seeking certain gifts for their seeming spiritual value, they should be functioning like a healthy body, caring for one another (especially weaker members), suffering with those who are suffering, and rejoicing with those who are honored.

12:27-31 *The body of Christ has a diversity of membership (gifts) but a mutuality of dependence.*

27   What was implicit in the preceding discussion is now again made explicit (as at the outset; cf. v.12). The metaphor of the human body is a reflection of Christ's body, and the members are the believers who make it up.

28   For the fourth and final time (cf. v.24), Paul reiterates the divine appointment of gifts in the body of Christ. Indeed, along with the major themes of diversity and unity, it is this feature which Paul seems to emphasize above all others; he effectively asserts that no one should 'rate gifts' or pursue one above another. God is the One who gives the gifts, just as He desires. He has *appointed* (τίθημι; put in place) each one in the church. His wisdom in body function is evident in the physical realm; He also provides for the spiritual body, the church. It is not for Christians to dictate to the Spirit which gifts they want, or which gifts should be possessed by all. The gift(s) which they have, they should be faithful to exercise.

Paul now lists gifts, beginning by numbering the first three, *apostles...prophets...teachers*. While some see the order being continued with *then...then* (ἔπειτα; BAGD, 284) for the next two gifts, *miracles* and *gifts of healing*, this is not certain. Regardless, here the 'order' of gifts stops, and it is doubtful in any case that Paul is trying to "value" the gifts, since he has gone to pains to show that weaker and less seemly members are just as important as those members who are more prominent. Instead, he is probably responding to some who had devalued the apostolic role, along with the prophetic and teaching gifts, below tongues and other more spectacular gifts. Apostles, prophets, and teachers were gifted people whose ministries were vital to the whole body of Christ. As such they stood apart from the other gifts.

It may be suggested that if the gifted offices of apostles and prophets functioned during the foundational period of the church (cf. Eph. 2:20), the gift of teaching (and evangelism; cf. Eph. 4:11ff) is vital in the ministry of the church today.

On the gifts of *miracles* and *healings*, cf. above on 12:9, 10. The gift of *helps* (ἀντιλήμψεις, used only here in the New Testament), or helpful deeds (cf. BAGD, 74) probably refers to 'deacon-like' ministry, performing physical tasks which aid and expedite the overall function of the body. Perhaps this gift is parallel to the gift of service (διακονίαν) in Rom. 12:7 (see Fee, 621).

The gift of *administrations* (κυβερνήσεις; used only here in the New Testament) is the ability to guide and direct the church. The noun from the same root is used in Acts 27:11 and Rev.18:17 of one who directs a ship. While this may be demonstrated in a person who fills an administrative role in a local church, the gift reflects more an inner wisdom rather than a managerial skill.

On *various kinds of tongues*, see 12:10.

29-30　　With a series of rhetorical questions, Paul drives home his point. All these gifts exist, and no one of them is for everyone. Diversity in the unity of the body is essential. Each question demands a negative answer (seven times Paul uses μὴ), and the English translation should reflect this (in this regard, the NASV [*All are not apostles, are they? All are not prophets, are they? ...*] is preferred over both the NIV and NKJV).

31a　　The opening phrase here can be read as indicative (*But you are earnestly desiring the greater gifts*; cf. NIV marg.), which certainly fits in with the Corinthian problem (they *were* desiring the gifts which they *thought* were greater), but is hard to justify grammatically, since Paul uses the same words (ζηλοῦτε δὲ) when he resumes his instruction in 14:1 (where it is clearly imperative). But why, if Paul has been stressing the equal need for all the gifts in the body, and has further emphasized repeatedly that all gifts are distributed sovereignly by God, would he here command the Corinthians to *earnestly desire the greater gifts*?

Most likely this refers back to the three gifts Paul listed first in verse 28 (apostles, prophets, and teachers). He wants the Corinthians to desire the exercise of intelligible gifts which edify the whole congregation the most (apostles, etc.).

In support of this view is Paul's instruction in chapter 14. Chapter 13 prepares the way for what follows: The Corinthians need to see the surpassing greatness of love beyond all the gifts. But when he gets to specific instruction in response to their desire for tongues, he emphasizes that they should seek the exercise of intelligible gifts (specifically prophecy) in their public meetings. The *greater gifts* here refer to those who speak intelligibly, and under apostles, none other ranks any higher than prophets. Therefore, his instruction to pursue prophecy (instead of tongues) in 14:1-25 is a natural extension of this command. On the one hand, this looks back to the gifted men he has listed (12:28), but on the other (since they do not usually have an apostle with them) it looks forward to the function of the gift of prophecy. This is one of the greater gifts, and its function is to be desired in the assembly.

31b   The Καὶ (*And*) beginning this phrase indicates that Paul is continuing on from his command to desire the functioning of the greater gifts. But before he launches into that discussion (14:1), his audience must first have the right attitude. The purpose of the gifts, after all, is to build up the body, and this is impossible apart from love. There were elements in the church at Corinth which thought of themselves as wise or strong or spiritual, and who needed to be repeatedly told that without an active concern for those who were not so wise or mature, but were weaker and not so gifted, any exercise of their giftedness would amount to no good. Therefore, as a foundation for his instruction in chapter 14, he wants them to be under the banner of love. For even if they follow his instructions there, yet lack love, it will profit them, and the church of Jesus Christ, nothing. This, then, is the *still more excellent way.*

13:1-13 *Love is essential to the exercise of spiritual gifts because of its superior character and permanence.*

13:1-3 [Love is essential to the exercise of spiritual gifts.]

13:1 Paul here (and in verses 2-3) makes his admonition personal: *If I...* He is no different than they; love is for all of us. The question often asked here concerns the meaning of *tongues of men and of angels.* It may be that the Corinthians thought their tongues were an angelic language, and Paul wants to counter the idea that this type of speaking can be effective without love. However, it is more likely that this is a *merism,* a figure of speech using two extremes (tongues of *men* and *angels*) to refer to 'any and all speech.' In other words, he is saying, "No matter what language I speak in—even an angelic one!—it makes no difference if I don't have love!" A *noisy gong or a clanging cymbal* may grab attention for a moment, but its sound is not pleasing.

There is no justification for equating 'ecstatic speech' with 'the tongues of angels.' The normal meaning of γλῶσσα (BAGD, 161) is a literal language (see above on 12:9-10). Paul spoke in human tongues (languages) often (14:18), but again, consistent with the meaning of tongues, this is a reference to known earthly languages.

2 If their favorite gift (tongues) was worthless without love, so too was Paul's favorite, *prophecy*! To 'top it up' even more, Paul throws in the highly desired gifts of knowledge and faith (*and know all mysteries and all knowledge; and if I have all faith, so as to remove mountains*). A person with this potent brew of gifts

might be considered an exceptional spiritual specimen by those in Corinth! Paul concludes that even if he were to have all of these, yet *not have love*, he would be *nothing*.

3 The gift of giving is not included in this letter (cf. Rom. 12:8), but is reflected here. Again, the absolute necessity of love is emphasized. Paul sets the bar high: *And if I give all my possessions to feed the poor, and if I deliver my body to be burned, but do not have love, it profits me nothing.* The most sacrificial giving, even to the point of martyrdom, apart from the presence of love, profits the giver nothing.

4-7 [Love is superior because of its selfless characteristics.]

4 Here ensues a list of verbs (love is an action!) which describe love (ἀγάπη). *Love is patient* (μακροθυμεῖ) and *kind* (χρηστεύεται; used only here in the New Testament). The cognate nouns are both fruits of the Spirit in Gal. 5:22, and parts of the 'new man' to "put on" in Col. 3:12. It is not surprising that these describe God's attitude of love for the lost world (Rom. 2:4).

These two positive descriptions of love are followed by eight negative ones. Love is *not jealous* (ζηλοῖ). This term expresses desire (12:31a; 14:1) in a positive sense, but also divisive envy (cf. NIV/NKJV) which afflicted the Corinthian congregation (3:4; cf. Gal. 5:20). Love does not envy that which belongs to another, whether a possession, or a gift, or an office.

Love does not brag (*boast*, NIV; *parade itself*, NKJV; περπερεύεται) refers to being consumed with one's own virtue (braggart, wind-bag; BAGD, 659). For the believer who understands the condition he was in when Christ saved him, this attitude is untenable (1:26-31; cf. Eph. 2:9). For one who is continuing to live with this attitude, let him never think that he is exhibiting love, and since he is not doing so, any gift that he may have been bragging about having will be of no profit, either.

Love *is not arrogant* (*proud*, NIV; *puffed up*, NKJV; φυσιοῦται).

This is precisely what Paul pointed out to the Corinthians in 8:1, where their knowledge of spiritual truth had led them to act in such a way that showed no concern or kindness for those who did not possess such knowledge. Knowledge puffs up; love builds up. The function of spiritual gifts is to edify the body; what is needed is for them to function with love.

5   Love *does not act unbecomingly* (*is not rude*, NIV; *does not behave rudely*, NKJV). The verb here (ἀσχημονεῖ; cf. 7:36, its only other occurrence in the New Testament) refers to shameful actions. The related adjective ἀσχήμων appeared in 12:23 to describe sexual organs. Love simply does not engage in things not fit for public consumption. The fact that the Corinthians were dragging their dirty laundry before the public in lawsuits (6:1-8) shows their need to grasp this aspect of love. Their lack of concern for one another in public worship in general showed their need to apply love there.

Love *does not seek its own;* it is not selfish. It seeks the good of others, not self. Paul showed this in his attitude toward those without the gospel (9:19-23; cf.10:24, 33). The Corinthians needed to show it in love feasts (11:21).

Love *is not provoked* (*easily angered*, NIV). This term (παροξύνω; BAGD, 634) occurs only one other time in the New Testament, in Acts 17:16, where it refers positively to Paul's spirit being stirred up to confront the idolatrous Athenians. Here it refers negatively to provoking others to wrath through irritation. It is therefore in the character of love to be 'thick-skinned.' Love is not easily led into a rage. Furthermore, love *does not take into account* (λογίζεται; 'let one's mind dwell on') *a wrong suffered.* It does not carry around grudges, and 'get even' with those who wrong it. Love will "turn the other cheek" (cf. Matt. 5:39). As personified in a godly man, this aspect of love means he will not be pugnacious (cf. 1 Tim. 3:3).

6   A succinct contrast shows that love has an ethical component as well. Love *does not rejoice in unrighteousness, but rejoices with*

the truth. Paul distinguishes between wrongdoing in general (ἀδικίᾳ; BAGD, 17f) and the element which exposes sin—the truth (cf. Rom 1:18). In the exercise of their gifts, the Corinthians must guard against replacing God's truth with their own experience. Already, they have evidenced a penchant for embracing unrighteousness (5:1-2; 6:1-20; 8:10-12) on the basis of flawed human wisdom. Furthermore, they have been reluctant to respect Paul's apostolic teaching. As a result, despite their giftedness, they are not being built up. A true love for God will result in an aversion to sin and a readiness to receive the truth.

7   Paul concludes his reflections on the character of love with four brief inclusive features. Love *bears all things* (NIV *it always protects*). The beauty of love is exhibited in its refusal to take advantage of another for its own gain. Love "throws a cloak of silence over what is displeasing in another person" (cf. στέγω; BAGD, 765f). Love *believes all things* and *hopes all things*. Perhaps this means that where there is love, one never loses faith and hope. An active love will face the deepest, darkest hours with an unshakeable expectation and anticipation of a good resolution. As love thus promotes faith and hope, it shows its superior nature to even those virtues (v. 13). Finally, love *endures all things* (NIV *always perseveres*). This quality, in addition to complementing the first in the verse, provides a hinge with the section to follow. Whatever may come, love will not fail. When everything else is gone, when all other virtues have fulfilled their purpose, love will remain. It "goes the distance." It is this feature of love to which Paul now turns his attention.

8-13   [Love is superior because of its permanence.]

8   So well has Paul prepared his readers for this subject, the opening phrase seems to be a conclusion statement from verse 7: *Love never fails*. But rather than a continuation of his discussion on the character of love, it soon becomes apparent that Paul is now

focusing on the infinite nature of love. He emphatically conveys this by contrasting the permanence of love with the ephemeralness of various gifts. While love continues, *prophesy...will be done away; tongues...will cease; knowledge...will be done away.* In general, Paul's message is simple: Gifts—as represented by these which the Corinthian Christians preferred—have a limit to their useful lives. For those who over-emphasized the gifts, the message is specific: 'You have been stressing that which is of passing significance instead of that which is eternal!' Paul is not saying that love is opposed to the exercise of gifts; rather, as important as the gifts are (and they *are* important, as chapter 12 has emphasized), they must never take precedence over the exercise of love.

Theological Note: The significance of Paul using a different verb, and the middle voice, in reference to tongues ("they will cease;" fut. mid. from παύω) has led some to suggest that Paul was communicating—cryptically, since it wouldn't apply for another generation at least—that while prophecy and knowledge would be done away (see vv. 9-10 below on the question of when this would occur), tongues would cease on their own (before prophecy and knowledge did). This entire discussion is speculative, and foreign to the focus and argument in this chapter. Paul is not here distinguishing between prophecy and knowledge on one hand, and tongues on the other. If he had wanted to, he surely would not have placed tongues in between the other two! Rather than burden this passage with a theological issue obviously alien to it, let those passages which speak directly to the gift of tongues and its application in the church today define our understanding.

9-10 With an explanatory γὰρ (*For*), Paul proceeds to demonstrate the temporal nature of gifts. "Now," he tells the Corinthians, "*we know in part, and we prophesy in part; but when the perfect comes, the partial will be done away.*"

Let us keep the issue of this passage firmly before us. Paul is illustrating the temporal nature of spiritual gifts, and does so by referring to the gifts of prophecy and knowledge. He states that what they presently know and prophesy is incomplete, and thus these gifts continue. But one day, prophecy will be fulfilled, their knowledge will be complete, and thus—then—these gifts will be done away.

Interpretive Note: The question which remains, and which this passage does not explicitly answer, concerns the time referred to by Paul's cryptic "when the perfect comes." Is he covertly referring to the completion of God's written revelation in the New Testament, which occurred some 40 years later? Or is he pointing to the yet-future return of Christ? While arguments have been made for each, in the end, the historical context of this letter rules out the former. On the one hand, the idea that Paul knew 'New Testament' revelation would one day be completed in written form for future generations is questionable. It certainly would've been the furthest thing from his mind! The 'Old Testament' canon wasn't finally settled until after Paul died. Every indication from his writings suggests that he anticipated the imminent return of Christ (cf. 1:8; 4:5; 6:2, 3, 14; 7:29ff; 9:24-27; 11:26; 15:22f, 51-58), not the nearly 2000-year period which has ensued. If this had been Paul's meaning, how would the Corinthians ever have derived it from the text? They were not concerned with written revelation or the cannon of scripture! Their concern was spiritual gifts, which were given by the triune God to contribute to the growth and maturing of the Body of Christ, until Christ returned (11:26). It is this future return of Christ to which Paul here refers.

---

11   To illustrate the distinction between the "now" when spiritual gifts are operative, and "then" when only love remains, Paul provides a simple analogy from his own life: *When I was a child, I used to speak as a child, think as a child, reason as a child; when I*

became a man, I did away with childish things. Paul is probably using the faculties of speaking, thinking, and reasoning to allude to the gifts of tongues, knowledge, and prophecy mentioned in verses 8-10. Just as the speech and mental processes of a child are fitting when one is a child, so too spiritual gifts like these are appropriate for the church *now.* Again, just as childish speech and thinking is unfit for a grown man, so too there will come a day when the spiritual gifts will be obsolete.

Interpretive Note: It is tempting to see in this analogy a veiled exhortation. With their emphasis on spiritual gifts, and their contrasting lack of love, Paul surely wanted the Corinthians to "grow up" spiritually, and stop emphasizing spiritual gifts at the expense of love. But even if this was Paul's desire, and even if the analogy 'fits,' we cannot arbitrarily import it into Paul's meaning. This analogy contributes in one specific way to Paul's overall argument: It illustrates the transience of the gifts, thus highlighting by contrast the permanence of love.

[N.B. Even more far-fetched is the suggestion that speaking, thinking, and reasoning as a child refers to the "immature period of the church" (that time before the completion of the New Testament writings), and that becoming a man and putting away childish things refers to the "mature" church (in possession of the written New Testament). As noted above, seeking to tie Paul's argument to the question of the completion of the canon is both anachronistic and foreign to his argument.]

---

12 The "now...then" contrast is here applied by Paul to himself and the Corinthian congregation. This is the evidence in their experience which confirms the fact that in the future there will be a time when spiritual gifts will no longer be functional. The reason (*For*) Paul knows this is true is that *now we see in a mirror dimly* (δι' ἐσόπτρου ἐν αἰνίγματι; cf. BAGD, 23), *but then face*

to face; now I know in part, but then I shall know fully just as I also have been fully known. The basic message is simple; while the present 'vision' of the church is imprecise and unclear ('dim;' Gk. αἴνιγμα, BAGD, 23, "riddle;" source for the English word 'enigma'), it will be perfect. The spiritual knowledge of believers in this life is represented metaphorically as an image dimly perceived in a mirror (see "mirror" in W.E. Vine, *An Expository Dictionary of New Testament Words*). While Paul's knowledge is only partial, it will one day be complete.

Interpretive Note: Paul's reference to seeing in a "mirror" is regarded by some as a veiled reference to scripture, based on the other New Testament use of this noun in James 1:23. Such a conclusion leaves one wondering why Paul never made this clear—especially since he knew the Corinthians' tendency to misapply his instructions (cf. 5:9ff). If any other text informs our understanding here, it is Paul's own words in 2 Cor. 3:18, which suggests this refers to "seeing" Christ imperfectly now, but "face to face" in the future (see Conzelmann, 227f). It is best, however, to see this as an appeal to something the Corinthians knew about. A local Corinthian industry manufactured mirrors, and this most likely explains Paul's usage of the figure (TDNT, 2:756; Fee, 647f).

---

13   The superiority of love, and thus its importance for the spiritual life of the Corinthian church, is now confirmed by Paul. The time will come when spiritual gifts will be gone; at that time love will stand alone. *But* they do not need to wait till then to exercise love, for *now abide faith, hope and love, these three.* These three Christian virtues embody the Christian life, reflecting dependence on God, anticipation of Christ's return, and fellowship with believers. Even among these essential virtues, however, there is a hierarchy: *the greatest of these is love.* There can be no argument; the Corinthian's lack of love was wrong. Nothing could take the place of it. Nothing—not even the most

spectacular spiritual gifts—could create unity and build up the body without love. This then is the still more excellent way. Paul is now ready to present his instruction concerning their misplaced emphasis on the gift of tongues.

Theological Note: The question of the permanence of certain spiritual gifts in the modern church has transformed Paul's instruction in this chapter into a battlefield which he never intended. By pursuing this issue in a context in which it is not addressed, both charismatic and non-charismatic evangelicals have exhibited a puerile abuse of biblical hermeneutics, and ignored the *heart* of Paul's message—the need for love. This passage neither confirms nor denies the presence of certain spiritual gifts, either in Corinth or today. It speaks only of spiritual gifts in a general sense, contrasting them with love, which is superior. The questions often debated here are directly addressed in other passages. For example, the question of some spiritual gifts being given for a foundational period of the church is explicitly informed in Scriptures like 2 Cor. 12:12, Eph. 2:20, and Heb. 2:3-4. Christians of all persuasions would do well to show more interest in what scripture can do to them, and less interest in what they can do to scripture!

Homiletical Ideas: Most pastors have encountered divisiveness of the church. Inter-church and intra-church divisions often cripple the effectiveness of Christians in the world. Sadly, the solution for many today is a bland embracing of "love" at the expense of biblical truth. In the end this is shown to in fact not be love, but lust. It is getting what we want, a façade of unity, but with the 'heart of truth' removed! Between theological divisions and ecumenism, the message of this chapter rises like a banner. It is a celebration of real love, without which any other gifts or knowledge or virtues are lifeless.

The message itself is not complex, but it is deep. The importance of love, its characteristics, and its permanence, should guide our lives. If a church apprehends these truths, the unity-in-diversity of the body which Paul set out as the pattern for the church (chapter 12) will be realized. But all three are important, and in their order. We must first accept the absolute importance of love (vv.1-3). We are then ready to consider the characteristics of love, and how they apply in our lives (vv.4-7). When this has happened, our lives will exhibit the priorities which will be perfectly realized only when we see Christ face to face (vv. 8-13). We will finally be ready to let everything else in our Christian experience take its place, recognizing the surpassing greatness of love.

Perhaps most important here is how *not* to preach this passage. Don't allow the message to be eclipsed by confusion over the cessation of tongues (v. 8), the meaning of terms like "perfect" (v10), and Paul's imagery in verses 11-12. These are popular issues for debate, but they are fruitless detours away from the message of this chapter. Those who have misconstrued the function of gifts and the ministry of the Spirit need to apprehend Paul's message here; only then will they be prepared to follow his teaching in chapter 14. Likewise, those who have quenched the Spirit in their Christian experience, content to cling to lifeless orthodoxy, need to apprehend Paul's message; only then will they begin to enjoy the fulfilling experience of the body of Christ spelled out in chapter 12.

14:1-25 *The Corinthians should desire the exercise of the gift of prophecy over tongues in church because prophecy edifies the body and convicts unbelievers, while tongues do not.*

14:1-5   [The Corinthians should desire the exercise of the gift of prophecy over tongues in church because prophecy edifies the body, while tongues do not.]

1   With a few well-chosen words, Paul sums up all he has been saying up to this point: *Pursue love, yet desire earnestly spiritual*

gifts (πνευματικά; cf. 12:1). His focus is the meeting of the church, in which the exercise of spiritual gifts was proper. He wants them to let love—both for one another and for the unsaved—control all they do (cf. διώκω, BAGD, 201; to strive for, seek after love). At the same time, with the controlling motivation of love, they should desire (ζηλόω; BAGD, 338) spiritual gifts used for the benefit of all. This was hardly happening in Corinth! Their lack of love and misapplication of gifts had fractured the body. They had forgotten that showing love includes being concerned about the edification of the body (8:1), and the exercise of spiritual gifts is for the common good (12:7-11).

Now, picking up on his admonition for them to desire the *greater* gifts (12:31), Paul addresses their particular area of need—the misuse and overuse of tongues. His advice is simple: I want you to desire the exercise of spiritual gifts in general— *but especially that you may prophesy.* Paul began this letter by thanking God that the Corinthians were not lacking in any gift (1:7). That sincere thanks is now tempered by the fact that the Corinthians were not using the gifts for the edification of the body. In short, they were emphasizing the wrong gift, tongues.

2   The reason Paul wants them to especially desire the exercise of the gift of prophecy in the assembly is that *one who speaks in a tongue does not speak to men, but to God.* There is no need to water this down, nor to make it say any more than it does. Paul assumes the sincere nature of the tongues-speaker, and says he is speaking to God (perhaps praises and thanksgiving; cf. 14:17; the contemporary idea of a "message in tongues" is baseless; Fee, 656). But since the language is foreign to all others present, he can be saying nothing to any of them; *no one understands!* In fact, even the speaker does not know what he is saying (v. 14)! Rather, *in his spirit* (or *the Spirit*) *he speaks mysteries.*

Interpretive Note: Whether Paul here refers to the Holy Spirit (RSV; cf. Fee, 656, "by the Spirit," and NEB, "he is...inspired"), the spirit of the man (NASV, NIV), or the spiritual realm (NKJV), is unclear. Regardless, it is clear that the gift of tongues to which he refers is the gift given *by the Spirit* (see 12:9-10, *kinds of tongues*), and not an unidentified spiritual language (Grosheide, 317). The reference to *mysteries* is not to be confused with the eschatological *mystery* (2:7; 15:51; cf. Eph. 3:1-13); there is no evidence that the tongues contained special information on God's spiritual program. The reference to *mysteries* (plural) in the New Testament (only in this epistle; 4:1, 13:2, and here) simply refers to things which are unknown. In this case, Paul means that the tongues-speaker is saying things that are outside the understanding of both himself (cf. v.14) and those listening to him.

---

3   On the contrary, *one who prophesies speaks to men for edification and exhortation and consolation.* The contrast is not that one is a valid gift and the other not, but that one results in understanding— and thus ministers to the needs of the hearers—while the other does not.

4   Paul now simplifies the contrast between tongues and prophecy. *One who speaks in a tongue edifies himself; but one who prophesies edifies the church.* To "edify oneself" means that one who speaks in a tongue "benefits" or "strengthens" only himself (οἰκοδομέω; BAGD, 558). This is not sarcasm (MacArthur, 372); nor is Paul suggesting a supernatural communication with God that bypasses the mind (Fee, 657). Rather, this edification may refer to a person being reassured that he possesses the Spirit (Grosheide, 319), or (more likely) encouraged by the knowledge that he is exercising his spiritual gift. Nevertheless, each gift has its intended time and place of expression, and tongues are *not* for the assembly (see below, v. 22). Prophecy *is* for the assembly, since it serves to build up the whole church.

5   Did Paul think the gift of tongues was worthless or meaningless? Hardly! Like all spiritual gifts, it was intended for the edification of the body. To emphasize this point, he opens with a statement of hyperbole: *Now I wish that you all spoke in tongues, but even more that you would prophesy.* Since Paul has already affirmed that the key to the correct functioning of the body is the diversity of roles among the members (12:12-30), he clearly is not suggesting all should exercise the same gift. Each believer is to exercise the gift he has been given by the Spirit, not seek someone else's gift. Rather, Paul is here contrasting the value of tongues with the surpassing value of prophecy. In the public worship of the church, *greater is one who prophesies than one who speaks in tongues, unless he interprets, so that the church may receive edifying.* We might paraphrase Paul here, "It would be nice if everyone had the gift of tongues (which, of course, all do not), but much nicer if everyone prophesied (of course, not all prophesy, either). Why? Because prophecy is beneficial for the whole assembly—much more than tongues, especially tongues that are not interpreted."

Interpretive Note: Whatever Paul may have thought about the misuse of tongues in the Corinthian church, he clearly was not interested in abolishing the practice of the gift. His interest is evident in his exception, *unless he interprets* (cf. v.13). Paul wanted the congregation to understand what was said, so that all could be edified.

14:6-19 [The reason tongues do not edify the body is because they are unintelligible, and thus have no meaning or purpose in the church meeting.]

6   With an emphatic *But now, brethren,* Paul begins a series of arguments and analogies designed to demonstrate why prophecy is preferred over tongues in the meeting of the local church. The contrast, as above, is between that which is intelligible and that which is not. His opening rhetorical question is transparent: *if I come to you speaking in tongues, what shall I profit you, unless I*

speak to you either by way of revelation or of knowledge or of prophecy or of teaching? There is no profit (cf. ὠφελέω, BAGD, 900; cf. 13:3; Matt. 27:24) in that which no one can understand! But prophecy—along with revelation (ἀποκάλυψις; cf. 2:10; 14:26), knowledge, and teaching, three other types of intelligible speech—is understood and appreciated.

7-9   Analogies from musical instruments (*lifeless things*) illustrate Paul's point. If a *flute or harp* is played, but *does not produce a distinction in the tones* (the different notes are not discernible), *how will it be known what is played?* This would be an embarrassment in a performance, but much more serious in another context: *For if the bugle produces an indistinct sound, who will prepare himself for battle?* The correlation is clear.

When the church is gathered together, unless what is said is in *speech that is clear* (εὔσημον; "easily recognizable"), *how will it be known what is spoken?* Similar to a bugler whose tones are indistinct, such a person *will be speaking into the air...*expending effort, but without any results. Intelligibility is critical.

Application: Christians, both individually and collectively, are under siege today. Society has embraced a worldview which eliminates God and enthrones self as the center of the universe. By removing God as Creator, and thereafter from education, morality, and government, mankind is left with no absolute truth. As society unravels, social engineers must blame someone to justify their worldview. Christians are viewed as impeding progress by 'poisoning the minds of people' with myths about God, preaching the message of sin, salvation, and judgment, and holding to biblical morals. As this battle intensifies, the Christian "army" is in desperate need of clear direction. Now, more than ever, just as the bugle must produce a distinct sound in battle, there is a need for clear communication of God's truth to His people.

10-12 To make sure the link between musical instruments and verbal communication is not lost on his audience, Paul turns from the sounds made by lifeless things to the sounds made by humans. He submits that there are probably *a great many kinds of languages* (φωνή is used to maintain the correlation with the musical instruments' analogy; cf. BAGD, 870f) *in the world, and no kind is without meaning.* Unlike instruments which produced an indistinct, and thus meaningless, sound, Paul allows that every language has meaning. This meaning, however, must be known by both speaker and hearer, or there is no communication. *If then I do not know the meaning of the language, I shall be to the one who speaks a barbarian, and the one who speaks will be a barbarian to me.* The Corinthians, living in a city through which merchants from around the world passed, would immediately understand Paul's meaning. Two people could be speaking, each in his own language, yet neither would be able to understand the other.

Paul's aim? *So also you* (cf. v.9), *since you are zealous of spiritual gifts, seek to abound for the edification of the church.* Speak that which can be understood, not that which will confuse.

Interpretive Note: Although Paul refers to known languages here, this does not on its own suggest he was classifying tongues as foreign languages. Even if he had he used γλῶσσα or διάλεκτος here, such an argument would simply go beyond what he is saying. Someone speaking a foreign language may make no sense to me, but he surely makes sense to himself! However, a person who speaks in a tongue doesn't even know what *he* is saying (v.14)! Paul's purpose is simply to affirm that intelligibility is essential in the public worship of the church, and hence uninterpreted tongues are meaningless. However, as a second line of reasoning, this may substantiate the lexical meaning of γλῶσσα as a known language (see above on 12:10).

13-14 With an inferential *Therefore*, Paul introduces his practical conclusion: *let one who speaks in a tongue pray that he may interpret*. Why? *For*, Paul adds, *if I pray in a tongue, my spirit prays, but my mind is unfruitful*. Uninterpreted tongues are, for Paul, totally worthless in the public worship of the church (cf. v.5). Only when there is an intelligible translation do tongues have any place (cf. v.28). Unlike intelligible gifts (like prophecy or teaching), there is no reason to think that God would give a "message" to the church through tongues (see above on v.2). The only content of tongues was evidently prayers and other expressions of praise, thanksgiving, and exaltation to God (vv.2, 13-17; cf. Acts 10:46).

Interpretive Note: When Paul writes that if he prays in a tongue, "my spirit prays," he does not mean that he has a special communion with God that bypasses the mind (cf. Fee, 657). Rather, he means that a person praying in a tongue may feel prayerful, and may have an attitude of praise and thanksgiving. Regardless of this, the prayer itself is still unintelligible, and thus meaningless.

---

15 *What is the outcome then? I shall pray with the spirit and I shall pray with the mind also*. Paul doesn't mean he prays two kinds of prayers—one intelligible, one unintelligible! This misses his point altogether. Spiritual gifts are for the edification of the church body, not the personal satisfaction of a believer in private. Whatever spiritually positive feelings one may gain from praying in tongues, this does not justify it. Paul declares that he will pray, engaging *both* his spirit and his mind. Similarly, he will *sing with the spirit and...with the mind also*. The first without the second is folly; the second without the first is futile.

Application: For many Christians, our problem is not a disengaged mind, but a dormant spirit. While it is easy to indict those who pray in tongues, and thus fail to pray with their minds, many believers have engaged their minds, but not their spirits! They hide their spiritual emptiness behind a façade of pious orthodoxy. It is sad that many believers have sought spiritual nurture in mindless utterances. It is also sad that other believers have, in avoiding the former, clung to biblical truth, yet grown lifeless spiritually.

---

16   Paul determines to pray and sing with both the spirit and the mind because (ἐπεὶ, *Otherwise*), he reasons, *if you bless in the spirit only, how will the one who fills the place of the ungifted say the "Amen" at your giving of thanks, since he does not know what you are saying?*

Translational/Interpretive Note: Paul's reference to the "ungifted" person has raised questions: Who is this unnamed person? Some think this is an "outsider" (unbeliever; RSV), but Paul seems to have in mind a member of the assembly. Others have suggested a "second-class Christian" somewhere between unbelievers and full-fledged Christians (cf. Fee, 672, n. 42), but there is no such thing. This is most likely a subtle reference to all the other believers in the assembly, who, when a person rises to give blessing and thanks to God in an unknown tongue and there is no interpreter, cannot affirm (*say the "Amen"* to) what he says, since they cannot understand him.

As throughout this section, Paul is concerned for intelligibility. Tongues without interpretation were meaningless; hence, no one could agree with the speaker.

17   Paul is willing to grant that the speaker is *giving thanks well enough*; regardless, *the other man* (that is, all others in the meeting) *is not edified.* After all is said and done, it is such edification for which the spiritual gifts are given. If tongues are not interpreted,

there is no way that they can build up the body, and they should not occur in the public worship of the church.

18-19   With a touch of the dramatic, Paul concludes his discussion of tongues and edification. He declares, *I thank God, I speak in tongues more than you all.* As an apostle, it comes as no surprise that Paul had been given an abundance of the sign gifts (cf. 2 Cor. 12:12). But when and where did Paul speak in tongues? Not in church!

He immediately makes this clear, with emphasis! He writes that *in the church I desire to speak five words with my mind, that I may instruct others also, rather than ten thousand words in a tongue.*

Clearly, Paul spoke in tongues somewhere other than the church assembly. Where? It is often suggested that this indicates Paul practiced private prayer in tongues (Fee, 674ff; Conzelmann, 238) while praying intelligibly in public worship. But is this consistent with the purpose of spiritual gifts?

As spiritual gifts were given by God to each one for the common good of the body (12:7), they each have a role in the proper growth and functioning of the church. Each spiritual gift finds its purpose in meeting the needs of the body. The idea that the gift of tongues was primarily for private prayer cannot be sustained in this light. So what was the intended context for tongues, and where did Paul speak them?

Some spiritual gifts, and gifted people, were specifically for the foundational period when the church was being established (e.g., apostles, prophets; cf. Eph. 2:20). Some gifts were given especially for the communication of truth within the body (prophecy, knowledge, teaching, exhortation). Some provided for the maintenance and growth of the church (helps, administration, giving, faith, service). Some were primarily useful for heralding the church's gospel to the world (evangelism, healings, miracles). It is in this final category that the gift of tongues seems chiefly to fit. The gift served as an attention-getter at Pentecost (Acts 2:4-13). Tongues were given for a sign, not to those who believe, but to unbelievers (1 Cor. 14:22). While confirmatory of the apostolic office (2 Cor. 12:12), tongues (speaking in unknown languages) served as divine authentication of the apostolic message (Heb. 2:3-4).

When and where did Paul speak in tongues? It was not in the public meeting of the church, nor a private prayer-language; most likely it was on his missionary journeys. Perhaps with those whose language he did not know, tongues was a sign to unbelievers (14:22). The fact that Paul goes on to provide rules for the practice of tongues in the assembly does not mean that was what Paul wanted. The practice of tongues-speaking in Corinth was out of control. Paul was satisfied to see it controlled; it could then serve its evangelistic purpose. Furthermore, by being controlled, the gift of tongues would become less prominent in Corinth, and in time cease to be a problem altogether (Orr/ Walther, 310).

14:20-25   [The Corinthians should desire the exercise of the gift of prophecy over tongues in church because prophecy convicts unbelievers, while tongues do not.]

20   With a reaffirmation of his readers' spiritual condition (*Brethren*; cf. 3:1), Paul exhorts them to grow up in their thinking: *do not be children* (παιδία) *in your thinking; yet in evil be babes, but in your thinking be mature.* The Corinthians had shown a penchant for confused thinking—a result of their failure to distinguish between God's and man's wisdom (see 1:18-25; 3:18ff; 8:1-3) which in turn resulted in them having a knowledge of truth, yet practicing evil. Evidently, their emphasis on tongues in church was yet another illustration of this. Paul wants them to mature in their thinking and avoid evil. In particular, he wants them to see that prophecy is preferred over tongues in the assembly. To that end, he provides one final argument.

21-22   To begin, Paul appeals to the authority of the scriptures (*the Law*); he cites Isaiah 28:11-12, then provides an explanation: *"By men of strange tongues and by the lips of strangers I will speak to this people, and even so they will not listen to me," says the Lord. So then tongues are for a sign, not to those who believe, but to unbelievers; but prophecy [is for a sign], not to unbelievers, but to those who believe.*

Why Paul refers to Isaiah 28 is debated. Some suggest (Fee, 679f; Barrett, 322f) that Paul was drawn to the quote only because of the occurrence of the words "other tongues" and the fact that these tongues did not result in the hearers believing (thus, they are of no value to them). The problem with this view is that Paul goes on to indicate that tongues *do* have value to unbelievers (they are a sign to them), but not in the gathering of believers. As a Pharisee trained in the teaching of the Law (Phil 2:5f), Paul would have been aware of the context of Isaiah 28. The prophet declares that because of their unbelief, God will speak to Israel through unintelligible (to them) languages (that of their Assyrian captors). This foreign tongue will be a sign to them that they are under His judgment (Lowery, 539).

The gift of tongues, Paul says, functions in a similar way, showing unbelievers that they have failed to hear God's message. It is a sign not to those inside, but those outside the church; "not to those who believe, but to unbelievers." Inside the church, among believers, prophecy is the preferred gift.

23   Paul now demonstrates the truth of his point with two contrasting hypothetical situations. The first setting has curious unbelievers entering a church in which all are speaking in tongues: *If therefore the whole church should assemble together and all speak in tongues, and ungifted men or unbelievers enter, will they not say that you are mad?* While tongues *outside* the church signify the failure of unbelievers to hear God's message, inside the church they exhibit confusion! Those who are unbelievers will be led to conclude that Christians are crazy (μαίνομαι = "out of one's mind;" cf. BAGD, 486; John 10:20).

24-25   On the contrary, *if all prophesy, and an unbeliever or an ungifted man enters, he is convicted by all, he is called to account by all; the secrets of his heart are disclosed.* The unbeliever who enters hears of the power and love of God. He becomes aware of God's holiness, and His righteous judgment on sin. He understands the need of his heart, and the great gift of God made available through Jesus Christ for that need. As a result, *he will fall on his face and worship God, declaring that God is certainly among you.* This is an admission by the outsider that what he has heard is true, and that he accepts it. With all speaking in tongues, he is confused; when all prophesy, he is converted. Paul's point is made: The Corinthians should desire the exercise of the gift of prophecy over tongues in church.

Practical Note: It is common for churches today to try to attract unbelievers to their services. Sometimes, though not always, this involves a "watering down" or "sugar-coating" of the message. This is viewed as an aid in reaching the lost—bringing the gospel down to their level. It is unlikely, however, that Paul would endorse it. In Corinth, a city with great spiritual need, no "show" of tongues is called for. No "bait" is used to lure outsiders to come. And if they did come, no adjustment in the message was made. Rather, that which profited the assembly of believers (prophecy; 14:3) was practiced. The result of this is "evangelism"! In short, Paul is saying that in the church assembly, the best "evangelism" is to expound the teaching of God, so that any unbelievers who come in will become aware of the difference between their spiritual condition and the spiritual condition of believers. When this happens, they become convicted of sin, and are drawn to the provision of Jesus Christ as Savior from their sin.

Homiletic Note: The fundamental message of this section is the desirability of prophecy over tongues in the public church meeting in Corinth. The *reasons* for this, however, remain important in the church today. Paul emphasizes two things: In the church, believers should practice that which edifies the body, and also serve to convict unbelievers. In Corinth, this meant that prophecy, not speaking in tongues, was needed. This was because prophecy was intelligible, while tongues were not.

In a modern setting, Paul's reasoning suggests some further applications. What activities (traditions) do churches practice which do not build up the body? Have we allowed ourselves to become like the Corinthians—having our favorite "gifts" (or gifted people) and emphasizing them, remaining comfortable in our secure identity, but avoiding those things which would challenge our lethargy?

On a personal level, does our witness for Jesus Christ sometimes confuse the gospel rather than clarifying it? Do we speak in "tongues" (spiritual language) which is confusing and unintelligible to unbelievers, or do we clearly communicate their need because of sin, and Christ's provision on the cross?

To a church which has lost its way (and to a large degree, the modern church has), we may derive two lessons from what Paul writes:

1) Pursue open and clear ways of communicating in the assembly which will result in believers being strengthened and challenged in their faith, and

2) Proclaim the deep truths of scripture which both edify believers and evangelize unbelievers, instead of a diluted message which will accomplish neither.

14:26-36 *The Corinthians should follow rules for conduct in the public meeting of the church that will build up the body.*

26   Paul's case for the exercise of the gift of prophecy in church instead of tongues is complete. He now turns his attention to the practical ramifications of this teaching. He rhetorically asks, *"What is the outcome then, brethren?"* (or "With this instruction in mind, how should it affect what we do?"; see v.15). *When you assemble, each one has a psalm, has a teaching, has a revelation, has a tongue, has an interpretation.* This may be a subtle way of suggesting what *should*

be going on in church (Fee, 690). It is more likely, however, that Paul is stating what was already going on in Corinth (Grosheide, 335). The believers had a deeply ingrained individualism, resulting in *each one* focusing only on his own gift, rather than on what was good for the body (Martin, *The Spirit and the Congregation*, p.78). Paul thus states the guiding principle which should govern the expression of all such gifts in church: *Let all things be done for edification* (14:5, 12). As verse 40 makes clear, edification requires that all things be done with propriety and order.

Translation Note: The NIV here (*All of these must be done for the strengthening of the church*) can be misleading. Edification (οἰκοδομὴν) *is* spiritual *strengthening*, but entails other elements as well (encouragement, conviction, instruction, etc.). Furthermore, the word order makes it sound like Paul was saying that an occurrence of *all* these things (psalms, teaching, revelations, tongues, interpretations) are necessary for the strengthening of the church. Paul's emphasis is not on having every gift represented in each service, but on having any gift which is used serving to build up the whole body.

27-28 While the exercise of any gift requires the proper time and place, Paul is concerned only with tongues and prophecy in this context. He begins by regulating the exercise of tongues in church. *If anyone speaks in a tongue, it should be by two or at the most three, and each in turn, and let one interpret.* The number of tongues-speakers is limited to prevent the gift continuing to dominate their meetings. Two guidelines are then added to insure these tongues edify the church. First, each one is to speak in turn (no mass participation); secondly, each message is to be interpreted. With this second guideline Paul returns to the issue of intelligibility (vv.1-25); the ability of all in the assembly to understand what has been shared is so important that *if there is no interpreter*, the tongues-speaker must *keep silent in the church*. Instead, he is to *speak to himself and to God*, perhaps to request the gift of interpretation for himself (v.13) so he might exercise his gift.

29 As tongues are restricted in the assembly, so too is prophecy. The initial wording is similar to verse 27: *And let two or three prophets speak, and let the others pass judgment.* Unlike with tongues, Paul is not here restricting them to two or three prophets in a given service. The omission of "at the most" (τὸ πλεῖστον; v.27) and the allowance that "you can all prophesy one by one" (v.31; cf. v.24) suggests that only two or three prophets should speak before the others pass judgment (Fee, 693). Passing judgment (cf. διακρίνω, BAGD, 185) may refer to the exercise of the gift of distinguishing of spirits (12:10), or simply signify a general time for all to assess how a new revelation stacked up against already-revealed truth (cf. Rom. 12:6).

30 *But if a revelation is made to another who is seated, let the first keep silent.* A prophetic message might be received before the church gathering, or during it. If one was standing and sharing, and another received a revelation at that time, the first one was to give way to the more recent prophecy.

31-32 This should not be a problem, because there was time for *all* to *prophesy one by one, so that all may learn and all may be exhorted.* Since *the spirits of prophets are subject to prophets*, there would be no difficulty in stopping or restraining a prophecy for a time. Unlike pagan seers who entered a state of "ecstasy" and were "carried away" in their delirium, those bearing inspired messages in the church are always under control.

33 By observing these guidelines, the Corinthian church would begin to reflect the character of God in their services—*for God is not a God of confusion but of peace.* Confusion (ἀκαταστασία; BAGD, 30) results when there is jealousy and selfish ambition (cf. Jas. 3:16), something the Corinthian church had plenty of! By yielding to the need for the whole body to be edified, they would instead promote peace. This was the standard to be observed *in all the churches of the saints.*

> **Interpretive Note:** Many commentators read this final phrase
> as the introduction to the following restriction on women speaking
> in the assembly (Grosheide, 341; Ralph Martin, *The Spirit and
> the Congregation*, 83; Orr/Walther, 311; MacArthur, 392; Lowery,
> 540), but this creates an awkward repetition—"in all the churches"
> followed in the same sentence by "in the churches" (Barrett, 330).
> Since Paul's other uses of such appeals in this letter always conclude
> a sentence or section (4:17; 7:17; 11:16; cf. Fee, 698), it seems best
> to read it so here.

34-35 Some commentators suggest that these verses may not be original
(Fee, 699-710; Conzelmann, 246; Barrett, 330-33). One problem
is a seeming contradiction between these verses and the assumed
prophetic role of women in 11:5 (Barrett). Others think the text
flows better if v.33 is followed directly by v.36, and that vv.34-
35 are really an intrusion into Paul's train of thought (Fee, 701f;
see Conzelmann, 246, who suggests that the entire section from
33b-36 is an interpolation). But in light of these arguments, one
is hard-pressed to imagine how these verses—if not original—
ever came to be an accepted part of the letter! There is *no* support
in the textual tradition for the omission of these verses. Frankly,
the real reason for deleting Paul's words here seems to be that
some today disagree with the apostle. Evangelical feminism has
caused many to gag on any restriction on the role of women in the
church. Paul had no such qualms, and the evidence supports the
authenticity of these two verses.

There is no difficulty in reconciling Paul's instruction here with
11:5. In the earlier passage, he indicated only that a woman should
have her head covered while praying or prophesying. Now, in the
context of restrictions on prophesying in the assembly, he writes:
*Let the women keep silent in the churches; for they are not permitted to
speak, but let them subject themselves, just as the Law also says.* That
Paul should dare to make such a seemingly absolute prohibition

is unacceptable to many Christians today. But perhaps the prohibition is not so absolute. While many reasons for Paul's words have been offered (cf. Ralph Martin, *The Spirit and the Congregation*, 85-87), one has been almost totally overlooked: Paul may have been addressing this restriction to married women *only*. A number of factors make this interpretation most likely (see Orr/Walther, 312f; Lowery, 541).

The word translated *women* (γυναῖκες; see γυνή, BAGD, 168) is used by Paul in this letter to refer to women in general (11:5-15), and specifically to unmarried women (7:34), engaged women (7:27), and married women (5:1; 7:2-4, 10-14, 16, 29, 33, 39; 9:5). Context determines the usage. The first clue that Paul is speaking only to *wives* here is his call for them to *subject themselves* (cf. ὑποτάσσω; BAGD, 847f). But to whom are they to subject themselves? Nowhere does Paul use this verb in relation to women in general; it is always directed to wives (Eph. 5:22; Col. 3:18; Titus 2:5). That he is speaking here to married women is further confirmed by what follows: *And if they desire to learn anything, let them ask their own husbands at home; for it is improper for a woman to speak in church.* Clearly, Paul is talking to wives!

Paul's instruction is that a wife sitting in church with her husband should honor him by keeping silent, reflecting her submissiveness. Other women are free to pray and prophesy with heads covered, in keeping with 11:1-16.

36   The role of women in the church was evidently a contentious one in Corinth (cf. 11:16), and there were also many who were less than supportive of Paul's apostleship. To prevent resistance to this instruction, Paul uses sarcasm to confront their arrogance (cf. 4:7ff). *Was it from you that the word of God first went forth? Or has it come to you only?* His point is obvious; they are neither the fountain nor the preserve of truth. They share a common source of knowledge with all the churches of the saints (v.33). Although they had an exalted view of themselves, they had not evidenced

spiritual wisdom. On this issue, they once again needed to stop fighting God, and start obeying Him.

14:37-40 *Paul declares that his instruction is from the Lord and the Corinthians should therefore desire prophecy over tongues, and order in all things.*

37-38   Paul now steps back from the specific regulations of the previous verses, and sums up all his comments concerning spiritual gifts in Corinth. Twice before in this letter he has confronted the Corinthians' delusion concerning their own capabilities. In 3:18, it was their perceived wisdom; in 8:2, their knowledge. Here, in keeping with the overall context, he confronts *anyone* who *thinks he is a prophet or spiritual* (πνευματικός; 12:1; 14:1; cf. 2:15).

Those who considered themselves spiritually adroit, yet were prone to confront Paul's teaching, were stopped short. Just as a test of a prophet in the Old Testament was the truth of his prophecy (cf. Deut. 13:1-5; 18:20-22), so too in the New Testament. The Apostle Paul spoke not his own words, but God's word, which is truth (John 17:17). Therefore, he could challenge those in Corinth who touted themselves as spokesmen for God and His people to *"recognize that the things which I write to you are the Lord's commandment."* In 7:25, Paul wrote that he had "no command of the Lord," but that he was giving "an opinion as one who by the mercy of the Lord is trustworthy" (cf. 7:40). This did not diminish the authority of what he said, however. Here he expresses this fact clearly; *if anyone does not recognize* that what he says as an apostle is the same as God's commandment, *he is not recognized* (ἀγνοεῖται).

Translation Note: The Greek word ἀγνοέω is variously translated. While it can mean to "not recognize" (NASV) or to "ignore" (NIV), these renderings suggest a willful disregard for and disobedience to Paul's instruction. Paul had other terms which would have

---

addressed this (cf. παρέρχομαι, Luke 11:42; 15:29; καταστρηνιάω, 1 Tim. 5:11; περιφρονέω, Tit. 2:15), but ἀγνοέω conveys the idea of one being "ignorant" (BAGD, 11; cf. NKJV; "agnostic"). Paul seems to be saying that if anyone (especially among those who think they are spiritual) is 'ignorant' of the authority of his words, the rest of the church should treat him as one who is ignorant.

39   What is the sum of Paul's instruction? First, addressing the issue of prophecy and tongues, he states that believers (*my brethren*) in Corinth should *desire earnestly to prophesy*. While this is the preferred gift, they are to *not forbid to speak in tongues*, assuming, of course, that there is an interpreter present, and other conditions are also observed. This verse effectively summarizes 14:1-25.

40   In order for any and all sharing of gifts in the church to result in edification, the guidelines in 14:26-36 must also be observed. Paul concludes, therefore, with an appeal that *all things be done properly and in an orderly manner*. To do something *properly* (εὐσχημόνως; BAGD, 327) includes the idea of acting in such a way that those outside the church would see Christ (Rom. 13:13; 1 Thess. 4:12). Perhaps Paul was thinking of 14:23ff when he included this.

With this summary Paul concludes his teaching on spiritual gifts in general, and the problem of the Corinthian misuse of tongues in particular. His teaching has been both gracious and firm. A correct understanding of spiritual gifts results in no gift being sought over others; instead, all gifts are divinely given to fulfill the needs of the body. Furthermore, without love, any exercise of gifts is fruitless and futile. With this in mind, however, the church as a whole should desire the exercise of those gifts in the public assembly which will both edify the body, and convict unbelievers. This means that prophecy is desired over tongues (though tongues are allowed, if there is an interpreter), and that all sharing must be done in a proper and orderly way.

Homiletical Note: As is often the case in this epistle, Paul's instructions find a ready context in contemporary Christianity. Christians often 'bounce' from one church to another, or one service to another within a church, all in pursuit of a certain worship experience. While pursuing excellence in worship is laudable, too often individual likes trump unity in the body. All that is done in the church should build up the body; therefore, guidelines, structure, and limitations are needed. Furthermore, the most profitable gifts for the body as a whole need to be given priority in the public gathering, not just those which individual worshippers may desire.

Distilled down to the basics, Paul's teaching in 14:26-40 is that 1) all things be done for edification (26), 2) any confusion be avoided (33, 40), and 3) in this area, as in all areas, the commandments of the Lord—not the cravings of the flock—be followed.

E. QUESTIONS CONCERNING THE RESURRECTION ARE DISCUSSED (15:1-58)

Paul now confronts an issue which was at the heart of the Corinthian problem. All their failings—divisions, pride, immorality, idolatry, taking each other to court—are a result of contaminating divine truth with human wisdom. This tendency is now again evidenced by some in the fellowship doubting the future resurrection of believers from the dead (15:12; cf. 6:13ff, where this view had disastrous results). Just how these believers came to this position is unclear (see Ralph P. Martin, 129; Fee, 715f), but one thing is sure: It was in part a result of them diluting God's revelation with human knowledge.

Paul has confronted their attraction to human knowledge throughout this letter (1:26-31; 2:5, 11-16; 3:18-23; 4:10; 6:5-6; 8:1; etc.). His oft-repeated *Do you not know...?* (3:16; 5:6; 6:2, 3, 9, 15, 16, 19; 9:13, 24) is his way of reminding them that while they have knowledge, there are many things they have failed to apprehend the things pertaining to God.

His decision to leave the discussion of the resurrection until the end of the letter is significant. It is no mistake that he both begins and ends this epistle with arguments concerned with the content of the gospel message. In 1:18-25, he showed that their divisions were caused by a misunderstanding of the gospel. Human wisdom taught that the message of *Christ crucified* was foolishness; Paul countered that while the gospel was foolishness to those who are perishing, it was God's power for those being saved (1:18)! At that point of the letter, however, he focused only on the *crucifixion* of Christ (1:17, 18, 23; 2:2).

Now, addressing the questions some in the church had concerning the bodily resurrection of believers, he again points to the gospel message—focusing here on the *resurrection* of Christ—to show the error of their thinking. Once again, mixing human wisdom with the gospel message does not result in clarity, but confusion. In this case, it is the blessed future hope of resurrection that is sacrificed on the altar of human knowledge.

Thus, beginning with a review of the gospel message, followed by logical and practical arguments, Paul reveals that their denial of the coming resurrection is not wisdom, but foolishness (1-34). This leads to a further discussion of *how* the dead will be raised (35-58). In response to fools (v.36) who denied it, Paul declares that the resurrection is of the *body*—but an imperishable, glorified, powerful, spiritual, heavenly body. This is the blessed hope, the final victory over death! Whatever the cost, therefore, we should thrive in working for the Lord, knowing that the resurrection is coming (58)!

15:1-34 *The future resurrection of believers is affirmed by showing its integral relationship to Christian faith in the gospel message, in the logical ramifications of Christ's resurrection, and in the current experience of believers.*

Paul's initial goal is to convince his readers that denying the future bodily resurrection of believers makes no sense. He "sets up" his argument by reminding his readers that the physical resurrection of Christ is central to the gospel message which he preached, and which they believed (1-11).

Having established this, he makes two logical arguments, one hypothetical, and the other historical. He first argues that *if* there is no resurrection of the dead, then Christ didn't rise, and therefore, the gospel is false (12-19). Conversely, *since* Christ has risen from the dead, the future bodily resurrection of all believers is must also be true (20-28).

Paul's final contention is that both his and their actions imply belief in a future resurrection (29-34). Why perpetuate the preaching of the gospel message if it provides no future promise? Why suffer for Christ and deny earthly pleasures if there is no reward coming? Why even avoid sin, if there is no resurrection—and thus no future judgment? But of course there is, and that is why the church continues to reach out to the lost, why Paul endures persecution, and why they should stop sinning.

1-11   [The historical bodily resurrection of Christ is central to the gospel message the Corinthians have believed.]

1-2   Paul begins his discussion of the resurrection by *making known to* his readers that the resurrection of Christ is a fundamental element of the *gospel*. The verb γνωρίζω ("to make known;" BAGD, 163) usually pertains to something previously unknown, but not so here. The Corinthians knew the gospel; in fact, they had *received* it, and were standing firm (ἵστημι; BAGD, 382; cf. 2 Cor. 1:24; John 8:44) in it. They need to be reminded of it, however, because the resurrection was central to it, and some of them, by denying the bodily resurrection of all believers, were tacitly denying the resurrection of Christ! This *had* escaped their notice. In order to build his case, Paul must first remind them of *"the gospel which I preached to you...by which also you are saved, if you hold fast the word which I preached to you, unless you believed in vain."*

What does Paul mean by the final conditional phrase, "if you hold fast the word which I preached to you, unless you believed in vain"? The Corinthians had *believed* and *received* his gospel message, and they *stand in* it (the perfect tense implies past action with continuing results). They clearly *are* believers! But does their 'final destiny'—eternal life—still depend on how they live? Is Paul saying that while believing the gospel saves us (perhaps only temporarily), we only *stay saved* if we "hold fast" to it?

This view arises from a misunderstanding of what being 'saved' means. Many wrongly equate it with salvation from hell. But the basic meaning of 'saved' (σώζω, v.2) is to be *delivered* or *preserved*. In the Bible, this deliverance can be from many different things (sickness, death, peril, demons, sin). In this context we must ask, *what* will the Corinthian believers be saved from if they "hold fast the word which I preached to you"?

Even a cursory knowledge of the circumstances in the church at Corinth provides the answer: The Corinthian believers were fighting (and losing) battles with sin. Paul wants them to be *saved* (delivered) from lives of defeat because of sin. The present tense (*you are [being] saved*) refers to their lives *now*, not in the eternal future. If the Corinthian believers do not hold fast to Paul's gospel—if they deny the resurrection of Christ—they will not be saved from the effects of sinful living that have plagued them.

What of the final phrase, *unless you believed in vain*? It is possible that Paul was anticipating his argument in verses 12-19. In this view, the Corinthians would have *believed in vain* ("to no purpose," εἰκῇ; cf. BAGD, 222) if the gospel they had believed were in fact *not true*. If Christ did not rise from the dead, then both Paul's preaching and the Corinthians' faith was *vain* (cf. v.14; without result or profit; κενός, BAGD, 427). If this is Paul's meaning, he wants the Corinthians to understand the importance of the doctrine of bodily resurrection; those who deny the doctrine of believers' future resurrection are actually undermining the salvation message they believed! *If their current view that there is no resurrection is correct, then Christ did not rise, which in turn means that they have believed in vain. If they are right, everything is a lie, and they cease to exist as believers altogether* (cf. Fee, 721).

But it is best to connect both parts of Paul's conditional phrase in verse 2. The intended goal of believing the gospel is not simply deliverance from hell, but victorious life here and now! If the Corinthians do not *hold fast* to the gospel Paul preached (the death and resurrection of Christ), their spiritual life will be stunted. They will have 'believed in vain' because that faith did not produce the ongoing victory and power and spiritual maturity which it could have. No wonder this gospel is "of first importance" (v.3) to Paul! It delivers from hell and bestows eternal life when first believed, and delivers from the pernicious effects of sin if we hold fast to it. We must get the gospel right!

3   Paul now proceeds to lay out his gospel message: *For I delivered to you as of first importance what I also received.* The gospel message Paul preached was the same one *he* had believed. It was this

which he, in a moment of blinding light on the Damascus Road, suddenly realized. In the form of a confession, he now outlines the content of that gospel. The first truth is that *Christ died for* (ὑπέρ; see Lexical Note below) *our sins*. Perhaps to remind them this message does not arise from human wisdom (cf. 1:18-25), Paul adds that it is *according to the Scriptures* (in accord with Old Testament teaching). Redemptive images are replete in the Old Testament. There were historical events (like the Exodus); there was the sacrificial system, with its offerings which forecast the Coming One who would take the place of guilty sinners. And there is Isaiah 53, the prophetic foretelling of the One who "bore the sin of many, and interceded for the transgressors" (Isa. 53:12). This was no human fable; it was God's redemptive plan, foretold in the events and prophecies of the Old Testament.

Lexical Note: The preposition ὑπέρ (*for*) with the genitive describes a person doing something *on behalf of* (representation) or *in place of* (substitution) another person. This latter meaning is common in references to Christ dying for sinners (Rom 5:6-8; 2 Cor. 5:14). But ὑπέρ here refers to Christ dying not for *sinners*, but for *sins*. In cases like this, the preposition means *for the sake of*. A good interpretive translation here is: *Christ died to deal with our sin* (cf. DNTT, 3:1196f; Barrett, 338). This is why He died for us (*in our place*); He took sin and its repercussions on Himself (2 Cor. 5:21; Gal 3:13).

---

4   That Christ actually died is verified by the fact *that He was buried*. This also underscores the *bodily* aspect of the resurrection, the second tenet of the gospel: Christ was *raised on the third day according to the Scriptures*. Perhaps the reference to Old Testament teaching here points to Psalm 16:8-11, to which Peter appealed in his sermon on the Day of Pentecost (Acts 2:24-32).

5   Finally, the proof of Christ's resurrection is *that He appeared to Cephas* (Peter), *then to the twelve* (designating the disciples, even though after Judas' death, there were only eleven). Paul's

purpose is not to give a complete record of Jesus' resurrection appearances; indeed, the first witnesses of the risen Christ are omitted (cf. Matt. 28:1-10; John 20:11-29). Perhaps he includes only Peter and the other disciples here because of their status in the early church.

6-7   But there *were* many other witnesses. Paul states first that the risen Christ *appeared to more than five hundred brethren at one time, most of whom remain until now, but some have fallen asleep* (died; κοιμάω, BAGD, 437; 7:39; 11:30; 15:18, 20, 51). The power of these witnesses was that they were *living*. The testimony of those who had died was one thing; having living eyewitnesses who could testify to seeing the risen Lord was strong evidence of its veracity. After this, there was the appearance *to James* (the Lord's brother; cf. Gal. 1:19), *then to all the apostles* (possibly referring to the ascension). Although all of Jesus' brothers probably believed in Him after His resurrection (Acts 1:14), James is singled out because of his prominent place in the early church (Acts 12:17; 15:13; 21:18; Gal. 2:9). Jesus' appearance to James may have resulted in him and the other brothers believing in Him as the Son of God, which they did not believe in His earlier ministry (John 7:5).

8   Linking himself to this apostolic line (those who had seen the risen Christ; cf. 9:1), Paul now adds his own encounter with the Savior (Acts 9:1-9). He describes his induction into this elite group as being *to one untimely born* (ἐκτρώματι; BAGD, 246), a pejorative term reflecting both his late meeting with the Savior (after the ascension), and the feelings of some in Corinth that he was not on a par with the other apostles. While defending apostolic authority (14:37), Paul accepted his insignificance; he was no more than a servant of Christ (4:1), a minister of and by the grace of God (15:10).

9   The mention of his apostleship leads Paul to a short digression (9-10). Instead of attacking, he agrees with his detractors: *For I*

am the least (ἐλάχιστος, BAGD, 248; cf. Eph. 3:8) *of the apostles, who am not fit to be called an apostle, because I persecuted the church of God.* While some in Corinth may have looked down on Paul because of a supposed lack of wisdom or power or spirituality, he saw himself as 'unworthy' of apostolic honor because of his persecution of the church. What claim did he have to preach the gospel? He had once persecuted those who preached it! But though he felt unworthy to be a servant of Christ, he was willing (and felt privileged) by God's grace to do anything in fulfilling that service (4:9-13; 9:15-23).

10   Paul knew he did not *deserve* to be saved, much less to be numbered among the apostles! He confesses that *by the grace of God I am what I am.* The privilege of serving Christ was as much a gift of God's grace as eternal life (cf. Eph. 3:7-8). But while salvation was not of works (Eph. 2:8f), serving Christ was (Eph. 2:10)! It follows that nothing motivated Paul more than faithfully discharging his duty as an apostle. He therefore announces that *"His grace toward me did not prove vain"* (it was not without profit or effect; cf. κενός, BAGD, 427). The reason it did not was that Paul *labored even more than all of them* (the other apostles). This was not for him any reason to boast, however, since in all he did, it was *not I, but the grace of God with me* (cf. 1:30-31; 3:6). Paul had been made an apostle by God's grace, and by God's grace had faithfully executed his duties. The Corinthians themselves, in fact, were the proof of it (9:2; 2 Cor. 3:2f).

11   His digression completed, Paul returns to his main point—the content of the gospel message. It is that message of the death and resurrection of Christ which both Paul and the other apostles *preach*, and which the Corinthians *believed*. This is what he wanted to establish in this paragraph, and is the basis for the argument which follows: It is logically absurd to accept the bodily resurrection of Christ from the dead, but deny the future resurrection of believers.

Homiletical Ideas: Paul wrote this paragraph primarily to set up the following argument against those who were denying the resurrection, but it has much to say on its own. Two issues in particular are vital, and should be addressed when preaching the passage.

The first is the *content* of the message, which is critical in light of the unclear gospel preaching today. To put it simply, the content of the gospel (good news) is that *Christ died for our sins and rose from the dead.* That message is the power of God which saves those who *believe* it (vv.2, 11; cf. 1:18, 21; Rom. 1:16-17). Those who add to or subtract from this clear presentation are distorting the gospel. There is no other gospel (Acts 4:12). In particular, those who add a requirement of baptism, perseverance, or good works in addition to faith are undermining the saving message (Rom. 4:4-5). The *minimum* requirement is also the *maximum* requirement: *Believe* on the Lord Jesus Christ, and you will be saved (Acts 16:31).

The second issue here involves our *conviction* of the truth of the gospel message. Is it possible that we, like the Corinthians, could believe in the resurrection of Christ, yet fail to apprehend what it means for us—both now and in the future? Not only is this true, it is pervasive. How much less sin (cf. v.33), and how much more joy and impact on the world might Christians have if they really lived like Christ was alive, and that they would someday live with Him (cf. 1 Thess. 5:9-11)?

The first thing a person must do with the gospel is to *accept* it by faith, believing in Jesus Christ as personal Savior. The second thing a person must do with the gospel is *hold to* its significance in everyday life, living in daily fellowship with the risen Lord. The first of these leads to justification; the second leads to sanctification and victorious life (cf. v.10). Both aspects are part of the teaching of this paragraph.

12-19   [Logically, if the doctrine of bodily resurrection is false, then Christ did not rise, and faith in Him is worthless.]

12   The trap has been set, and Paul now walks the Corinthians straight into it. *Now if Christ is preached, that He has been raised from the dead* (and as Paul has just rehearsed, this is what he preached, and they believed), *how do some among you say that there is no resurrection of the dead?* The gospel message was nothing without the resurrection; if Christ was not risen, there was no *good news*. A crucified and buried Christ might evoke adulation and praise from devout followers, but if that is the end of the story, He is no different from a myriad of spiritual leaders throughout history. Only a *risen* Christ stands apart from the rest.

The Corinthians all professed this; but they had failed to see that by denying the resurrection of the dead, they were also tacitly denying the resurrection of Christ.

13   It is this logical connection Paul wants them to see, so he announces it (the first of three times; cf. vv.15, 16): *But if there is no resurrection of the dead, not even Christ has been raised.* If what they say about the resurrection of the dead is true, then what they believe about Jesus Christ is false!

14   And what difference does it make *if Christ has not been raised?* Two results which strike at the heart of their faith: First, *our* (Paul's and the other apostles') *preaching is vain*, and secondly, *your* (the Corinthians') *faith also is vain* (κενός; cf. v.10 above). Why is this so?

15-16   In the first place, Paul and the other apostles, as those who have preached this gospel, *are even found to be false witnesses of God, because we witnessed against God that He raised Christ whom He did not raise, if in fact the dead are not raised.* Paul preached Christ was risen; if what the Corinthians said about there being no resurrection was true, then Paul's message was false! Both cannot be right. *For if the dead are not raised, not even Christ has been raised!*

17-19 Worse yet are the results for the Corinthians themselves! For *if Christ has not been raised, your faith is worthless* (empty, useless, powerless, lacking truth; μάταιος; BAGD, 495; cf. 3:20); *you are still in your sins.* A false gospel, no matter how sincerely preached or how firmly believed, can never save. So if Christ did not rise, they have no past salvation, and no future hope! Of course, this means that *those also who have fallen asleep* (died; cf. 15:6) *in Christ have perished.* To be "in Christ" (ἐν Χριστῷ) is Paul's way of identifying believers (1:2, 30; 2 Cor. 5:17). To "perish" (ἀπόλλυμι, BAGD, 95) refers not to the end of physical life, but to eternal death (cf. DNTT, 1:464); it is the antithesis of eternal life (John 3:16; cf. 2 Thess. 1:8-9). The scalpel of Paul's logic has fully exposed the cancer of their theology. No one would quarrel with his conclusion: *If we have hoped in Christ in this life only, we are of all men most to be pitied* (most miserable of all men; cf. ἐλεεινός, BAGD, 249; Rev. 3:17). Their doctrine may have grown out of human wisdom, but it led to spiritual despair.

Homiletical Ideas: What difference would it make if Christ had in fact not risen from the dead? Besides losing the Easter holiday (the meaning of which has long since been eclipsed by bunnies, baskets, and colored eggs), would it make any difference? Paul answers with a resounding "Yes!" in this paragraph, and Christians need to be reminded of the centrality of the resurrection to our present (and future) lives regularly.

But beyond this, Paul's argument forces us to assess our convictions in two areas. First, do we *really* believe Christ rose from the dead? It is clear that Paul believed in the resurrection of Christ from the dead as an actual event—not an existential "spiritual" idea with no historical veracity. It is not uncommon for Christians today to talk about "what Christ means to me," but the real meaning of Christ's resurrection is that those who believe in Him are saved forever. This is based not on feelings or impressions, but on the fact that it really happened in human history. (Christian singer-songwriter Don

Francisco's *He's Alive!* captures well the emotion we should feel as we contemplate the reality of the resurrection.)

Secondly, do we *really* believe in the future resurrection of *our* body? If so, what difference will that make in how we live? Modern science has conditioned us to question the supernatural, and some Christians—while accepting the truth of Jesus' resurrection—may waver when it comes to their own future resurrection. After all, it sounds like something a Hollywood New Age guru might espouse! *The resurrection of Christ two thousand years ago we can believe; but what about us, and today?* Paul forces us in this paragraph to shed the artificial distinction between our experience and Christ's. If we doubt our own resurrection, we have not yet understood the full significance of Christ's resurrection. Christ's resurrection guarantees our future resurrection. It therefore removes the doom of physical death as the finality of our existence (15:51-57). It keeps our focus on the eternal, not the temporal. And it gives us a proper perspective on this life, and the next (cf. Phil. 1:20-23; Col. 3:1-4). How much more would we be willing to face danger and endure hardship for Christ if we lived like we believed in our own resurrection? Songwriter Bill Gaither has put it well:

> *Because He lives, I can face tomorrow;*
> *Because He lives, all fear is gone;*
> *Because I know, He holds the future,*
> *And life is worth the living, just because He lives.*

20-28   [Logically, since Christ has indeed risen from the dead, those who have believed in Him will also be raised at His second coming.]

20   The despair of verses 12-19 now gives way to a joyful proclamation of the resurrection of Christ and all believers in Him. Paul had been arguing that *if* there is no resurrection, then not even Christ had been raised. But of course, Christ *had* risen, a fact which both he and the Corinthians believed. It was verified

by numerous appearances, some of the eyewitnesses still living (vv.5-8). Just as the Corinthians' denial of the resurrection of the dead implied Christ had not risen, so too the fact that Christ had risen proved that the resurrection of the dead was in fact true. So Paul announces (in contrast to the hypothetical *if Christ has not been raised* in vv.14, 17), *But now Christ has been raised from the dead,* (*and has become;* NKJV) *the first fruits* (v.23) *of those who are asleep* (cf. v.18; lit. *have fallen asleep* [perfect tense]).

"First-fruits" (ἀπαρχὴ; BAGD, 81) is a technical term which referred to sacrificial offerings. According to Old Testament Law, the firstborn of animals (cf. Exod. 22:29-30) and first-fruits of the field were given to God (Exod. 34:26; Lev. 23:9-14; Deut. 26:2), anticipating the bountiful harvest season ahead. In the New Testament, the term means simply the "first" of many. Early Jewish believers were a "kind of first fruits" of all believers that would follow (Jas. 1:18). Initial converts in a region were called the first fruits of that area (16:15; Rom. 16:5; cf. 1 Clem. 42:4. Here, Paul refers to Christ as the first of many who will rise from the dead, the anticipation of a "bountiful harvest" of saints! His resurrection is God's guarantee that those who have fallen asleep in Christ (v.18) will rise. The future resurrection of believers is as sure as the past resurrection of Christ.

21-22   The reason (signaled by "For," γὰρ) Christ's resurrection insures the resurrection of all believers is now explained; *since by a man came death, by a man also came the resurrection of the dead.* Paul then makes his reference specific: *For as in Adam all die, so also in Christ all shall be made alive* (ζωοποιέω; cf. BAGD, 341f).

How did death enter the world? Through the sin of Adam. The results of this sin have impacted all mankind; *through one man sin entered into the world, and death through sin, and so death spread to all men, because all sinned* (Rom. 5:12).

Scripture is clear that no one can avoid sinning (Eccl. 7:20; Rom. 3:10-12, 23; 1 John 1:10). While Adam had the ability not to sin, and by so doing to experience immortality, when he disobeyed, both he and the entire human race *lost* the ability not to sin. Mankind thus fell under a collective death penalty (Gen 2:17; 3:19; Kistemaker, 549).

This highlights why it was necessary for Christ to come in flesh as a man (cf. 1 John 4:2). In order to reverse the effects of the fall, the problem of sin had to be addressed. Since it was through a man that sin entered the world, so too it was through a man that the sin problem would be dealt with. This God accomplished in Christ; *He made Him who knew no sin to be sin on our behalf, that we might become the righteousness of God in Him* (2 Cor. 5:21). In Adam (*the first man*; v.45), sin had entered into the world, and death through sin (Rom. 5:12ff). In the man Christ Jesus (*the last Adam*, v.45; cf. Rom. 5:15; 1 Tim. 2:5), sin and death were defeated; His resurrection from the dead was the end of their reign (Rom. 5:13).

Theological Note: Paul's statement that *in Christ all shall be made alive* is not endorsing the Universalist doctrine of the ultimate salvation of all men. The 'dead' of whom Paul speaks are those who have died *in Christ* (v.18). To paraphrase Paul, "For as *all those who are* in Adam all die, so also *all those who are* in Christ all shall be made alive." To be "made alive" points to the future resurrection, which is the guarantee to all who have received by faith the free gift of eternal life, made available to all by the death and resurrection of Christ, but only received by those who believe in Him.

It should also be noted that, while all who die will be resurrected, some to life, and others to judgment (cf. John 5:28f), this is not Paul's point here. There is a resurrection of the unsaved dead (Rev. 20:11-15); Paul is concerned only with *believers* who have died (cf. 1 Thess. 4:16).

23   Why is the resurrection of believers so certain? Because it is an

integral part of the sequence of events that will culminate in the end of time. The resurrection of Christ, as well as of those who are in Christ, is part of this sequence. *But each is resurrected in his own order: Christ the first fruits* (v.20), *after that those who are Christ's at His coming.* Again, Paul is not giving detail about future resurrections here (cf. Charles C. Ryrie, *Basic Theology* [Wheaton: Victor Books, 1986], 518, for a concise overview of future resurrections). He is showing that the future resurrection of believers is just as much a part of redemption history as is the past resurrection of Christ. When Christ returns, he will take those who are His to be with Himself (John 14:3). No time frame is given for this resurrection, but already a period of nearly 2000 years has elapsed (cf. Bruce, 146).

24   After this *(then) comes the end.* Again, no time frame is given (cf. εἶτα; BAGD, 233f), which is not surprising, since it was not Paul's purpose to explain end-time events. Those who use Paul's failure to mention the millennial kingdom here as grounds for denying it (Kistemaker, 552) do so without basis. Paul is not giving a comprehensive review of end-time events. His concise commentary in v.23 concealed a period of already nearly 2000 years; why not a kingdom of 1000 years here (Lowery, 544)? In fact, it is this *kingdom* which Christ *delivers up...to the God and Father.*

Christ's earthly kingdom reign is the culmination of God's program to exalt Jesus Christ. It was God's plan which sent Christ to the cross (Acts 2:23). It was God who raised Him from the dead (Acts 2:24, 32). It is God who has highly exalted Him (Phil. 2:9-11). In the Millennial Kingdom, this exaltation will be realized on earth. At the end of the thousand years, Christ will hand over His kingdom to God the Father, who gave it to Him. This will happen *when He has abolished all rule and all authority and power.* The terms *rule, authority,* and *power* represent spiritual forces of darkness. Scripture affirms that Christ will abolish (καταργέω) Satan and his evil minions at the end of His earthly millennial reign (cf. Rev. 20:7-10).

25-26   Associated with this final victory is the abolishing of the greatest enemy, death. The defeat of death was sealed when Christ rose from the dead (2 Tim. 1:10), but it will be the last foe finally abolished by Christ. *For He must reign until He has put all His enemies under His feet. The last enemy that will be abolished is death.* While Paul here distinctly states that Christ's final victory over His enemies is yet future, other passages (Eph. 1:20ff; Col. 2:10) suggest this has already taken place. The solution is likely that the ultimate victory of Christ over sin and death was *sealed* at His resurrection, but will finally and fully be *realized* only at the end. Paul anticipates that which is sure in the Ephesians and Colossians passages (proleptic, or prophetic use of the aorist and present tenses, respectively). God's victory over the last enemy, death, is not in doubt; it will occur at the end of the Millennial Kingdom (cf. Rev. 20:11-15). Paul's point in all this, of course, is to illustrate that Christ's resurrection directly guarantees the future resurrection of all who are in Christ.

27   The reason Christ must reign until all enemies, including death, are abolished, is because (γὰρ) *He* (God the Father) *has put all things in subjection under His* (Christ's) *feet.* This citation from Ps. 8:6 indicates that God has already decreed this final outcome. What began at Christ's resurrection will be completed at the final resurrection of all who are in Christ.

This does not mean, however, that God the Father will be subject to Christ. Paul provides a brief commentary on the Psalmist's words: *But when he* (the psalmist) *says, "All things are put in subjection," it is evident that He* (God the Father) *is excepted who put all things in subjection to Him* (Christ).

28   At the end, *when all things are subjected to Him* (Christ), *then the Son Himself also will be subjected to the One* (God the Father) *who subjected all things to Him, that God may be all in all.* When God's redemption history is finally completed and the last enemy has been abolished, God's will and design for all things will be restored. Fallen mankind will be saved, and be God's inheritance

of saints (Eph. 1:18), spiritually raised from the dead and seated with Christ in the heavenly places (Eph. 2:1-6), an eternal exhibition of His great grace in the ages to come (Eph. 2:7). All this is *to the praise of the glory of His grace, which He freely bestowed on us in the Beloved* (Eph. 1:6). Satan's destructive reign of sin and death in this world will be done. The long wait of all creation to be set free from the bondage of sin will be over (cf. Rom. 8:19-22). The stunning closing scene reveals the integral place of the future resurrection of believers, and the absurdity of denying it, as some in Corinth were.

Homiletical Ideas: When Christians get their eyes off Christ and on themselves, they lose sight of the wonder of all that has been accomplished through His death and resurrection. Likewise, when we get our eyes off of God's redemptive promises and on to the times in which we live, we soon lose hope. In this paragraph, Paul calls us to look back, and to look forward. Both the past and the future are part of the same redemption program of God, and they are both equally sure. Historical evidence verifies the resurrection of Christ (cf. 15:3-8); since it is true, it follows that we who are in Christ will also be raised. It is as good as done!

There are a number of ways to approach this passage. One is to focus on the resurrection of Christ: How does it affect the believer's future? The answer is that it is a paradigm of our own coming resurrection. Christ was "the first-born from the dead" (Rev. 1:5), the "first-born among many brethren" (Rom. 8:29).

Another way to convey Paul's message here is to focus on God's redemptive plan: How does God view history? God sees everything from the vantage point of eternity. The entry of sin into the world condemned it to death, a penalty which He laid on His own Son in order to purchase redemption for all creation. All that He has done is to the praise of the glory of His grace, which has been poured out for our benefit, not because we are in any way worthy, but because of His great love. It is the resurrection of Christ which exhibits God's eternal master plan for reversing the power, penalty, and presence of sin in His creation. To borrow from C.S. Lewis' tale *The Lion, the Witch, and the Wardrobe*, the death of Christ dealt with the "Deep Magic from the Dawn of Time" (the Law), but the resurrection showed God's "Deeper Magic from Before the Dawn of Time."

Reminders of coming resurrection should not be left for Easter! Faith is the assurance of things hoped for (Heb. 11:1). Remind believers of Christ's resurrection, and how it guarantees their future resurrection.

29-34   [The present actions of Corinthian believers and the sufferings of Paul are senseless if there is no future bodily resurrection of believers.]

For all practical purposes, Paul's argument is complete at verse 28, and he could have ended his discussion there. But he instead appends a brief section dealing with baptism for the dead and suffering, leading to a closing appeal for them to live life with the reality of resurrection in mind.

29   By opening this verse with Ἐπεὶ (*Otherwise*), Paul connects this new section with the implications of the resurrection of Christ for believers in vv. 20-28 (Kistemaker, 560). Like a row of dominos which each fall in turn, the resurrection of Christ results in all the events listed—in particular, of course, all those in Christ being made alive (v.22). Paul here returns to those in Corinth who deny the resurrection, and asks two rhetorical questions. We might paraphrase verse 29, "*If the dead are not raised at all... what will those do who are baptized for the dead*, and *why...are they baptized for them* at all?!" Indeed, the practice makes no sense, and that is exactly Paul's point.

But to what is Paul referring? Dozens of explanations exist for the background and meaning of Paul's reference to *those...who are baptized for the dead*; some are impossible, and none is beyond doubt.

Perhaps some Corinthian Christians had adopted pagan ideas and imported them into the church (Hoehner, 544; Barrett, 363). The Corinthians had a magical view of baptism (see 10:2) which could have encouraged this. Of course, even if Paul did have this in mind, using their erroneous actions for his argument is no endorsement of them! On the other hand, Paul's use of the third person plural (*those...they*) could suggest he is referring to a baptism for the dead practiced by those outside the church (but this weakens his argument).

If the actions to which Paul refers were not of pagan origin, other explanations may be correct. Perhaps he had in mind those who were baptized "in place of" or "for the sake of" (ὑπὲρ; cf. BAGD, 838f) saints who had died. We might paraphrase, "If the dead are not raised at all, what will those who take their place in ministry do (when trials come)? Why expose new converts to danger and hardship, if there is no resurrection?" This interpretation ties in well with Paul's final question in v.30 (cf. Findlay, 930f).

Theological Note: Throughout Church History, various teachings have suggested ways for the living to minister vicariously for the dead. 2 Maccabees 12 refers to Jews who were slain because of idolatrous actions. Their comrades, upon discovering this, prayed to God *that the sin committed might wholly be put out of remembrance* (v.41). Such prayer for the dead is a part of Roman Catholic ritual, a logical consequence of their doctrine of purgatory. The Church of Jesus Christ of Latter Day Saints (Mormons) has a similar doctrine of a "second chance" following death, and teach—alongside the requirement of baptism for salvation—a vicarious baptism for the dead (which they base in part on this verse). No 'second chance' is taught in Scripture, which makes it clear that *it is appointed unto men to die once and after this comes judgment* (Heb. 9:27).

It should be added that Paul disallows any inclusion of water baptism as part of the gospel in this letter (1:14-17). In no way can Paul's comments here be used to support an idea of one person's action substituting for another.

30   With the antecedent condition of verse 29 still in force (*If the dead are not raised at all*), Paul adds one final rhetorical question: *Why are we also in danger every hour?* Why expose themselves to persecution and constant hardship if there is no resurrection? Denying the resurrection was the same as denying the gospel (vv. 12-19), and if the gospel is false, suffering for it is certainly the height of stupidity!

But beyond this, Paul reveals here the motivation of rewards which motivated the apostles to sacrificial service for the gospel. This is not to imply that their *only* motivation for service was gaining recognition or reward before Christ; Paul has indicated otherwise already (9:19-23; 10:33). But the anticipation of receiving an imperishable prize when he stood before His Savior clearly *was part* of Paul's motivation to endure hardship (9:24-27; 2 Tim. 4:6-8; cf. Heb. 12:1-2). Those who deny rewards as an incentive for faithful Christian living think this promotes pure motives, but they only "provide a theological loophole which the self-righteous aspect of our nature rather hastily welcomes" (R. T. Kendall, *When God Says "Well Done!"* [Christian Focus Publications Ltd, 1993], p.8).

31   Having brought himself into the discussion, Paul takes the opportunity to remind them of his own sufferings. *I protest, brethren, by the boasting in you, which I have in Christ Jesus our Lord, I die daily.* For Paul, the Corinthians—like others who had believed through his ministry (cf. 2 Cor. 1:14; Phil. 4:1; 1 Thess. 2:19-20)—were a source of great pride, not as if he had done it himself, but because of what God had done through him (1:30-31). It was knowing that his ministry for Christ had resulted in their salvation that encouraged him to go on, even if standing for

the gospel meant facing the reality of death on a daily basis (Fee, 769). And this was no idle claim. Over and over again, Acts records the abuse, imprisonment, beatings, and near escapes he endured on his journeys. Indeed, on at least one occasion, he was stoned and left for dead (Acts 14:19-20)!

32   Paul wants to emphasize the connection between the reason for his willingness to suffer for Christ and the resurrection of believers. *If from human motives I fought with wild beasts at Ephesus, what does it profit me?* Of course, the answer is "Nothing!" The approval of men is fraudulent and fleeting; that which matters is the praise which comes from the Lord (4:3-5).

Interpretive Note: Paul's reference to fighting with wild beasts (θηριομαχέω) at Ephesus may be a metaphor for his encounters with enemies of the gospel there (cf. Acts 19:28ff; Ironside, 501). A similar passage in Ignatius' Letter to the Romans (5:1) reads: "From Syria all the way to Rome I am fighting with wild beasts, on land and sea, by night and day, chained amidst ten leopards (that is, a company of soldiers) who only get worse when they are well treated."

To emphasize his point, that resurrection is a motive for godly living and sacrificial service, Paul now affirms the opposite. *If the dead are not raised, let us eat and drink, for tomorrow we die.* Because of the resurrection, Paul elected to spend his life preaching the gospel, with the result that he faced death daily. But if there is no resurrection, Paul suggests (borrowing his words from Isa. 22:13) they all indulge in the feeding frenzy of the world, satisfying their fleshly lusts, since the future is nothing but a dead end (cf. Luke 12:19). In effect, Paul says here, "If there is a resurrection, living (and possibly dying) for Christ makes sense. If there is no resurrection, life is nothing but a desperate, meaningless journey to death."

33   But of course, there is a resurrection, so what we do in this life does matter in the life to come (cf. 4:5). The denial of the resurrection was another case of the 'wise' Corinthians being deceived by their own fallacious reasoning. So Paul instructs them, in light of the coming resurrection, *Do not be deceived: "Bad company corrupts good morals."*

There were probably many ethical reminders Paul could have inserted here. What precise problem he had in mind with this statement is not clear. The Corinthians had evidenced, however, a penchant for "seasoning" apostolic teaching with a generous dose of worldly wisdom, with the result that both their doctrine and practice had gone terribly wrong. They needed to distance themselves from the "bad company" of the wise, mighty, and noble in Corinth who were perishing (1:26-29); such ties were corrupting their spiritual lives. As a central example of the effect these ties had on them, it is likely that their denial of the resurrection had resulted in much of their aberrant behavior (Fee, 773).

34   What should they do? Paul is quick to draw his argument to a practical conclusion. *Become sober-minded as you ought, and stop sinning.* The first imperative here means "to come to one's senses" or "be awake" (cf. ἐκνήφω; BAGD, 243; 1 Thess. 5:8). The adverb δικαίως (BAGD, 198) can mean "as you ought," but more likely here has its usual meaning of "uprightly" or "in uprightness." It is unlikely Paul would tell the Corinthians to wake up, as you ought; rather, he wants them to "wake up to uprightness, and stop sinning" (cf. NKJV). They have been alert to the thinking of the world for too long; it is time for them to start paying attention to God's truth, and—as a result—to stop sinning. For Paul, the two are inextricably tied together.

They need to do this, because (*for,* γὰρ) *some have no knowledge of God.* By hobnobbing with the world and letting it corrupt their message and morals, they had failed to confront those living in Corinth with the gospel. This failure to fulfill their ultimate commission was inexcusable. Paul's conclusion, *I speak this to your shame* (cf. 6:5), might better be rendered, "Shame on you!" They had let the world impact their lives, instead of letting their lives impact the world. "Wake up!" Paul says, "and start living the way you should. Then you will be able to bring others to a knowledge of God."

Homiletical Ideas: This concludes Paul's defense of the resurrection of believers. He has shown the connection between the future and the past (the resurrection of believers and the resurrection of Christ are inextricably linked). Here, he turns his attention to the present. In customary fashion, he caps off his doctrinal discussion with an appeal to related or resulting moral issues. What we have here is practical instruction resulting from an affirmation of the resurrection.

Unfortunately, as Fee has noted (775), the difficulty in knowing what to do with verse 29 has resulted in a strange silence in the church in regard to this paragraph. This is tragic, since many Christians today—like the Corinthians—are more interested in doctrinal debates than how they should live (cf. 8:1). This passage, dealing implicitly with the issue of rewards, is a key source of motivation for Christians to live pure and sacrificial lives for the Lord.

The question Paul is answering in this paragraph is: *What incentive is there to live a godly life (and suffer for Christ as a result)?* The answer? If there is no resurrection, *none!* If there is no resurrection, there is no meaning; we all might as well go out, get gorged, get drunk, and die. But if there is a resurrection, we have the incentive of *rewards!* Someday, in the resurrection, we all will receive our evaluation and praise from God (4:5). As a result of this knowledge, we should avoid bad company, which corrupts good morals, stop sinning, and start paying attention to what God has prepared for us (cf. Eph. 2:10). Only then will each of us—and the church as a whole—have an impact on those who have no knowledge of God.

Christians are to be a "living gospel" for the world to see. Our lives are to proclaim the reality of the good news. If we are living with the resurrection in mind, we will be tools of the Spirit to convict unbelievers of sin, righteousness, and judgment (cf. John 16:8-11).

Wesley once told a group of young preachers, "You have nothing to do but save souls." Paul would have agreed (cf. 7:16; 9:19-23; 10:33). May we all, with our future day of reckoning in mind, live in such a way that we will win as many to Christ as possible.

15:35-58 *The future resurrection of believers is affirmed by explaining how it will occur and what its results are.*

35 [The future resurrection of believers was mocked as absurd by those who denied it.]

Paul's argument showing the necessity of the resurrection to everything from the gospel message to motivation for living for Christ is complete. His concluding admonition in vv. 33-34 was directed at the Corinthians' readiness to accept secular ideas and ways of thinking, ignoring what he had taught them, or conforming it to worldly wisdom. But Paul knows his argument, however convincing, will not end the debate. The Corinthians had shown a stubborn contempt for his previous instruction, and this would be no different. Furthermore, Paul undoubtedly knew that while his logical and theological arguments were compelling, another question had to be answered: *How are the dead raised?* Or, more specifically, *with what kind of body do they come?* This, of course, was the issue. How could any sane person explain the resurrection of a dead, decayed corpse?! Up to this point, Paul has been talking about the resurrection of the *dead* (θάνατος and νεκρός appear 12x in vv1-34). But in verse 35, with parallel questions, he changes focus. The first question refers to the *dead* (νεκροί); the second introduces the term *body* (σῶμα), which dominates the rest of the chapter (see also σὰρξ, *flesh*, vv.39, 50). For Paul, the two questions are one; the resurrection of the dead is a *bodily* resurrection, and this is the sticking point for his readers.

The question of this was probably used to end debates on the resurrection. With condescending incredulity, one who denied the resurrection would say, "So you think there is a resurrection of the body. Explain how this is going to happen! Will heaven be populated with skeletons and rotting corpses?!" The question did not invite a response so much as it ridiculed the opponent. It did nothing to establish the validity of the "no-resurrection" position, but sought to establish it by default, mocking any who believed in the resurrection. In effect, it raised a basic philosophical question: How can something which dies (and decays) come back to life? As with the gospel message (1:18), Christian doctrine here is foolishness to the world. The absurdity of the idea to the natural man (2:14) weakened the conviction of the saints in Corinth. Paul now sets about explaining how the resurrection will occur.

36-38   [The future bodily resurrection of believers is affirmed through an analogy with seed that are planted.]

36   The no-resurrection position was the opinion of choice among the wise in Corinthian society, and they mocked those who believed in it as fools. Paul therefore responds in kind: *You fool!* Such a comeback indicates this was no trivial matter to him. They had been deriding those who held to his teaching; now he would deride them for their ignorance (cf. ἄφρων; BAGD, 127).

To those who skeptically asked, "How are the dead raised?" Paul replies, "Take a look at a seed!" *That which you sow does not come to life* (ζῳοποιεῖται; cf. v.22) *unless it dies.* While the question of how the body will be resurrected is not addressed until verse 51 (except for a passing comment in v.38), Paul here simply states that such an event is nothing bizarre. It is, in fact, a normal occurrence in nature.

37   Furthermore, *that which you sow, you do not sow the body* (σῶμα) *which is to be, but a bare grain, perhaps of wheat or something else.* Two further facts concerning the resurrection are now gleaned from the seed analogy. First, every reader would know that when

you put a grain of wheat in the ground, you get wheat from the ground. That is, you reap the same kind that you sow. This illustrates the continuity between that which exists before death and after resurrection. But Paul explicitly emphasizes something else all his readers would know, that when you sow a grain of wheat, you don't want to get that grain back in the same form at harvest! You expect to get wheat, to be sure, but in a different and improved form! The analogy is clear; the seed "body" is related to, but different from, that which is "resurrected" after it is sown. So too, the naked (γυμνός, BAGD, 167f) body of man which is laid in the ground is related to—but different from—that which is resurrected.

38   What the Corinthian doubters failed to take into account was God, who has made resurrection "routine" in nature. *God gives* each seed, when it is planted, *a* (new) *body just as He wished, and to each of the seeds a body of its own.* To those who doubt the viability of resurrection, Paul simply points to God. The implication is that just as "resurrection" is exhibited in God's visible creation, which we can observe in this life, so too it is a feature of His unseen creation, which we will only experience in the life to come.

39-41   [The future bodily resurrection of believers is affirmed through an analogy with different kinds of earthly and heavenly bodies.]

39   How can a resurrection body be the same, yet also different? Having introduced God's creative hand and the diversity of His creation into the discussion, Paul now elaborates on His sovereign design in giving different kinds of bodies (*just as He wished*) to different creatures. The *flesh* (bodies) of all creatures on earth is *not the same*; there are *men, beasts, birds,* and *fish*. Each body is a body of flesh, yet each is different, suited to its own environment. This distinction in kind anticipates the distinction between our present bodies and those we will have in the resurrection. Both are physical, but as vv. 42-44 make explicit, this does not mean there are no distinctions.

40   The distinctions, in fact, are summed up in the word *glory* (δόξα). All bodies do not have the same "glory," as is illustrated in the contrast between *heavenly bodies and earthly bodies*. These *heavenly bodies* are not angels (Findlay, 935; Morris, 225), or resurrected bodies (cf. vv. 47-49), but the sun, moon, and stars (cf. v. 41). The *glory of the heavenly* bodies is different from *the glory of the earthly* bodies. The beauty and wonder of heavenly objects is very different from that of earthly creatures.

41   Furthermore, even among the heavenly objects, *there is one glory of the sun, and another glory of the moon, and another glory of the stars; even star differs from star in glory*. Paul is here pressing the point of the analogies of earthly creatures and heavenly objects. There is infinite variety in God's creation; the splendor of one thing is different from that of another. So why limit the resurrected human body to that which presently exists (Bruce, 151)?

42-49 [The future resurrection of believers is affirmed through a contrast between the character of the present body and the resurrected body.]

42   A seed is changed into something very different (although related) when it is sown. Its new "body" (v. 38) is given by God, who has created many creatures and heavenly objects, each with its own unique character. *So also* ("in the same way"), *the resurrection of the dead* human body results in it being changed, and given a new character appropriate to the time and place in which it exists.

       Not all humans will die (cf. v. 51; 1 Thess. 4:15, 17; 5:10), but all have a body that is *perishable* (φθορᾷ). In contrast, the resurrection human body will be *imperishable* (ἀφθαρσίᾳ). Unlike the idea of reincarnation, Christians are not doomed to an endless cycle of life and death. From the moment of faith in Jesus Christ, the believer has eternal life (John 5:24; Rom. 6:23; 1 Tim. 1:16; 1 John 5:11-13). In the resurrection, all who have eternal life will receive a body that is likewise eternal. In fact, nothing perishable will exist in the resurrection (v. 50). Even the prize which Christians seek is imperishable (9:25)!

Theological Note: The possession of eternal life is a present reality for the Christian. In Col. 3:3, Paul states that believers "have died" and that their "life is hidden with Christ in God." This is eternal, imperishable, spiritual life, but we who possess it presently live in temporal, perishable, natural bodies! The two are incompatible, as our present bodies are totally unsuitable for our ultimate destiny. In the resurrection, our glorified bodies will be united with our already-raised and perfected spiritual souls in heaven (Col. 3:4; Kistemaker, 573). In that day, "the creation itself also will be set free from its slavery to corruption into the freedom of the glory of the children of God" (Rom. 8:21)!

---

43   Because the present body is perishable, it was viewed as "second-rate" by the Corinthians; it was something God would "do away with" (6:13). But Paul here exposes their error. Instead of destroying the body, God changes it from a body of *dishonor* into a body of *glory*; it no longer is a body characterized by *weakness*, but one of *power*.

44   Finally, the present *natural body* (σῶμα ψυχικόν; a body suited to the natural world in which we live; BAGD, 894) will be *raised a spiritual body* (σῶμα πνευματικόν; a body suited to the spiritual world of the resurrection). Paul is not saying we will be immaterial spirits in the resurrection; that would make the designation *spiritual body* a nonsensical concept. Rather, we will be *spiritual*. Some Corinthians already thought of themselves as spiritual, but their concept was flawed. Being spiritual did not mean rejecting or disregarding the body; it meant having a body which operated spiritually. Paul states that *there is a natural body*, and *there is also a spiritual body*. In the resurrection, believers will have a spiritual body, a body that is characterized by Spirit control and the fruit of the Spirit (Gal. 5:22-23).

Another way to say this is that our resurrection bodies will reflect the risen Christ, and bear His image (49). Christ's resurrected body was spiritual. He wasn't an immaterial phantom (cf. Luke 24:39); the disciples recognized him and touched his body. Rather, his body was perfectly suited to spiritual life in heaven. When He returns in glory and we see Him, we will be fully like Him (Col. 3:4; 1 John 3:2). It is to this future reality that Paul now turns.

Application: Believers are often urged to reflect Christ in their lives, or to become "more Christ-like." This is really just a call for us to start living now like we will live in heaven. The process of becoming "like Christ" began at salvation and will culminate at His Second Coming. In the present, the Spirit is working to make us more like we will be in the resurrection. The glory we will perfectly reflect then can be increasingly reflected in our lives now as we give our *bodies* over to the Spirit's control (2 Cor. 3:18; Rom. 12:1-2). To put it another way, we were declared righteous by God when we trusted Christ as Savior, and we will be actually righteous when we are with Christ in glory; but we will receive the crown of righteousness at that time (2 Tim. 4:8) only if we have "loved His appearing"—i.e., lived our lives with His coming in view, progressively becoming more like Him. We should emulate Enoch, who "walked with God, and was not, for God took him" (Gen. 5:24). Apparently, he was so spiritual that he passed directly from this life to the next. By reminding ourselves that what we do in this body is important, not irrelevant, we can look forward to an experience of enhanced joy in the coming resurrection of believers.

45-49   [The future resurrection of believers is affirmed through a contrast between Adam and Christ.]

45   Paul's normal practice, as evidenced through this letter (1:19; 2:9; 3:19f), was to refer to Scripture to support his instruction. Using the same terms with which he began v.42 (οὕτως καὶ, *So also*),

he borrows from Gen. 2:7 to illustrate the difference between the present human body, and the body believers will have in the coming resurrection. The reference to *the first man, Adam,* and *the last Adam* (Christ) builds on the earlier mention of these two in verses 21-22. Because of Christ's resurrection, those who faced death in Adam could receive the promise of resurrection through faith in Christ. And just as Christ's resurrection is the guarantee of resurrection for all believers, so too His resurrection body is the prototype of the body with which all believers will be raised. Adam *became a living soul* (ψυχὴν ζῶσαν; the cognate adjective ψυχικόν describes our present bodies in v. 44); Christ *became a life-giving spirit* (πνεῦμα ζῳοποιοῦν; He both gives the life and defines the type of body in which it is lived). The essence of Paul's message is that just as Adam had the prototype natural (soulish) body (which is perishable), Christ was raised with the prototype spiritual body (which is imperishable), which all believers will be raised with. The perishable body that is "sown" (in this life) will be raised in the life to come as an imperishable body.

46   For those who thought they could achieve this supernatural spiritual existence now, Paul makes it clear that this cannot be. There is an order to everything. A seed must be planted before it grows into a new plant (v.36ff); so too *the spiritual* (body) *is not first, but the natural; then the spiritual.* In the present, we bear the image of the natural, not the spiritual.

47   Borrowing once again from Gen. 2:7 ("the Lord God formed man of the dust of the ground"), Paul states that *the first man* (Adam) *is from the earth,* and therefore *earthy* (lit. "made of earth"). On the contrary, *the second man* (the Lord; see NKJV) *is from heaven.* While it is possible to see this as referring to origin, Paul is probably (as in the following verses) contrasting the character of the present body and the resurrection body (Fee, 792f). The present body, epitomized in Adam, is made out of dust; in other words, it is perishable. That which comes from the ground returns to the ground (Gen. 3:19). The resurrection

body, as embodied in Christ, is of heaven; in other words, it is imperishable. That which comes from heaven (John 3:13) returns there.

48   What does this mean for us? First, as long as we live in this life, we have the same characteristics as our prototype, Adam. Adam was *earthy, so also* we are *earthy*. The NKJV translation here is good: "As was the man of dust, so also are those who are made of dust." On the other hand, "as is the heavenly Man, so also are those who are heavenly." We can reflect 'heavenly' characteristics in this life, since we have already received His new life. But "we have this treasure in earthen vessels" (2 Cor. 4:7); only when we experience the "redemption of our body" (Rom. 8:23) in the resurrection will we be able to fully live out the spiritual life which God has prepared for us.

49   The second application which Paul draws from the contrast between Adam and Christ is that *just as we have borne the image of the earthy* (Adam), *we shall also bear the image of the heavenly*. To borrow from verse 22, just as it is true that all who are born in this life are mortal, and die (who would challenge that?), it is also true that all who are born *again* will be raised immortal, never to die (no one should challenge that!).

50-58   [The future resurrection of believers is affirmed by the revelation of a mystery.]

50   In a summary and restatement of all he has said to this point, Paul declares *that flesh and blood cannot inherit the kingdom of God; nor does the perishable inherit the imperishable*. The two statements are parallel, and form one conclusion. The physical body, in its present form, is ill-equipped for the coming spiritual world. While it is related to the resurrection body, it is also different from it, like a seed is related to, yet different from that which it becomes (v. 38). By referring to the time after the resurrection as *the kingdom of God* (4:20; 6:9-10), Paul points to the commencement of the eternal state (cf. v. 24). When time

itself is no more, then this flesh and blood, this perishable body, will be changed.

51   The question largely unanswered in the entire discussion to this point is, "How are the dead raised?" (v.35). The present perishable body is not fit for the spiritual environment; it must change. How will this occur?

Paul's answer is to *tell* them a *mystery*, meaning that he is going to reveal to them something that was previously unknown (see above on 2:7). This revelation is that *we shall not all sleep, but we shall all be changed*. Paul's use of the inclusive "we" probably reflects his expectation that he was live to see the Lord's return. Not all believers will die (κοιμάω, BAGD, 437; cf. 15:6, 18, 20) before the Lord comes, but whether they do or not, before they enter the presence of God the bodies of all will be transformed (ἀλλάσσω; BAGD, 39).

But what does it mean that we will be *changed*? The term sometimes means to *exchange* one thing for another (Rom. 1:23), but here reflects its more common meaning, to *alter* the character of someone or something (Gal. 4:20). In some way, the body will be changed. We will not receive a body unrelated to our present one, but in some way, the nature and qualities of our bodies will be different.

52   Unlike a progressive transformation "from glory to glory" (2 Cor. 3:18) which believers can experience in this life, the change when we enter the kingdom of God will happen *in a moment* (ἄτομος; BAGD, 120; an indivisible instant of time), *in the twinkling of an eye* (the time it takes your eye to blink)! This will occur when *the last trumpet* sounds, a clear reference to the rapture of the Church, when Christ returns for those who are His own, and the events of the End commence (Matt. 24:31; 1 Thess. 4:16). At this time, *the dead will be raised imperishable, and we shall be changed* (1 Thess. 4:13-17). For those who thought it too much to imagine God raising the bodies of dead believers, Paul makes

it clear that the real miracle of resurrection is changing our perishable bodies—whether alive or dead—into imperishable bodies. From the moment of birth, our bodies are on a course leading to death. It is this biological reality that will be turned on its head in the resurrection.

53   This is the change that is imperative. Since our *perishable (body)* is not suited for the kingdom of God (v. 50), it *must put on the imperishable.* To put it another way, *this mortal [body] must put on immortality.*

The idea of "putting (something) on" or "clothing" oneself (NIV) is used by Paul only here (and v. 54) in this letter, but it is common in his other epistles, where it describes three stages in our spiritual lives. By receiving Jesus Christ as personal Savior, we have "clothed ourselves" with Christ (Gal. 3:27). This illustrates the fact that we are in Christ; when God looks at us, He sees not our old sinful self, but Jesus Christ. This is the basis for our eternal security.

Unfortunately, our old self, with its tendencies, is not immediately eradicated, so we are elsewhere exhorted by Paul to lay it aside and "put on the new man" (Eph. 4:24), or to "put on Jesus Christ" (Rom. 13:14). While this process should continue throughout our Christian lives, it will never be complete until we stand in glory. It is only then that we will fully "put on" Jesus Christ, in a spiritual, imperishable body (cf. 2 Cor. 5:1-4).

54   What is the essential result of the resurrection process, moving from our present *perishable* bodies to *imperishable* ones, and from the realm of the *mortal* to *immortality?* Paul answers by adapting a prophetic announcement in Isaiah 25:8: *then will come about the saying that is written, "Death is swallowed up in victory."*

As Paul logically argued in verses 20-28, the final result of the resurrection of Christ would be the ultimate abolishment of death (v. 26). Now, coming by way of an explanation of the kind of body believers will be raised with, he arrives at the same conclusion. As long as we are in this body, our "earthly tent" (2 Cor. 5:1), we are in "slavery to corruption" (Rom. 8:21). Death wields her awful power in this life, but her reign is short-lived (Rom. 5:17). *When* we have been raised in immortal spiritual bodies, death (the last enemy) will be *swallowed up* ("made extinct;" cf. καταπίνω, BAGD, 416) in the victory that is ours in the resurrected Christ.

55   With a loose adaptation from Hosea 13:14, Paul raises a taunt toward death: *"O death, where is your victory? O death, where is your sting?"* While death has its "sting" and "victory" in this life, it is always under the sovereign control of God. In Hosea 13, God is calling on Death and Sheol to do their worst to a disobedient Israel. In our passage, God's power over death is again seen, but now (with the wording slightly changed) in a mocking display of death's impotence in the coming kingdom of God. Will death any more be the ultimate enemy? No! The power of God, shown in His raising Jesus Christ from the dead (Eph. 1:19f), has also secured our resurrection (Eph. 2:4f). It is as good as done. That is why, although our full experience of resurrection life is still future, we can join in the "taunt" today!

56   The answer to the rhetorical questions of verse 55 is now provided, and with it we are brought back abruptly from the future into the present. Where is the sting of death? *The sting of death is sin.*

Death is here personified as an insect with a poison stinger of sin in its tail. It is sin that makes death so awful. Sin breaks our fellowship with God, and makes our appointment with Him (at death) a terrible expectation. Gone is the experience of Adam and Eve in the Garden of Eden when, as sinless but mortal beings (for they had not eaten of the tree of life; cf. Gen. 3:22-24), they had no fear of death. They walked with God in the cool of the day (3:8). While not yet suited for heavenly life, "death" for them was more a moving from this world to the next than the final terminus it has since become. This is death without the sting of sin. Take away sin, and death is disarmed, so as to be no longer hurtful (Calvin, 64). But as Paul and his readers knew all too well, sin is a present reality in this life, and the sting of death with it.

The *power of sin* which exacerbates its effect on us *is the law.* Apart from the law, sin has no power. This is because the law arouses our sinful passions, resulting in deeds of death (Rom. 7:5). At the same time, the law makes us aware of our sin (Rom. 7:8-11), thus resulting in guilt before God. It imprisons us, on one side prompting us to do that which we know is wrong, and on the other condemning us for doing it! Well might we echo Paul's cry in Rom. 7:24: "Wretched man that I am! Who will set me free from the body of this death?"

57 The answer to that question is found in the resurrected Savior, Jesus Christ. We are powerless against the juggernaut of law-sin-death on our own, *but thanks be to God, who gives us the victory through our Lord Jesus Christ!* Paul invites his readers to claim the victory that is theirs in Christ; although they still exist in this life, and the resurrection has not yet come, the victory is already real. It was secured in Christ's resurrection, and will be realized at Christ's return. But it can also be experienced in this life when Christ reigns in our lives.

58 Because the resurrection is sure, he urges believers (*my beloved brethren*) to *be steadfast, immovable, always abounding* (περισσεύω, "doing more and more") *in the work of the Lord, knowing that your toil is not in vain in the Lord.* Too often we get consumed with our present lives and forget about the life to come. With this future now clearly in focus, Paul invites us to reconsider our priorities in this life. The subject of rewards (and judgment) for believers appears often in this letter (3:10-17; 4:1-5; 9:15-27), and for Paul is a significant motivation for us to work for the Lord. Those things which we do for Him are not in vain ('without profit;' cf. κενός, BAGD, 427). They will bring a reward—not in this life, but at the Judgment Seat of Christ.

Homiletical Ideas: The subject of the resurrection is a happy one. Who wouldn't want to hear about a time (although eternity can hardly be called a "time") when sin and death will be no more, where our broken-down bodies will be immortal?! In a nutshell, Paul is simply affirming the future bodily resurrection of believers by answering the two questions of verse 35. But in addition to this basic content, there are a number of themes which are ripe for application to the lives of believers.

For example, there is the theme of reaping what you sow. This principle is illustrated in a seed that is planted, and applied to the resurrection body (which is likewise related to our present bodies; 36-38). But it also appears in the final application, where—because of the resurrection—our work for the Lord will also reap a reward. While we look with anticipation toward the day of our Lord's return, we therefore should also remember that what we do for Him *now* will have great importance then.

The distinction between our present *natural* bodies which are *perishable*, and our future *spiritual* bodies which are *imperishable*, is also significant. While this passage is dealing with the absolute immortality of the spiritual body in the resurrection, a similar principle applies in our present lives. Just as our spiritual (sinless) bodies will never die, so too, by living for Christ now, we may lengthen our lives. Obedience to the Lord is the basis of long life (Deut. 4:40; Ps. 91:16; Prov. 3:16); on the contrary, sin results in death (Ezek. 18:20; Rom. 6:23a; Jas. 1:15). It is, of course, wrong to arbitrarily apply this principle, but the principle is a valid one. How many suffer anxiety-filled and abbreviated lives through failure to obey God's Word?

Finally, the grace of God shines brightly in the wonderful assurance that is evidenced in this passage. Forgotten are the woes which filled earlier chapters; instead, Paul urges us all to 'see' the wonderful future that *is* ours through Jesus Christ. One look at our broken-down bodies should remind us that neither our resurrection, nor our salvation, depends on what we do. God will give us a spiritual body, not because we deserve it, but because of His grace. We are assured of final victory not on the basis of our faithfulness, but because of what our Lord Jesus Christ has done for us. The "sentence of death" we have in our present bodies should be a daily reminder to us "to not trust in ourselves, but in God who raises the dead; who delivered us from so great a peril of death, and will deliver us, He on whom we have set out hope" (2 Cor. 1:9-10).

CONCLUDING RESPONSES, COMMENTS, EXHORTATIONS, AND SALUTATION (16:1-24)

16:1-4 *Paul instructs and exhorts the Corinthians to lay aside money for the saints in Jerusalem.*

Paul is sometimes regarded as being hard and impersonal (at least early in his ministry), based in part on his treatment of John Mark at the beginning of his second missionary journey (cf. Acts 13:13; 15:36-40). This charge ignores much of his work, and his concern for the well-being of believers everywhere he went. His appeal for financial help for suffering Christians in Jerusalem, a theme reflected in other letters and travels (Galatia mentioned in v1; cf. 2 Cor. 8:1 [Macedonia and Achaia] and Rom. 15:26), reflects his heart for people.

1 Paul's opening *Now concerning* (Περὶ δὲ) signifies that he is responding to another issue raised in the Corinthians' letter to him (see Introduction to the commentary, and comments introducing chapters 7-16 above). This question about *the collection* (λογεία; used only here and in v.2 in the New Testament) *for the saints* (in Jerusalem, v.3), however, hardly compares with the weighty issues discussed in the previous chapters (marriage questions, fellowship with idolaters, the role of women in the church, the denigration of the Lord's Table, misuse of spiritual gifts, and denial of the resurrection). Unlike all those other issues, Paul does not need to correct any wrong practice or teaching here. But it is a reflection of the importance Paul placed on this issue that he included it alongside those other issues. Paul had *directed* (cf. διατάσσω, BAGD, 189) *the churches of Galatia* to give, and now he instructs the Corinthians to do the same.

2 His instruction is straightforward: *On the first day of every week* (κατὰ μίαν σαββάτου; cf. σάββατον, BAGD, 739,2.a.) *let each one of you put aside and save, as he may prosper, that no collections be made when I come.* This is one of only two explicit references in the New Testament to Christians meeting on the first day of the week (cf. Acts 20:7). There is little doubt, however, that this was the normal day for corporate worship and the breaking of

bread. The early church remembered Christ's death (through the Lord's Supper) and resurrection (by meeting on the day He rose; cf. Matt. 28:1; Mark 16:2; Luke 24:1; John 20:1) at the same time. On this day, when they remembered the price Christ paid for their salvation, they were admonished to also remember their less-fortunate brothers.

The prescribed way to do this was to *put aside* (τίθημι can mean "deposit;" cf. BAGD, 816) *and save* (θησαυρίζω; BAGD, 361). The terms are almost synonymous; both indicate an intentional gathering and storing up of assets. This should be in direct proportion to each one's financial success. There is no mention of a tithe; Paul exhorts them to consider how they have been blessed by God, and to set aside accordingly. There is no coercion here; his appeal is for voluntary, cheerful giving (cf. 2 Cor. 9:7). If they do this, he won't have to "drum up support" and take a special offering for the Jerusalem church when he comes. Furthermore, by having the matter on their hearts for a lengthy period of time, their gift would certainly be far greater.

3-4   As to who would deliver this gift *to Jerusalem*, Paul is content to let the Corinthians handle that; they should pick their own team (*whomever you may approve*), who will *carry your gift* (Paul would not handle the money). Perhaps this would make them feel more personally involved in the relief effort, and more at one with their Judean brothers in Christ. Although translations differ, it seems likely that Paul would write *letters* to accompany those who the church chose to carry their gift. Paul was unsure whether it would be *fitting* (proper; cf. ἄξιος, BAGD, 78) for him *to go* along. Perhaps this indecision on his part reflects a gracious attitude toward those in the church who he knew had personal problems with him, and might be unhappy being represented by him. If so, it also surely reflects his commitment to do nothing to upset, and thus thwart, the fund-raising effort.

Homiletical Ideas: This passage speaks directly to the issue of Christian giving. Ministers are reluctant to talk about giving, wanting to avoid appearing mercenary, a negative characterization that is reinforced by a few well-known charlatans, and Hollywood depictions of religious leaders who 'fleece the flock.' Paul did not shrink away from this subject, however, making the collection of monetary gifts for needy Christians a common appeal in his letters. The principles in these verses need to be taught. Christians should 1) lay aside gifts for the Lord's work and people *weekly* (in addition to the offering they give for the regular needs of the local church); 2) they should give generously, in proportion to their income; and 3) they should communicate with those they are supporting.

16:5-9 *Paul informs the Corinthians of his plans to visit them after completing his ministry in Ephesus.*

5 Three times in this letter, Paul has mentioned in passing his plan to come to Corinth and visit them (4:18-21; 11:34; 16:3). Now he provides more details about his plans. He will visit them *after* a trip *through Macedonia.* That is, instead of immediately sailing across the Aegean to deal with them, he will stick with his original plans to visit the other churches in Macedonia on the way. Knowing that much of what he had written would not find immediate acceptance among some in Corinth (to say the least!), Paul was probably happy, in any case, to give them a 'cooling down period.' The Corinthians viewed themselves as 'a cut above' other churches, not to mention the apostles (4:6-13)! By refusing to alter his travel plans, Paul infers that he does not share that view; they are no more important than any other church.

6 The duration of his visit is uncertain, but he wants them to know that *perhaps* ("if possible;" cf. τυγχάνω, BAGD, 829) he will *stay with* (παραμενῶ; cf. BAGD, 620) them for an extended time, perhaps *even spend the winter* (which wouldn't be the best time to travel anyway). The purpose for staying on, *that you may send*

me on my way wherever I may go, anticipates that after spending time together, their differences will have been resolved, and the church will give him some support and encouragement when he leaves.

7   After reading his letter to this point, some may have thought that Paul would never want to see them again! Despite their problems, however, Paul is not coming "just because he had to." He makes it clear that his casual-sounding "perhaps I will stay with you" in the previous sentence did not reflect a lack of concern. Rather, *I do not wish to see you now just in passing; for I hope to remain with you for some time, if the Lord permits* (ἐπιτρέπω; cf. 14:34). Perhaps it is not too much to see in Paul's words here a 'subliminal message': "You Corinthians have exaggerated your own significance and put others down, but I won't do the same to you. I want to spend enough time with you to restore your fellowship with the Lord and with me. I pray that God will permit me to do so."

8-9   In addition to the delay in his arrival caused by him going through Macedonia, Paul adds that he will *remain in Ephesus until Pentecost*. This is because *a wide door for effective service has opened to me, and there are many adversaries*. A thrilling account of Paul's experiences in Ephesus during this time is found in Acts 18:24-19:41. Pentecost came in the spring, a natural time to travel.

The precise sequence of events which transpired after the writing of this letter is not clear (see Introduction). It is likely that the situation in Corinth was so bad, Paul had to make an unplanned "sorrowful" visit (2 Cor. 2:1) shortly after sending this letter. Following this visit, while still based in Ephesus, he wrote his "sorrowful letter" (2 Cor. 2:4). Shortly after sending Titus with that letter, Paul left Ephesus for Troas, where he waited in vain for Titus to return from Corinth with news (2 Cor. 2:13). After going on to Macedonia, Titus finally met back up with him, and gave him the good news he was waiting for: The Corinthian church had responded to his instruction (2 Cor. 7:6, 13-16). This prompted Paul to write 2 Corinthians. Connecting this with Luke's account of Paul's third missionary journey, we learn that Paul gave "much exhortation" to the churches in Macedonia before arriving in Corinth (Acts 20:2). He spent three months (probably winter) there, then in early spring, wanting to reach Jerusalem by the Day of Pentecost (Acts 20:16), planned to sail directly to Syria. A Jewish plot against him (probably to be carried out at sea) caused him to return through Macedonia instead (20:3).

Homiletical Ideas: Two principles for those in ministry are implicit in Paul's comments here. First, Paul did not 'fly by the seat of his pants'; he planned his ministry carefully. This is in contrast to some Christians in ministry who are always "waiting on the Lord" or "seeking God's will"—which often amounts to doing little or nothing, waiting for God to 'move' them. Paul didn't wait; he planned! From all indications, those plans were changed by the Lord. That is always His prerogative. It is our responsibility to have a plan of action, then let the Lord direct our paths (cf. Jas. 4:13-17). Proverbs 16:1 says: *The mind of man plans his way, but the Lord directs his steps.*

Second, Paul writes that "a wide door for effective service" has opened at Ephesus, then adds that "there are many adversaries." An "open door" obviously doesn't mean everything will go smoothly, or that there will be success. It may mean hardship and persecution. Difficulties in ministry are not God 'closing a door' of service for Him! Indeed, trials in ministry are God's way of maturing us, and if endured, they result in praise and honor when Christ returns (Jas. 1:2-4; 12; 1 Pet. 1:6-7). God desires diligence, whatever the cost!

16:10-12 *Paul comments on potential visits by Timothy and Apollos, and exhorts the Corinthians to treat Timothy well.*

10   The discussion of his own plans to visit Corinth reminds Paul that he sent *Timothy* to visit churches in Macedonia (cf. Acts 19:22), and that he would soon be coming to Corinth (4:17). Would Paul's uncompromising instruction in this letter cause them to turn on his emissary? He warns them to *see that he is with you without cause to be afraid!* Whether he was actually concerned for Timothy's physical safety is uncertain, but he reminds them that Timothy *is doing the Lord's work, as I also am.*

11   More likely, Paul feared that some in Corinth would treat Timothy with the same contempt they had shown him. He therefore adds that no one should *despise him* (ἐξουθενέω; treat him with contempt; cf. 6:4; BAGD, 277). Rather, they should *send him on his way in peace, so that he may come to me; for I expect him with the brethren.* Paul's fatherly concern for Timothy, which is reflected in his letters to him (cf. 1 Tim. 2:1, 18; 2 Tim. 1:2-6; 2:1), is easy to see here. He watches over him closely, and the message for any malcontents in Corinth is clear; if they treat Timothy badly, he will hear of it, and hold them personally responsible.

12   If Timothy, as Paul's representative, might receive a chilly welcome, Apollos was the opposite. Did those who were "of Apollos" (1:12) request him to come? Paul's use of Περὶ δὲ (*Now concerning;* cf. Fee, 823f), his customary way of responding to something they had written, suggests this may be the case. Considering Apollos' oratorical skill (Acts 18:24), and Paul's lack of it (1:17; 2:1), he might have been welcomed. But although Paul *encouraged him greatly to come...with the brethren* (perhaps with Stephanas, Fortunatus, and Achaicus; v.17), Apollos had declined. Why he was unwilling to come is unknown. He may have simply wanted no part in fueling any ongoing division in the church. However, it is likely that he was engaged in serving the Lord elsewhere, since Paul adds that he would come *when he has opportunity* (εὐκαιρέω, cf. BAGD, 321).

Homiletical Ideas: What a shocking indictment of a church are Paul's words in verses 10-11! Paul warns them not to give Timothy any reason to be afraid, and exhorts them not to despise him! Before we 'polish our halos' with Corinthian rags, however, we might consider our own tendencies. The church is fragmented and divisive in much of the world today. How do we treat those with whom we disagree? Our response may be complicated by the presence of churches that garble the gospel and 'tickle ears' (1 Tim. 6:3-5; 2 Tim. 4:3-4), and cults that usurp the name of Christ to mislead the ignorant (Matt. 24:11; 24-26; 2 Pet. 3:1-3). We need godly wisdom, and must avoid rash judgments, even when we must differ. Paul's admonition to love in 13:1-3 (and in v.14 below) is applicable here! Although the Corinthians had problems with Paul, he wanted to keep the lines of communication open. There is a lesson and example here for all believers.

16:13-18 *Paul exhorts the Corinthians to faithfulness and love, and to be in subjection to those who have devoted themselves for ministry to the saints.*

13-14   With five successive imperatives, Paul exhorts the Corinthians to set their spiritual house in order. They must first *be on the alert* (keep awake; be watchful, vigilant) for influences in society which would erode their spiritual foundation. Similarly, they must *stand firm* (στήκω; BAGD, 767f) *in the faith.* The wealth, wisdom, and wiles of Corinth had so polluted everything from their gospel to their morals, they were deluded, thinking themselves to be spiritual royalty (4:7-8) when they were really a spiritual nursery (3:1-2)! They needed to examine themselves to see if they were "in the faith" (2 Cor. 13:5). This has nothing to do with whether or not they are saved, but whether they are following God or men! To stand firm in the faith does not merely mean to hold to a set of doctrines; it means to steadfastly trust what God says over what men say.

If they were going to do this in the midst of Corinthian society, they would also need to *act like men* (be manly, courageous; cf. ἀνδρίζομαι, BAGD, 64) and *be strong*. In 3:3-4, Paul called them "mere men"—men who acted like spiritual babies (3:1)! Here he urges them to be "real men"—believers who will stand firm against the world.

Finally, they must show *love*. In worldly eyes, they may have seemed "manly," but showing love would require all the courage and strength they could muster.

15-16 In concluding his epistles, Paul often warned his readers to avoid people who were unteachable or divisive (cf. Rom. 16:17-20; 2 Thess. 3:6-15; 2 Tim. 4:14-15; Titus 3:10-11), or conversely, encouraged them to submit to those who ministered to them (1 Thess. 5:12-13). Perhaps because most of this letter has addressed negative issues, we find the latter here in his concluding remarks.

A lengthy parenthesis in verse 15 introduces *the household of Stephanas* (cf. 1:16), who *were the first fruits of Achaia* (among the first Christians in Corinth), and who *have devoted themselves for ministry to the saints*. Stephanus was 1) a spiritual leader at home, 2) not a new convert (his faith had stood the test of time), and 3) was devoted to the ministry of the church. These characteristics reflect some of the qualifications of an elder (cf. 1 Tim. 3:1, 4-6). It is this kind of man that Paul urges them to *be in subjection to*, along with *everyone who helps in the work and labors* (perhaps an allusion to deacons). If only the Corinthians had followed the spiritual men in their midst (cf. 2:15) instead of the so-called wise or gifted (in their own eyes), they would have avoided many of their problems.

17-18 Paul is genuinely delighted (*I rejoice*; cf. χαίρω, BAGD, 873f) *over the coming of Stephanas and Fortunatus and Achaicus* for two reasons. First, *they have supplied what was lacking on your part*. Paul is not cryptically suggesting the Corinthians had failed him in any way; rather, this is his way of recognizing these men for providing something on behalf of the whole church (cf. Phil. 2:30, where Epaphroditus 'represented' the church in Philippi by helping Paul in Rome). The men Paul mentions here had brought him the Corinthian church's letter, which re-opened the lines of communication with them. Secondly, *they have refreshed my spirit and yours*. Good friends from a far country are like cold water to a weary soul (Prov. 25:25). Perhaps these men had brought some good news, but whether they did or not, their fellowship was greatly appreciated. Anyone serving on the mission field will readily attest to the great joy that accompanies any correspondence or visits from the folks back home. The visit of these men had forwarded the work of the church, and for that, the Corinthians should *acknowledge* ("give recognition to;" cf. ἐπιγινώσκω, BAGD, 291) them.

Homiletical Ideas: These verses provide a brief summary of biblical teaching on church leadership; verses 13-14 tell us the kind of men the church needs, verse 15 gives us an example of such a man, and verses 16-18 instruct the church to recognize such men.

16:19-24 *Paul's salutation includes greetings from fellow saints and a final exhortation for them to love the Lord.*

19 Many of Paul's letters include closing greetings, reflecting his desire that believers see themselves as part of a universal body (cf. 12:13). Paul repeatedly reminds the Corinthians that his ministry to them is as part of a much larger community, made up of all the (local) churches (cf. 1:2; 4:17; 7:17; 11:16; 14:33; 16:1). So it is no surprise that he includes greetings from *the churches of Asia* (a general salute), and "hearty greetings" (cf. πολύς; BAGD, 688) *in the Lord* from *Aquila and Prisca* (or *Priscilla*), along *with the church that is in their house.*

Households played a significant role in the development of the early church, both in Jerusalem following Pentecost (Acts 2:46), and in Paul's ministry (Acts 16:15, 31-34; 1 Cor. 1:16; 16:15). Religious instruction normally occurred at home (1 Cor. 14:35; Eph. 6:4), so it was natural for the teaching meetings of the local church to be based there as well (cf. Acts 5:42; 20:8, 20; Rom. 16:5; Col 4:15; Philem. 2).

Aquila and Priscilla were well-known to those in Corinth, having once been residents of the city (Acts 18:1-3). They served with Paul in many capacities, continuing his work in Ephesus while he went to Jerusalem at the end of his second missionary journey (Acts 18:18-21), and in particular, teaching Apollos (who soon after went to Corinth) "the way of God more accurately" (Acts 18:26-28).

20   This summary greeting is echoed in other letters of Paul (Rom. 16:16; 2 Cor. 13:12-13; 1 Thess. 5:26). Greetings are included from *all the brethren* (from Christians everywhere), and in customary fashion, they are exhorted to *Greet one another with a holy kiss* (a culturally appropriate way of expressing their special relationship as members of Christ's body).

21   Paul's personal *greeting* is written *in my own hand*, again a common practice at the close of his letters (cf. Gal. 6:11; Col. 4:18; 2 Thess. 3:17). If Paul dictated this letter to an amanuensis, as on other occasions (cf. Rom. 16:22), he took the pen in hand to write this personal word. Such an act both confirmed his authorship (2 Thess. 3:17), and perhaps added a touch of authority to his words (cf. Philem. 19).

22   Drawing on this authority, Paul adds that *if anyone does not love* (have affection for, like; cf. φιλέω, BAGD, 859) *the Lord, let him be accursed* (ἀνάθεμα; cf. Rom. 9:3; Gal. 1:8f). This is the only time Paul uses φιλέω in reference to believers loving the Lord (his only other use of the word is in Tit. 3:15); the conditional clause indicates the possibility that some in the Corinthian church have no affection for Christ (Kistemaker, 611). The meaning of the judgment enjoined (*let him be accursed*) is debated, making any conclusion as to Paul's precise meaning

tenuous at best. However, under no circumstances was Paul inviting the Corinthians to judge one another as to their relative love for the Lord, or excommunicate those who didn't measure up (MacArthur, 488)!

The Corinthians had an abundance of self-appointed "fruit inspectors" who divided the church on the basis of works or merit. Why would Paul, after seeking to thwart such divisiveness in his letter, now encourage it at its close?! Judgmental attitudes have plagued the church throughout her existence, and many believers today exist in a spiritual quagmire of doubt as a result of their eternal salvation being made dependent on their works. This is not Paul's desire.

To be "accursed" or "anathema" (ἀνάθεμα) meant to be 'dedicated to destruction' (DNTT 1:414-15). While it is often viewed as synonymous with 'cursed in hell,' Paul is not here suggesting that a Christian who lacks affection for Christ is eternally condemned. Rather, this is a strong way of saying, "Don't hang out with these guys! Don't listen to them! Separate from them!" Those who reject his gospel (see Gal. 1:8-9), or those who reject his teaching (and are thus out of fellowship with the Lord), should be treated as such. In effect, he returns to the first half of the letter. He reiterates that those who deviate from his gospel by mixing it with human wisdom (1:18-2:5), and those who engage in depraved practices (cf. 5:1-2; 6:1-20), should be excluded from fellowship.

Paul knows, of course, that ultimate judgment lies with the Lord, not with him, or anyone in Corinth (4:5). Perhaps an awareness of this fact leads him to write *Maranatha* ("O Lord, come!" NKJV/NIV). Even what we can never fully know, the eyes of Christ will fully expose (cf. 3:13; 4:5).

23-24 As he began the letter, so he ends it, drawing their attention to *grace*. Paul wants the *grace of the Lord Jesus* to be active in their midst. The more they understand what they have freely received in Christ, the less they will be distracted by the society in which they live. More than any other word, grace expresses what God has done, and what He will do, for believers in Jesus Christ (Fee, 839).

However harsh his words had seemed at times, Paul's heart was never filled with anything but love for the Corinthians. It was his love which would not allow him to abandon them to their own foolishness, and which eventually took much of his time and attention. This is a positive and appropriate finale to his letter: *My love be with you all in Christ Jesus. Amen.*

Homiletical Ideas: Although not the "final word" on any church doctrine or practice, Paul's closing comments reveal his deep concern for believers. He wants them to be unified (19-20; not just on a local level, but as part of a universal Body of Christ). He wants them to be devoted to the Lord in love, looking forward to His coming (21-22). Finally, he wants them to fully grasp the wonder of God's grace, which would in turn motivate love and purity (23-24).

CONCLUSION

As a first-year seminary student many years ago, I had a class in basic theology—anthropology and angelology. Being exposed for the first time to in-depth theological study was tedious for many students. Each class period, the professor reserved the last fifteen minutes or so for questions. One day, a student near the back, frustrated with what seemed like endless minutiae, raised his hand.

"Prof, why do we have to know this stuff? Wouldn't it be better for us to learn *practical* truths that could help us in our ministry?"

The professor responded as if he had been waiting all his life for a student to ask that question. The essence of what he said has stuck with me ever since. "What you believe will affect everything in your life. It will affect the priorities you choose, the person you marry, the career you pursue. It will determine the habits you form, the way you love your wife, and the way you raise your children. Going through life without knowing what you believe is like getting a ticket for a train without knowing where it is going. Nothing is more practical than knowing what you believe, because that will determine how you live your life!"

One of the most tragic deficiencies in the church today is in the area of theology. Over the last thirty years, the theological quotient of church leaders has declined, creating a vacuum of practical truth for Christians. So many today do not know how to live their lives, because they have no foundation in biblical truth. Church leaders follow the winds of societal change, accepting whatever our depraved culture embraces. Believers are left in a subjective quagmire of moral and ethical options, and the church, instead of confronting the world, is impotent to respond in a day of unprecedented evil.

A cursory look at New Testament history suggests that Christians in Corinth faced a similar challenge to what we face today. Advances in human knowledge, the encroachment of immoral and unprincipled behavior in the church, and an undermining of the institution of marriage, all threatened to derail the fledgling congregation. It is into this context—and thus into our own—that Paul penned First Corinthians.

The practical impact on the church had been dramatic. Mixing worldly wisdom with divine truth resulted in a toxic spiritual poison that led them to compromise the gospel, and in turn created divisions which weakened the church from within. Correcting this fundamental problem was central for Paul. He 'bookends' his letter with a trenchant attack on those who pursue the 'wisdom of men' instead of the 'foolishness of God' (chapters 1-4), and in that wisdom deny the heart of the gospel, the resurrection (chapter15). How tragic that in these last days, history is repeating itself, as 'wise' theologians and church leaders market a gospel which eclipses the work of Christ by injecting the works of man into the salvation formula.

It is not surprising that in conjunction with a loss of appreciation for the pristine grace of God in salvation, we are experiencing a moral decline in the church. The unambiguous teaching of Scripture, when clouded by worldly wisdom, creates confusion: 'A fog in the pulpit is a mist in the pew!' Christians flounder between legalistic moralism and licentious indulgence. Any pastor who has ministered over the last few decades has watched it happen: Millions of Christians wander through life like 'sheep without a shepherd,' and marriage—the institution on which Paul focused in 1 Corinthians 7, is once again unraveling. As Yogi Berra would say, 'It's *déjà vu* all over again!'

First Corinthians is an inspired guidebook for Christians who are making their way through treacherous waters of modernity, seeking to live out an unwavering commitment to grace and godliness. Without compromising God's gracious gift of eternal life in the gospel, Paul directs believers to live life with eternal rewards in view, remembering that God will judge both motives and actions. He confronts the arrogance and heartlessness of self-righteous religion, and instead exhorts us to 'do all to the glory of God.'

Like a kaleidoscope with seemingly endless beauties, the more one looks at First Corinthians, the more one sees the wonder of God's grace.

Unsullied by man's corrupting wisdom, it enables us to avoid the pitfalls of moral decline, warns us of the dangers of human pride, and guides us in the pursuit of holiness. Here, then, is an ever-timely theological and practical treatise on the Christian life.

Therefore, my beloved brethren, be steadfast, immovable, always abounding in the work of the Lord, knowing that your toil is not in vain in the Lord. (1 Corinthians 15.58)

www.ingramcontent.com/pod-product-compliance
Lightning Source LLC
Chambersburg PA
CBHW051413090426
42737CB00014B/2644